O9-AIG-298

BACKCOUNTRY ALASKA

"Where The Roads End...
The Real Alaska Begins."

Volume 13, Number 2 / 1986
ALASKA GEOGRAPHIC®

The Alaska Geographic Society tabletop
version of The Alaska Wilderness MILEPOST™.
A digest-sized guidebook for
backpacks or briefcases.

The Alaska Geographic Society

To teach many more to better know and use our natural resources

Editors this issue: Juli Chase, Kris Valencia
Contributing Editor: Rollo Pool
Editorial Assistance: Fay Bartels
Editor: Penny Rennick
Associate Editor: Kathy Doogan
Designer: Sandra Harner

ALASKA GEOGRAPHIC®, ISSN 0361-1353, is published quarterly by The Alaska Geographic Society, Anchorage, Alaska 99509-3370. Second-class postage paid in Edmonds, Washington 98020-3588. Printed in U.S.A. Copyright© 1986 by The Alaska Geographic Society. All rights reserved. Registered trademark; Alaska Geographic, ISSN 0361-1353; Key title Alaska Geographic.

THE ALASKA GEOGRAPHIC SOCIETY is a nonprofit organization exploring new frontiers of knowledge across the lands of the polar rim, learning how other men and other countries live in their Norths, putting the geography book back in the classroom, exploring new methods of teaching and learning — sharing in the excitement of discovery in man's wonderful new world north of 51°16'.

MEMBERS OF THE SOCIETY RECEIVE *Alaska Geographic®*, a quality magazine which devotes each quarterly issue to monographic in-depth coverage of a northern geographic region or resource-oriented subject.

The cover — *Community of Tenakee Springs, reached only by seaplane or boat, is a popular southeastern Alaska vacation destination for residents and visitors alike. (Rollo Pool, staff)*

Previous page — *Alaska cotton rims tundra pond near the headwaters of the Susitna River in the Alaska Range. (George Wuerthner)*

Facing page — *Village of Gambell, framed by drying racks for walrus hide and meat. The hide will be used to make a traditional Eskimo boat. (© Chlaus Lotscher)*

MEMBERSHIP DUES in The Alaska Geographic Society are $30 per year; $34 to non-U.S. addresses. (Eighty percent of each year's dues is for a one-year subscription to *Alaska Geographic®*.) Order from The Alaska Geographic Society, Box 93370, Anchorage, Alaska 99509-3370; (907) 563-1141.

MATERIAL SOUGHT: The editors of *Alaska Geographic®* seek a wide variety of informative material on the lands north of 51°16' on geographic subjects — anything to do with resources and their uses (with heavy emphasis on quality color photography) — from Alaska, northern Canada, Siberia, Japan — all geographic areas that have a relationship to Alaska in a physical or economic sense. We do not want material done in excessive scientific terminology. A query to the editors is suggested. Payments are made for all material upon publication.

CHANGE OF ADDRESS: The post office does not automatically forward *Alaska Geographic®* when you move. To ensure continuous service, notify us six weeks before moving. Send us your new address and zip code (and moving date), your old address and zip code, and if possible send a mailing label from a copy of *Alaska Geographic®*. Send this information to *Alaska Geographic®* Mailing Offices, 130 Second Avenue South, Edmonds, Washington 98020-3588.

MAILING LISTS: We have begun making our members' names and addresses available to carefully screened publications and companies whose products and activities might be of interest to you. If you would prefer not to receive such mailings, please so advise us, and include your mailing label (or your name and address if label is not available).

About This Issue: This issue of *ALASKA GEOGRAPHIC®* has been excerpted from the premier issue of *The Alaska Wilderness MILEPOST™*, a compendium of information about the communities and attractions in Alaska's Bush. *The Alaska Wilderness MILEPOST™* incorporates information from *The MILEPOST®*, *ALASKA®* magazine, *The ALASKA ALMANAC®*, and previous issues of *ALASKA GEOGRAPHIC®*.

We thank the many fine photographers who contributed their work, as well as the local governments, Native corporations, postmasters, teachers, and hundreds of other individuals who provided information on community questionnaires.

We also thank the following for their assistance:

The U.S. National Park Service; U.S. Postal Service; U.S. Forest Service; U.S. Bureau of Land Management; U.S. Bureau of Customs, U.S. Coast Guard, 17th District; U.S. Fish and Wildlife Service; U.S. Bureau of Indian Affairs; U.S. National Oceanic and Atmospheric Administration.

State of Alaska — Division of Tourism; Office of Enterprise; Division of Marine Highway Systems; Department of Transportation and Public Facilities; Department of Fish and Game; Division of Mining; Division of Parks and Outdoor Recreation; Office of History and Archaeology; Department of Community and Regional Affairs; Division of Alasks State Troopers; Division of Fire Prevention; Alaska Court System; Department of Education; Division of Occupational Licensing; Department of Health and Social Services; Department of Revenue, Division of Public Services and Alcoholic Beverage Control Board; Alaska State Museum; University of Alaska Museum; Department of Environmental Conservation; Department of Labor, Division of Research and Analysis; Division of State Libraries; University of Alaska, Arctic Environmental Information and Data Center and Cooperative Extension Service.

The Alaska Municipal League; Anchorage Telephone Utility; Rural Alaska Community Action Program; Alaska Professional Hunters Association; Alaska Air Carriers Association; Museums Alaska, Inc.; Nova Riverrunners of Alaska; Tanana Chiefs Council; Alaska Wilderness Guides Association; Channel Flying Inc.; Exploration Holidays and Cruises; Kodiak Area Chamber of Commerce; Valdez Chamber of Commerce; Alaska Wilderness Sailing Safaris; Kodiak Island Borough; City of Cordova; Alaska Discovery Inc.

TABLE OF CONTENTS

Bush Living/6

Bush Travel/10

Southeast/14

Southcentral/ Gulf Coast/48

Alaska Peninsula/ Aleutians/86

Bering Sea Coast/114

Arctic/172

Interior/196

From the President

Where the roads end is where Alaska begins. The folks who only see the metropolitan centers, the supermarkets and the superhighways, don't even get a good smell of the real Alaska. That's a compounding of berries and Hudson's Bay tea on untrammeled tundra, kelp and popweed and clams and decaying driftwood on a thousand beaches.

It's the sound of harsh and cold Bering Sea breakers dumping on the lonely western shore. It's the sound of waterfalls tumbling a thousand feet from Southeast snowfields and marmots whistling from the heights. It's clamoring geese, kreeking eagles and whirring hummingbird wings.

It's the endless expanses of sea where the waves march backward in great heaving swells to the Orient . . . where the peaks rise vertically from your feet to the heavens . . . everywhere things growing . . . browns, reds, shiny black and myriad shades of green.

To know this land is to love it. In this book we have put together some needful facts on how to get there, what to expect when you arrive and a lot of questions answered that you'll be glad somebody finally put together in one book.

We've done one copy for the packsack and another for your coffee table. It's our Alaska and we're happy to share it with you.

Sincerely,

Robert A. Henning,
President

Introduction

More than 200 communities and an almost equal number of attractions are covered in the following pages, most accessible only by air or by water. Highways cover only a third of Alaska; the rest of the state comes under the heading of Bush. And it is this vast land of varying geography that *The Alaska Wilderness MILEPOST*™ covers. In tackling this immense subject, we first divided it into the six distinct natural regions that make up the state of Alaska: Southeast; Southcentral and the Gulf Coast; the Alaska Peninsula and Aleutian Chain; the Bering Sea Coast; the Arctic; and the Interior. Of these six major regions, the Bering Sea Coast can be further divided into three subregions: Bristol Bay; Yukon-Kuskokwim; and Seward Peninsula and Norton Sound. Under each of these headings are described first the communities and then the attractions of the region.

Left — *Residents of St. Lawrence Island, located in the Bering Sea, stop their boat near a sea cliff that is home to hundreds of murres.* (©*Chlaus Lotscher*)

Upper right — *Winter grips the small community of Unalakleet (population 784) located on Norton Sound in northwestern Alaska. (Division of Tourism)*

Right — *Hiker in Gates of the Arctic National Park dumps water from her boots after crossing an icy stream. (George Wuerthner)*

Far right — *Forest Service public recreation cabin at Lake Eva on Baranof Island is equipped with decks and ramps for easy access by the handicapped. (U.S. Forest Service)*

BUSH LIVING

If we were to draw a boundary around Alaska's major towns and cities, separating them from the rest of this country, we would find that most of Alaska is in the "Bush." The bush lifestyle does not meet any easy, pat definition. A bush community typically is one that can be reached only by air, water or trail. It could be a Native village, a fishing village, a logging or mining camp. A quick definition of a bush town might be: "Any settlement that doesn't have community electricity, medical facilities, or a Sears Catalog Sales Office." (Anyone who has lived away from the large cities understands the importance of those three amenities, especially when there is the need for a spare part or new jeans.) But even this definition is far from accurate, since public and corporate funds have brought community electricity, water and sewage systems to many bush towns and helped build medical clinics (although they may be staffed by a single nurse practitioner).

Bush living ranges from the independent, no-frills, subsistence lifestyle of a settlement like Kupreanof or Skwentna to the wilderness setting with urban amenities of hubs like Fort Yukon. There are also roughly two degrees of bush living: living in a bush settlement or living remote even from a small village.

Bush living may be part geography and part frame of mind. Those living in the Bush are there by choice, by design and by habit. Some are escaping the city or escaping other people. To others, bush living is the only lifestyle they have ever known.

Author Ray Tremblay *(Trails of an Alaskan Trapper)* went to the Bush in 1949 to become a trapper. He first sought out a retiring trapper, who gave Ray his opinion of what someone needed to make it in the Bush.

"The primary tools were good health, job interest, single or married, and without children. I questioned him about children, and he reminded me that he was forced

Snow covers winter camp in Kotzebue Basin. (Mark Ocker, reprinted from ALASKA GEOGRAPHIC®)

Modern dish antenna at village of Kotlik. (Staff, reprinted from ALASKA GEOGRAPHIC®)

7

into town the next year because his children were now school age. Trapping would no longer be a full-time occupation for him. The secondary requirements were more subtle and harder to define and varied with individuals. They involved one's ability to adjust to the solitary existence as a permanent condition, weighing the rigors of life against the rewards, learning to play the game before enthusiasm faded, and avoiding the traps of our gadget-ridden civilization."

Times have changed since then. There are a few who adhere to the old ways of trapping, but now there are airplanes and snowmobiles that can go farther and faster than snowshoes. Small villages now have schools, and for families homesteading away from a village there are correspondence courses. Even some "gadgets" have crept into the bush lifestyle, most notably television.

But there is still a simplicity and sharing in Alaska's far-flung communities that keeps them whole and draws new residents. And many old customs and habits of community life endure, although the form may change.

There was a time when the only form of communication in the Bush, besides the mail, was by radio. Teachers, weather observers and others in far-flung communities kept regular schedules to talk with airlines, hospitals and the like — a system that was hardly private since most of Alaska could tune in. Today, most villages have at least one public phone and the number of phones in

Woman uses ulu *to split walrus hide.*
(Richard Harrington, reprinted from
ALASKA GEOGRAPHIC®)

private homes is increasing. But Bush message programs on commercial radio stations remain a popular means of getting a quick message to someone in an isolated location.

One of the inventions of northern bush living that has been sustained through the years of modernization is the cache, a sort of elevated closet. The concept of this contraption is to keep animals out of the contents, whether it's food, building materials or other supplies. Usually a cache is built as a tiny house or platform on a single delimbed tree. The caches are above a bear's 10- to 15-foot reach above the ground. Several feet of sheet metal is wrapped around the lower portion of the tree to thwart squirrels and the like.

Major events in the smaller rural communities continue to be the arrival of the mail plane and — for communities on the Far North coast — the arrival of the first barge in the spring.

For the many smaller settlements around Ketchikan a welcome visitor was a cargo vessel that delivered goods and supplies and sometimes mail — despite the increasing competition from airplanes and an expanding road system. At Christmastime, crews decorated the small ship from stern to bow with strings of lights. Coming through the evening darkness of Clarence Strait, Sea Otter Sound or Kasaan Bay, she was recognizable for miles, if not by the multicolored lights then by the speakers blasting Christmas carols across the water.

Bush living breeds a spirit of self-sufficiency, but also a spirit of neighborliness. While there may be occasional friction between old-timers and newcomers, the visitor to the Bush will still find — more often than not — that the coffee pot is on and the latchstring is out.

Left — CB radio is often used for communications in remote areas. (Staff, reprinted from ALASKA GEOGRAPHIC®)

Lower left — Three-wheeled ATVs are popular in Gambell and many other villages. (Chlaus Lotscher, reprinted from ALASKA GEOGRAPHIC®)

Below — A cache is a necessity in some areas to keep food and other supplies away from raiding animals. (©Kirk Beckendorf)

BUSH TRAVEL

Since the growth of commercial aviation in the 1930s, the far-flung communities and remote areas of Alaska's Bush have become more easily accessible. Jet aircraft and smaller bush planes provide transportation to the most isolated destinations. Nome is a two-hour plane ride from Anchorage or Fairbanks; Barrow is an hour and a half by air from Fairbanks. Avid bird-watchers fly 800 miles from Anchorage to the Pribilofs. Air travel in the Bush can be expensive, however, and visitor facilities may not be readily available.

Tour companies offer some travel packages to the Bush, which — although perhaps no more economical than an individual itinerary — do take care of meals and accommodations. The major bush communities served by tour companies are Barrow, Kotzebue, Nome and the Pribilofs. Package tours to

Some outfitters offer horseback trips through the Alaska Range. (©Kirk Beckendorf)

Katmai National Park and some other remote areas are available, too.

Commercial lodges offering meals and accommodations are found in many bush areas, from Misty Fiords to the Brooks Range. Most specialize in sportfishing or hunting, or offer simply the "wilderness experience."

Guides and outfitters are available to help visitors to the Bush, whether for hiking, canoeing, camping or hunting. There are a variety of options, from the more expensive fully-guided trip in which everything is taken care of (meals, lodging, equipment, transportation, etc.) to an unguided trip in which perhaps only transportation and some equipment is provided.

Whether with a tour or traveling independently, most visitors will spend time in at least one Native village. Although village life has changed in recent years, author Lael Morgan *(Alaska's Native People, ALASKA GEOGRAPHIC®)* points out that "it is still possible to find a village where no one over 35 except the postmaster speaks English, still

Boots and socks dry by a campfire after a rainy day of hiking. (©Chlaus Lotscher)

Air transportation is vital in the Bush. A floatplane brings a teacher and supplies to Lime Village. (Staff, reprinted from ALASKA GEOGRAPHIC®)

possible to find villages without house locks, and still possible to find villages where hunters share their meat."

Not too long ago, many homes in small Native villages had no electricity. Now they may have satellite television and VCRs. But life is still hard in these villages and traditional customs endure. Lael Morgan recalls, "I heard Native people making fun of Outsiders because they said 'thank you' so often when talk is cheap. If you really want to thank someone you must *do* something that shows appreciation." Smaller villages may or may not have formal lodging facilities and their general stores may carry only limited stocks of food (shelves can be bare in some areas in the spring before the barges arrive). If there is no lodge, visitors may be able to pay a local family or the schoolteachers for room and

board. Campers are generally welcome to set up their tents in or near a village, but permission should always be asked first.

Respect for local lifestyles, customs and the privacy of others is essential when visiting Native villages. The village chief or mayor or the community council office is the best place to get general information. Information about accommodations and conditions in villages may also be gleaned from the bush airlines that serve them. It is a good idea to write the village before a trip for permission and/or to make arrangements for accommodations. Some smaller communities are making an effort to encourage tourists, while others discourage Outsiders.

Visitors to bush villages should be aware of local ordinances and local attitudes. Many bush communities prohibit or restrict to some

degree the sale and importation of alcoholic beverages. Photography is generally acceptable if done with consideration for the residents; ask permission before photographing individuals or their homes.

Local transportation is usually by snow machine, boat or three-wheeler, although larger communities may have a few cars and trucks. Visitors usually can hitch a ride with local people to and from the airport or other destinations, but it is considerate to offer remuneration.

One potential area for friction which all visitors to the Bush should be aware of is interference with local subsistence activities. Subsistence hunting, fishing and trapping are permitted on national park and refuge lands and can include free-ranging activities as well as stationary camps and traplines. Land around a community may be owned by a Native corporation which restricts or charges for recreational activities on that land. In areas where game is scarce and the local people depend heavily on subsistence, hunting for sport can cause resentment. Trip planning should include contacting federal agencies and villages about planned routes. While en route, avoid disturbing camps (even if they look abandoned), fish nets, traps or other subsistence gear.

There are more than 200 million acres of public lands in Alaska — national parks and preserves, monuments and wildlife refuges, state parks and game refuges, and Bureau of Land Management lands — nearly all located in the Bush and most offering unique opportunities for hiking, camping, river running, wildlife viewing, hunting or fishing.

There are few established hiking trails on these lands; most hiking is cross-country. This means visitors should have a good knowledge of map and compass use and exercise low-impact hiking and camping techniques. It also means visitors must expect the unexpected. A heavy downpour or glacial runoff from high summer temperatures can cause a stream that is ankle-deep in the morning to be a hip-deep torrent in the afternoon. Changes in the weather and miscommunication with bush pilots also have wrought unpleasant surprises. A party of hikers once spent several days stretching out their food supply and trying to get comfortable in some willow trees while waiting for flood waters to subside and their bush pilot to show up. A rapid thaw had swollen a nearby river, flooding their camp and the surrounding country during the night. Inexact instructions to the bush pilot on when and where to pick them up delayed their rescue.

Obvious, but bearing repetition, is the reminder that this is remote country. Suffi-

Mosquitoes carpet a traveler's hat in Noatak National Preserve. (John and Margaret Ibbotson, reprinted from ALASKA GEOGRAPHIC®*)*

cient supplies of food and clothing should be brought along, even if there are villages in the vicinity. Fuel is also an important consideration, since Alaska's tree line is erratic and dead wood may not be available for fires. Clothing should be warm enough to guard against hypothermia, the number one killer of outdoor recreationists, and adequate enough to protect against that plague of man and beast — the mosquito.

Mosquito eggs hatch in water, so Alaska — with its many thousands of square miles of marshy tundra and lakes — is prime breeding ground. Mosquitoes are active from early spring to late fall. In some locations along the coast, no-see-ums are the major biting insect pest from about June through August. Snipe flies are a troublesome pest in certain mountainous localities as far north as the Alaska Range. These insects, which are present from late June to early August, have a painful sting. Black fly season starts in May and lasts until freezeup. Insect repellents containing diethyl-meta-toluamide are effective against mosquitoes, but the best protection against all insects is clothing that covers as much exposed skin as possible.

A much bigger and far more dangerous hazard encountered when traveling the Bush are bears. Black or brown bears are found just about everywhere in the state. Minimize the chance of a potentially dangerous confrontation by avoiding places where bears are likely to be found, such as salmon spawning streams, berry patches during berry season, and bear trails. Hikers should let bears know they're headed their way by wearing a bell, singing, carrying a can of rattling stones, talking loudly or otherwise making noise. When photographing bears, use a telephoto lens — a long one.

After all the talk about the inconveniences

Hikers should exercise caution and common sense when crossing streams. (George Wuerthner)

of Bush travel, why do people go there? Perhaps, as publisher Bob Henning notes, to get "a good smell of the real Alaska." Or watch the northern lights dance where there are no lights from a city to distract. Or to see bears, wolves, moose and other wildlife, which are so much more abundant away from the highway. Or maybe it's because this vast place offers a sense of another time. A time governed not by clocks, but by the rhythm of the tides and the seasons. A time when man was one with nature.

SOUTHEAST

Southeastern Alaska — often called The Panhandle — is a unique region where industry, transportation, recreation and community planning are dictated by its spectacular topography: A multitude of islands, inland mountains that rise sharply from the sea to snowcapped peaks, and glaciers that creep slowly down steep-walled, U-shaped valleys.

A rainwashed and verdant land, Southeast stretches nearly 600 miles from Dixon Entrance north to Icy Bay. Many millenia of geological activity has sculpted more than a thousand islands in this region, including Prince of Wales, third largest in the United States at 2,231 square miles. The narrow strip of mainland is isolated from the rest of North America by the Saint Elias and Coast mountain ranges. Mount Saint Elias (18,008 feet), Mount Vancouver (15,700 feet), Mount Fairweather (15,300 feet) and other lofty peaks make the Saint Elias the highest coastal range in the world.

Warmed by ocean currents, Southeast enjoys mild temperatures averaging around 60°F in summer. An occasional heat wave may reach the high 80s. Winters are cool, with alternating snow, rain and sunshine; January temperatures average 20° to 40°F. Subzero winter temperatures are uncommon. It rains a lot here, from 80 to more than 200 inches in some places. It is wettest in late fall, driest in summer. Communities receive 30 to 200 inches of snow annually, but more than 400 inches of snow falls on the high mountains each year.

The heavy rainfall and mild climate encourage timber growth. Three quarters of Southeast is densely forested, primarily with western hemlock and Sitka spruce, with some red cedar and Alaska yellow cedar. Lush ground cover includes the thorny devil's club, as well as the more friendly blueberries, huckleberries, mosses and ferns.

This is prime habitat for Sitka black-tailed deer, wolves and bears. Brown bears inhabit the mainland and the "ABC islands" — Admiralty, Baranof and Chichagof (which have no wolves). Black bears occur on other forested islands, as well as the mainland. Mountain goats, lynx, wolverines, foxes, mink, river otters, porcupines, marten, scattered populations of moose and an assortment of small mammals range throughout Southeast. The region boasts the largest bald eagle population in

Layers of mountain ridges recede into the distance on the east side of Sitka Sound. (Staff)

A dramatic example of Southeast Indian totemic art. (Division of Tourism)

Southeast

Location

Cartography by David A. Shott

N

Gulf of Alaska

Pacific Ocean

Wrangell-St. Elias
National Park and Preserve
Malaspina Glacier
Icy Bay
Yakutat Bay
Yakutat
Alsek R.

Saint Elias Mountains

Haines Highway

Chilkoot Trail

Klondike Highway 2

Skagway

Haines

Coast Mountains

○ Eldred Rock
Light Station

**Glacier Bay National
Park and Preserve**

Glacier Bay

○ Point Sherman
Light Station

Taku River

○ Sentinel Island
Light Station

Excursion Inlet
Gustavus ■

*Point
Retreat
Light Station*

Auke Bay ■

Icy Strait

Funter Bay

■ **Juneau**
■ **Douglas**

*Cape Spencer
Light Station* ○

*Cross
Sound*

Elfin Cove ■

Hoonah

Stephens Passage

■ **Hawk Inlet**

Tongass National Forest

Pelican ■

**Eight
Fathom
Bight**

**Tenakee
Springs**

■ **Hobart Bay**

Chichagof Island

Corner Bay ■

Admiralty Island

■ **Angoon**

*Fairway Island
Light Station* ○

*Five Finger Islands
Light Station* ○

*Windham
Bay*

Baranof Island

Cape Fanshaw

*Kruzof
Island*

Baranof ■

Mt. Edgecumbe ▲

■ **Sitka**

St. Lazaria Island

Kake ■

**Alaska Maritime
National Wildlife
Refuge**

Sitka Sound

*Biorka
Island*

Goddard ■

Kupreanof ■
Petersburg ■

*Kupreanof
Island*

*Mitkof
Island*

Stikine River

Kuiu Island

*Zarembo
Island*

■ **Wrangell**

*Wrangell
Island*

Port Walter ■

■ **Point Baker**
■ **Port Protection**

Etolin Island

Port Alexander ■

Whale Pass ■

Unuk R.

*Cape Decision
Light Station* ○

**Coffman
Cove** ■

○ Lincoln Rock
Light Station

Edna Bay ■

■ **Tokeen**

*Prince of Wales
Island*

Behm Canal

Thorne Bay ■

**Meyer's
Chuck** ■

Neets Bay ■

Kasaan ■

Loring ■

Klawock ■
Craig ■ **Hollis** ■

Clarence Strait

Revillagigedo Island

■ **Ketchikan**

**Trocadero
Soda Springs** ■

○ Guard Island
Light Station

Hydaburg ■

Dolomi ■

Metlakatla ■

*Annette
Island*

○ Mary Island
Light Station

*Dall
Island*

*Duke
Island*

Tree Point
Light Station ○

Canada / United States

Wilderness Areas of Tongass National Forest

Admiralty Island National
Monument

Tracy Arm-Fords
Terror Wilderness

Misty Fiords National
Monument

Stikine-LeConte
Wilderness

Russell Fiord
Wilderness

Endicott River
Wilderness

Petersburg Creek-Duncan
Salt Chuck Wilderness

West Chichagof-Yakobi
Wilderness

South Baranof
Wilderness

Tebenkof Bay
Wilderness

South Prince of Wales
Wilderness
Maurelle Islands Wilderness
Warren Island Wilderness
Coronation Island Wilderness

the world and its waters are home to a variety of fish and marine mammals, including humpback whales that winter in the Hawaiian Islands. Sea lions rest on the rocky shoreline, Pacific white-sided dolphins somersault out of the water, and speeding Dall porpoises swim off the bows of visiting boats.

Access to and within Southeast is by air or water. Islands and mountainous terrain make construction of highways between most communities impossible. (Haines, Skagway and Hyder are the only communities connected to the inland highway system.) Instead, a variety of watercraft — from small skiffs to the big car-carrying state ferries — connects communities. The state ferry system connects all major Southeast ports and some smaller communities, as well as Prince Rupert, British Columbia, and Seattle, Washington. Many communities have scheduled air service, from jets to floatplanes, and charter floatplanes can reach virtually any location.

More than 95 percent of the land in Southeast is under federal jurisdiction. About 73 percent of

Southeast lies within Tongass National Forest, largest national forest in the United States. The forest serves as a recreational haven — although largely undeveloped — for hiking, hunting, fishing and camping. It is also a resource for one of Southeast's major industries, timber harvesting, which supplies pulp mills and sawmills in several communities.

Fishing and fish processing comprise the region's second major industry. Salmon is Southeast's most abundant product from the sea. Crab, shrimp, halibut, herring and cod also are harvested commercially.

The third major industry is government, most of it in Juneau, the state capital. Tourism is a big contributor to the economy and mining is gaining increased importance with development of a world-class molybdenum mine near Ketchikan and a base metals mine on Admiralty Island.

Of the approximately 61,000 people in Southeast, about 75 percent live in the larger communities of Juneau, Ketchikan, Petersburg, Sitka and Wrangell. The remainder are settled in medium-sized communities like Skagway and Haines; small logging communities like Coffman Cove and even smaller commercial fishing settlements like Funter Bay; on remote homestead parcels or in seasonal logging camps; and in predominantly Native villages like Kasaan. Of the total population, more than 20 percent are Native, mostly Tlingit, Haida and Tsimshian Indians.

The Tlingits and Haidas, famous for their totem poles and potlatches, occupied southeastern Alaska long before Captain Commander Vitus Bering discovered Alaska in 1741. The first significant white populations arrived with the gold rush of 1898, when thousands of gold seekers threaded their way through the Inside Passage to Skagway, bound for the Klondike goldfields and Alaska's Interior.

Imperial Russia controlled Alaska from the early 19th century until the United States purchase in 1867. The extensive Russian fur trading empire was centered in Sitka, capital of Alaska from Russian times until 1900, when the government was transferred to Juneau. Commercial interests

The many channels of the Stikine River form a pattern against the rich green of its delta. (Rollo Pool, staff)

in Southeast had declined along with the fur trade after 1867, but furs were soon replaced by salmon. The first cannery was established at Klawock in 1878, and dozens more followed, accompanied by sawmills, trading posts and all the trappings of industry and settlement.

Although a seemingly insignificant piece of real estate hanging off the bulk of the state, Southeast is possessed of deep beauty, wrapped in a green and misty mantle. Southeast moves to the gentle rhythm of the tides. Southeast's evergreen aromas are fresh and sweet. Its sounds quickly muffled by the forested envelope in a hundred shades of green. Southeast has rushing jet liners, a few pockets of sophistication, but most of this watery land is simple, rustic, unmarked by man. A land of peace.

The Communities

ANGOON, located on the west coast of Admiralty Island, 55 miles southwest of Juneau, 41 miles northeast of Sitka. **Elevation:** Sea level. **Transportation:** Scheduled ferry service;

scheduled seaplane service from Juneau. **Population: 470.**

Visitor Facilities: Angoon has two motels, Kootznahoo Inlet Lodge and Raven Beaver Lodge, and the Favorite Bay Inn bed-and-breakfast. Food service and supplies are limited to The Surf deli and the Angoon Trading Co. grocery. Fishing and hunting licenses may be purchased locally. Charter fishing boats and rental canoes are available. Limited gas and diesel available. Transient moorage at boat harbor.

Angoon is a long established Tlingit Indian settlement at the entrance to Kootznahoo Inlet. It is the only permanent community on Admiralty Island. On Killisnoo Island, across the harbor from the state ferry landing, a community of mostly summer homes has grown up along the island beaches. The lifestyle of the primarily Tlingit town is heavily subsistence: fish, clams, seaweed, berries and venison. Fishing, mostly hand trolling for king and coho salmon, is the principal industry. Unemployment in Angoon is high throughout the year.

The scenery of Admiralty Island draws many visitors to Angoon. All but the northern portion of the island was declared a national monument and is managed by the U.S. Forest Service. There is a USFS campground located near the state ferry landing. Kootznahoo Inlet and Mitchell Bay near Angoon offer a network of small wooded islands, reefs and channels for kayaking. Wildlife includes many brown bears, Sitka black-tailed deer and bald eagles.

Local residents can provide directions to the interesting old Killisnoo graveyards, located both on the island and on the Angoon shore of the old Killisnoo settlement, which once was one of the larger communities in southeastern Alaska.

COFFMAN COVE is located on the northeast coast of Prince of Wales Island, 53 miles north of Klawock, 42 miles southeast of Wrangell and 73

Colorful and unique Tlingit ceremonial hats are displayed on a table at an Angoon potlatch. (Staff)

miles northeast of Ketchikan. **Elevation: 10 feet. Transportation:** By road, boat and daily floatplane service from Ketchikan. **Population: 199.**

Visitor Facilities: Limited. Meals may be obtained at the Greentree Cafe. Convenience foods and other goods are available at The Riggin Shack general store. Hunting and fishing licenses may be purchased locally.

Coffman Cove is a family logging community, one of the largest independent camps in Southeast. Owned and operated by Mike and Leta Valentine, the camp has been in operation in this area for about 15 years. Housing is in mobile homes. Recreation includes hunting (deer and bear), good fishing in area lakes and streams, boating, hiking, and also television and VCRs. Coffman Cove's pioneer lifestyle and clean, safe environment were featured on ABC's "20/20" program in 1984, prompting a deluge of mail from around the country from people wishing to move here. While Coffman Cove does have fresh air, clean water and other advantages, residents point out the disadvantages of seasonal work, a faltering timber industry, and a lack of some conveniences taken for granted by people in larger communities.

CRAIG is on the west side of Prince of Wales Island, 31 road miles west of Hollis and 60 air miles west of Ketchikan. **Elevation: 10 feet. Transportation:** Charter floatplane from Ketchikan; by road from ferry landing at Hollis. **Population: 907.**

Visitor Facilities: Overnight accommodations at

Evidence of a recent rain lingers on the main street of Angoon. (Staff)

the Haidaway Lodge. There are restaurants and bars, two supermarkets, a general store, liquor store, gift shop, a laundromat with showers, clothing and hardware stores, gas stations, beauty salons and a bank. Fishing and hunting licenses may be purchased at the bank. There are two local fishing charter services. Marine repair available at the marina, and other major repair services available in town. Most types of fuel available. Transient moorage at the city harbor.

Craig was once a temporary fish camp for the Tlingit and Haida people of this region. In 1907, with the help of local Haidas, Craig Millar established a saltery at Fish Egg Island. Between 1908 and 1911, a permanent saltery and cold storage facility, along with about two dozen homes, were built at the city's present location and the settlement was named for its founder. Commercial fishing accounts for about half of the employment in Craig today. There is also employment in government, construction and timber.

Craig has become a service center for Prince of Wales Island, which is drawing an increasing number of visitors each year for its sportfishing and wildlife, both made more accessible by the expanding island road system. Crab Bay, within Craig city limits, is one of the major resting and feeding areas for migratory waterfowl and shorebirds in southeastern Alaska. At low tide, visitors can hike around Cemetery Island, beachcomb and explore tide pools.

DOLOMI, located in Port Johnson on the southeast side of Prince of Wales Island, 20 miles from Metlakatla, 27 miles from Ketchikan, due east of Hydaburg. **Elevation:** Sea level. **Transportation:** Charter seaplane from Metlakatla or Ketchikan; by boat. **Population:** 200.

Visitor Facilities: None. Originally a mining town established around the turn of the century, Dolomi is now a floating logging camp owned by Long Island Development, which provides a bunkhouse and cookhouse for residents. Emergency accommodations, meals and diesel fuel may be available.

EDNA BAY is located at the southeast end of Kosciusko Island off the northwest coast of Prince

Above — *Logging camp of Coffman Cove. (Rollo Pool, reprinted from* The MILEPOST®*)*

Below — *A floatplane waits in the mist at the dock at Craig. (Rollo Pool, staff)*

of Wales Island, 45 miles north of Craig, 90 miles northwest of Ketchikan. **Elevation:** Sea level. **Transportation:** By boat or floatplane. **Population:** 80.

Visitor Facilities: None. A state land sale community, Edna Bay is primarily a commercial fishing village (a fish buyer is in the bay in summer).

EIGHT FATHOM BIGHT, located in Port Frederick on Chichagof Island, is southwest of Hoonah at the western end of the bay, 60 air miles from Juneau. **Elevation:** Sea level. **Transportation:** By boat or seaplane. **Population:** 200.

Visitor Facilities: None. Eight Fathom Bight is a privately operated logging camp. This area was the setting for Louis L'Amour's novel *Sitka.* Just west of the logging camp is a short portage to Tenakee Inlet, an ancient route used by the Tlingits and later the Russians and still used today by visiting kayakers and canoeists. There is excellent fishing for king salmon and halibut in summer and early fall. Also lake and stream fishing for silver salmon and Dolly Varden in the fall.

ELFIN COVE, at the northern tip of Chichagof Island, 70 miles west of Juneau and 33 miles northwest of Hoonah. **Elevation:** 20 feet. **Transportation:** By seaplane or boat. **Population:** 28 in winter, 100 in summer.

Visitor Facilities: A seasonal community which serves as fish buying and supply center for fishermen, Elfin Cove has a hotel, the Elf Inn, which accommodates 12 persons and has a cafe. Louie's Place (rental cabin) accommodates six. Elfin General Supply has groceries and fishing gear and houses the public laundry and showers; Elfin Wet Goods sells liquor; and Radar Marine has boat electronics (sales and service) and marine hardware. Boats may be rented and gas and diesel are available at the fuel dock. Fishing and hunting licenses and charters are available locally. Transient moorage at the community dock.

This protected, flask-shaped harbor was originally called "Gunkhole" by fishermen anchoring here. Its safe anchorage and proximity to the Fairweather fishing grounds made this spot a natural for fish buyers and as a supply point for fishermen. Ernie Swanson built a store, restaurant and dock here in the late 1920s and renamed it Elfin Cove after his boat, the *Elfin.*

It is a seasonal community, active during the fishing season when local businesses serve the commercial fishing fleet. In winter, most of the residents migrate south or to Juneau. While most local people are fishermen or depend on the commercial fishing industry for a living, the area's scenery, fishing and other recreation are drawing an increasing number of tourists and three lodges offer food, lodging and sportfishing during the summer. There is year-round bottom fish and halibut fishing and clamming. There is also salmon fishing in season. Local activities include berry and mushroom picking, hiking and cross-country skiing.

Several attractions are within an hour's boat ride.

Company cannery operates here in summer, and the company store (also known as Coho Mercantile) stocks clothing and some other supplies. Hunting and fishing licenses may be purchased. Transient moorage at Excursion Inlet Dock; diesel and gas at Excursion Inlet Cannery dock.

FUNTER BAY, located 19 miles southwest of Juneau at the north end of Admiralty Island. **Elevation:** Sea level. **Transportation:** By boat or floatplane. **Population:** 10 to 20.

Visitor Facilities: Admiralty Inn wilderness lodge offers food and lodging for six guests from mid-May to September. Hunting and fishing licenses may be purchased at the lodge in summer. There are two public docks and two coves in the bay for anchoring small boats.

An important anchorage and the site of an abandoned cannery and gold mine, this area is the proposed site of a state marine park. There are some summer cabins at Funter Bay. Most of the permanent residents are commercial fishermen. Excellent area fishing for salmon and halibut. There is a three-mile trail to Bear Creek and a seven-mile trail to Mount Robert Barron; both are unmaintained.

GUSTAVUS, at the mouth of the Salmon River on the north shore of Icy Passage off Icy Strait, near the entrance to Glacier Bay, 48 miles northwest of Juneau. **Elevation:** 20 feet. **Transportation:** Year-round charter air service from Juneau; jet service in summer; private boat. **Population:** 218.

Visitor Facilities: Lodging in summer at Gustavus Inn, W.T. Fugarwe Lodge, Salmon River Cabin Rentals, Glacier Bay Country Inn and Glacier Bay Lodge. The lodges and inn serve meals and there is a cafe in town. Groceries and hardware may be purchased at the Mercantile. Fishing and hunting licenses also available. Fishing charter services are operated out of the area lodges. Diesel, propane and regular gasoline are available at Gustavus; marine fuel available at Bartlett Cove in Glacier Bay (approximately 12 miles). Automobiles, boats and charter aircraft may be rented. There is a car mechanic in Gustavus. Public moorage at state-operated dock and float.

Homesteaded in 1914, Gustavus began as a

Gustavus Inn operates one of the original homesteads at Gustavus. (Rollo Pool, staff)

small agricultural community. Today, Gustavus caters to sport fishermen and visitors to Glacier Bay National Park, who deplane here and are bused to area accommodations. The Gustavus Inn is one of the original homesteads and still maintains a large kitchen garden. There is good berry picking in the area and fishing for salmon, halibut and trout. Local residents also recommend bird watching, hiking and kayaking.

HAINES is on the upper arm of Lynn Canal, 80 air miles northwest of Juneau, 13 nautical miles southwest of Skagway and 150 road miles south of Haines Junction, Yukon Territory. **Elevation:** Sea level. **Transportation:** Scheduled air service from Juneau; scheduled ferry service; connected to the Alaska Highway by the Haines Highway. **Population:** 1,154.

Visitor Facilities: As a mainline port on the state ferry system and one of two Southeast communities connected to the Alaska Highway (the other is Skagway), Haines has complete visitor facilities.

A Presbyterian missionary named S. Hall Young established a mission at the present site of Haines in 1881. By 1884 there was a post office here and

Glacier Bay National Park is an hour's skiff ride; Port Althorp Bear Preserve is 40 minutes away by boat, and the abandoned Port Althorp cannery is a 20-minute skiff ride as is the World War II George Island Coastal Rifle Station.

EXCURSION INLET is located 38 miles northwest of Juneau, due east of Gustavus, at the mouth of Excursion Inlet off Icy Strait. **Elevation:** Sea level. **Transportation:** By boat or seaplane. **Population:** 350 in summer, 2 in winter.

Visitor Facilities: None. Excursion Inlet Packing

as placer gold mining began in the Porcupine District, about 36 miles upriver from Haines, the town became an important outlet. The Klondike gold rush of 1898 brought an influx of white gold seekers, and in 1904, the U.S. government established Fort William H. Seward, which was renamed Chilkoot Barracks in 1922 and deactivated in 1946.

Fishing was one of the initial industries in the early days, and remains as a commercial industry and as a visitor attraction. Visitors may explore the town's early history at Fort Seward or visit the Sheldon Museum with its Russian and Indian artifacts. The Southeast Alaska State Fair is held in Haines in August.

HAWK INLET is located on the northwest coast of Admiralty Island, 25 miles southwest of Juneau. **Elevation:** Sea level. **Transportation:** Charter floatplane or boat. **Population:** 4.

Visitor Facilities: None. A former salmon cannery, Hawk Inlet is now owned by a private mining venture. The only permanent residents are the caretakers. There is fishing for salmon, halibut and Dungeness crab, good deer hunting and lots of brown bears.

HOLLIS is located on the west coast of Prince of Wales Island on Twelvemile Arm, 25 road miles east of Klawock, 35 miles west of Ketchikan. **Elevation:** 20 feet. **Transportation:** By ferry from Ketchikan; by road; charter floatplane.

Visitor Facilities: None. The ferry from Ketchikan that serves Prince of Wales Island docks at Hollis. There are a boat ramp, dock and floats for moorage.

Hollis was a mining town with a population of 1,000 from about 1900 to 1915. In the 1950s, Hollis became the site of Ketchikan Pulp Company's logging camp, and served as the base for timber operations on Prince of Wales Island until 1962, when the camp was moved to Thorne Bay. Recent state land sales have spurred the growth of a small residential community here.

The state ferry Chilkat *unloads near Hollis.* (© *Walt Matell, reprinted from* The MILEPOST®)

HOONAH, located on the northeast shore of Chichagof Island, is about 40 miles west of Juneau and 20 miles south across Icy Strait from the entrance to Glacier Bay. **Elevation:** 30 feet. **Transportation:** Scheduled and charter air service from Juneau; twice weekly state ferry service in summer. **Population:** 803.

Visitor Facilities: Food and lodging at Huna Totem Lodge. Hoonah also has grocery and general stores, a bank, and laundromat with showers. Fishing and hunting licenses may be purchased here. There are two registered hunting guides and charter fishing may be arranged through the lodge. Major marine repair, gas and diesel are available. Transient moorage at the city harbor. The marina here is a popular layover for boaters awaiting permits to enter Glacier Bay.

Canneries established in the area in the early 1900s spurred the growth of commercial fishing, which remains the mainstay of Hoonah's economy. During the summer fishing season, residents work for nearby Excursion Inlet Packing Company or Thomson Fish Company in town. Halibut season begins in May and salmon season opens in midsummer and runs through September.

Subsistence remains an important lifestyle here, and many families gather food in the traditional way: catching salmon and halibut in summer, shellfish and bottom fish year-round; hunting deer, geese and ducks; and berry picking in late summer and fall.

HYDABURG, located on the southwest coast of Prince of Wales Island, 36 road miles from Hollis, 45 road miles from Craig, 50 air miles west of Ketchikan. **Elevation:** 30 feet. **Transportation:** Scheduled seaplane service from Ketchikan; by road or by boat. **Population:** 371.

Left — Historic Fort William H. Seward at Haines. (Rollo Pool, staff)

Sunlight touches a row of homes at Hoonah. (Rollo Pool, staff)

Totem poles mingle with telephone poles at Hydaburg. (Vicki Burgess, reprinted from ALASKA GEOGRAPHIC®)

Aerial view of Juneau, the state capital. (Division of Tourism)

Visitor Facilities: Fran Sanderson's boarding house provides rooms and meals. Meals are available at the Tide's Inn; groceries at the DoDrop In or Esther's Place; hardware and sundry items at Dot's Den. Hydaburg is "dry"; liquor is not sold locally. Crafts, such as Haida Indian carvings and baskets, may be purchased from residents. Marine machine shop and fuel available at harbor. Diesel and gas are available in town. Moorage at city floats.

Hydaburg was founded in 1911 and combined the populations of three Haida villages: Sukkwan, Howkan and Klinkwan. Hydaburg was incorporated in 1927, three years after its people had become citizens of the United States.

Most of the residents are commercial fishermen, although there are some jobs in construction and the timber industry. Subsistence is also a traditional and necessary part of life here. Hydaburg has an excellent collection of restored Haida totems. The totem park was developed in the 1930s by the

Civilian Conservation Corps. There is also good salmon fishing here in the fall.

JUNEAU, located on Gastineau Channel opposite Douglas Island, 91 nautical miles south of Haines. **Elevation:** Sea level. **Transportation:** Daily scheduled jet and commuter air service; state ferry service. **Population:** 23,729.

Visitor Facilities: As capital of Alaska and the largest city in Southeast, Juneau has all services.

Juneau got its start with the discovery of gold in 1880 by Joe Juneau and Dick Harris and the town boomed with the ensuing gold rush. By 1900, given Juneau's growth, it was decided to move Alaska's capital to Juneau. Transfer of government functions occurred in 1906. Today, government (federal, state and local) comprises an estimated half of the total basic industry. Dubbed "a little San Francisco," Juneau is a picturesque city overlooking Gastineau Channel and backed by the steep slope of Mount Juneau.

The city and area offer a number of attractions. There are downtown walking tours to see the government buildings and Governor's Mansion. The Alaska State Museum has excellent historical and cultural displays. Several charter boat and plane operators offer sightseeing and fishing trips, or visitors may see the countryside on foot from one of the Forest Service hiking trails in the area. There are bike paths to Douglas and to Mendenhall Glacier. Mendenhall Glacier is about 13 miles north by car from downtown Juneau. On Douglas Island, Eaglecrest ski area offers skiing in winter and chair lift rides in summer.

KAKE, located on the northwest coast of Kupreanof Island, is 40 air miles and 65 nautical miles northwest of Petersburg and 95 air miles southwest of Juneau. **Elevation:** Sea level. **Transportation:** Scheduled seaplane service from Petersburg or Juneau; state ferry from Petersburg and Sitka. **Population:** 574.

Totem stands in front of the tribal house at Kasaan on Prince of Wales Island. (Staff, reprinted from ALASKA GEOGRAPHIC®)

Visitor Facilities: Food and lodging at the Newtown Inn. Some hardware, clothing and other supplies available at three local groceries. Hunting and fishing licenses are sold locally. Laundromat available. There is a car mechanic and all types of fuel are available. Public moorage at city floats.

This is a permanent village of the Kake tribe of the Tlingit Indians. Its residents have historically drawn ample subsistence from the sea. However, with the advent of a cash economy, the community has come to depend on commercial fishing, fish processing and logging. The city's claim to fame is its totem, reputedly the world's tallest totem pole at 132 feet, 6 inches.

KASAAN, located on the east side of Prince of Wales Island, southeast of Thorne Bay. **Elevation:** Sea level. **Transportation:** Charter floatplane or boat. **Population:** 70.

Visitor Facilities: Overnight accommodations with cooking and laundry facilities are maintained by Kavilco Inc. in remodeled buildings that were originally used as bunkhouses by the salmon cannery until 1953. Diesel and gas are available. Moorage may be available at the public floats and dock.

Kasaan was founded as a copper mine site, where a sawmill and general store were established around 1900 and a salmon cannery was built in 1902. Members of the tribe of Haidas living at Old Kasaan, located south of Kasaan on Skowl Arm, relocated to New Kasaan, site of the mine and cannery. The copper mining company went bankrupt after four years, but the cannery continued to operate sporadically — with a half-dozen different owners — until 1953. The community has revitalized somewhat in recent years with the incorporation of the village under the Alaska Native Claims Settlement Act, but jobs are still scarce. As one resident puts it, "most people fish or are retired." Residents are heavily dependent on the subsistence lifestyle; fishing for salmon, halibut and bottom fish (in July, the whole village goes up to Karta Bay for subsistence fishing); hunting for deer; trapping for mink and marten; going out for black seaweed in April and May; and gathering clams (which are plentiful), some shrimp and Dungeness crab. The valuable timberland owned by Kavilco holds promise for economic improvement, and the community is hoping for a connecting road system to the rest of the island.

A 1,300-foot boardwalk leads from the harbor to a gravel footpath, which leads another half mile through the village to a totem park. Kasaan Totem Park contains a number of totems from Old Kasaan. Kasaan is only a few miles away from the Karta River, a favorite of sportsmen. Kavilco, however, does not allow camping on its land for fear of forest fires. Residents also fish in front of the village; watch for killer whales going up the bay; and watch the great numbers of eagles that soar overhead. The village community house hosts a number of community dinners.

KETCHIKAN, located on the southwest side of Revillagigedo Island on Tongass Narrows, 235 miles south of Juneau. **Elevation:** Sea level. **Transportation:** Scheduled jet service, commuter and charter flights; state ferry service. **Population:** 12,705.

Above — *Cruise ship* Sun Princess *docked at Ketchikan. (Rollo Pool, staff)*

Below — *Hiker crosses Settlers Creek near Ketchikan. (Rollo Pool, staff)*

Visitor Facilities: As Alaska's first port of call for northbound cruise ships and state ferries, and the state's fourth largest city, Ketchikan has all visitor facilities and services.

Originally a Tlingit Indian fish camp, the first salmon cannery was built here in 1897. With the discovery of gold nearby in 1898, Ketchikan became a booming little mining town. The fishing industry peaked in the 1930s, then bottomed-out in the 1940s with overfishing. As fishing reached a low point, the timber industry expanded. Today, fishing remains a major industry, a pulp mill operates at Ward Cove, and tourism is becoming increasingly important.

Ketchikan's history is highlighted in several local attractions. Creek Street is the town's infamous former red-light district. Dolly's House, a one-time brothel, is now only a museum. A local theater group presents the musical comedy *Fish Pirate's Daughter,* which portrays Ketchikan's early history and some of its spicier moments. Totem Heritage Cultural Center houses 33 totem poles and fragments retrieved from old Tlingit and Haida Indian villages. Two other collections of totems are found at Saxman Totem Park, about two miles south of town, and at Totem Bight State Park, 10 miles north of town.

Popular with visitors is the Deer Mountain Hatchery, within walking distance of downtown. One of the busiest hiking trails in Ketchikan is the Deer Mountain Trail, a three-mile climb which gives trekkers an excellent vantage of downtown Ketchikan and Tongass Narrows.

A number of tour operators in Ketchikan offer trips to Misty Fiords National Monument, located 30 miles east of town and accessible only by boat or floatplane.

KLAWOCK, on the west coast of Prince of Wales Island, is 24 road miles west of Hollis, 7 road miles north of Craig and 55 air miles west of Ketchikan. **Elevation:** Sea level. **Transportation:** Scheduled air service from Ketchikan; by boat or by road. **Population:** 532.

Visitor Facilities: Accommodations and meals at Fireweed Lodge and Prince of Wales Lodge. Rental cabins and RV spaces at Log Cabin Sports Rental. Gas, groceries, laundromat, banking and other supplies and services are available locally. Klawock is "dry"; liquor is not sold. Fishing and hunting licenses may be purchased. Fishing

Klawock boasts a fine collection of totems. (Division of Tourism)

charters available through local lodges and the sports rental outlet. Major repair services include marine engines, boats and cars. Cars and boats may be rented. All types of fuel available. Transient moorage at floats and dock.

Klawock originally was a Tlingit Indian summer fishing village; a trading post and salmon saltery were established here in 1868. Ten years later a salmon cannery was built — the first cannery in Alaska and the first of several cannery operations in the area. The local economy is still dependent on fishing and cannery operations, along with timber cutting and sawmilling. A state fish hatchery is located on Klawock Lake, very near the site of a salmon hatchery that operated from 1897 until 1917. Klawock Lake offers good canoeing and boating.

Recreation here includes good fishing for salmon and steelhead in Klawock River, salmon and halibut fishing in Big Salt Lake, and deer and bear hunting. Klawock's totem park contains 21 totems — both replicas and originals — from the abandoned Indian village of Tuxekan.

KUPREANOF is located on the northeast shore of Kupreanof Island, across from Petersburg. **Elevation:** Sea level. **Transportation:** Primarily by small boat from Petersburg. **Population:** 51.

Visitor Facilities: None. Formerly known as West Petersburg, Kupreanof incorporated as a second-class city in 1975, mostly to avoid annexation by the city of Petersburg and preserve its independent and rustic lifestyle. A small sawmill was started here in 1911 by the Knudsen brothers, and in the 1920s the Yukon Fur Farm began raising foxes, then mink; both the mill and fur farm operated into the 1960s. Today, Kupreanof has no industrial base or commercial activities. Most residents are self-employed or work outside the community. Subsistence activities also contribute to each household.

Boardwalks and trails connect most of Kupreanof, and residents also use skiffs to travel around the community. Kupreanof is adjacent to the Petersburg Creek-Duncan Salt Chuck Wilderness Area.

METLAKATLA, located on the west coast of

Commercial fishing provides a livelihood for Metlakatla residents. (Rollo Pool, staff)

Annette Island, 15 miles south of Ketchikan. **Elevation:** 110 feet. **Transportation:** Charter seaplane service; state ferry from Ketchikan. **Population:** 1,300.

Visitor Facilities: Permit required from the community's tourism department for long-term visits. Food and lodging at the Taquan Inn. Supplies and fuel available from local stores. Transient moorage at boat harbor; marine gas at fuel dock, marine repairs at cannery in season.

Metlakatla was founded in 1887 by William Duncan, a Scottish-born lay minister, who moved here with several hundred Tsimshian Indians from a settlement in British Columbia after a falling out with church authorities. The new settlement in Alaska, which Congress granted reservation status and title to the entire island in 1891, prospered under Duncan, who built a salmon cannery and sawmill. Today, fishing and lumber continue to be the main economic base of Metlakatla. The community and island also retain the status of a federal Indian reservation, which is why Metlakatla has the only fish wheels to trap salmon in Alaska.

(Floating fish traps were outlawed by the state 25 years ago.)

This well-planned community has a town hall, a recreation center with an Olympic-size swimming pool, a bank and post office. The Metlakatla Indian Community is the largest employer in town, with retail and service trades the second largest. Many residents also are commercial fishermen. Subsistence remains an important resource to residents, who harvest seaweed, salmon, halibut, cod, clams and waterfowl.

Attractions include the Duncan Museum, the original cottage occupied by Father William Duncan until his death in 1918. A replica of the turn-of-the-century William Duncan Memorial Church, built after the original was destroyed by fire in 1948, is also open to the public.

MEYERS CHUCK is located on the northwest tip of Cleveland Peninsula, 40 miles northwest of Ketchikan. **Elevation:** Sea level. **Transportation:** Floatplane or private boat. **Population:** 52.

Visitor Facilities: None. Visitors may arrange for food and lodging in private homes. The only retail store, the "Muskeg Market," carries some general merchandise and liquor and has gas pumps dockside. Marine gas, diesel and regular gasoline are available. Fishing and hunting licenses may be purchased at the market. Open moorage at the community dock.

The early history of Meyers Chuck is a bit hazy, although records suggest that white settlers began living here in the late 1800s, and the community was probably named after one of these early residents. (The name, too, is a bit hazy: there has been some argument whether it was Meyer, Myer, Myers or Meyers. Longtime resident Leo C. "Lone Wolf" Smith favored Myers Chuck. "Chuck" is a Chinook jargon word, usually applied to a salt water body that fills at high tide.) The natural harbor and the large Union Bay cannery nearby — which operated from 1916 to 1945 — attracted fishermen to the townsite in the 1920s and postal service began in 1922. Today, most residents make their living fishing and supplement their income by working outside the community or depend on subsistence. There is good fishing for salmon, crab, clams, red snapper and halibut. There is deer and duck hunting and also trapping. Several retired people also make their homes here. There is not much here in the way of traditional tourist attractions. The chief attractions, according to Robert Meyer, are "the lovely sunsets and scenery."

PELICAN, on the northwest coast of Chichagof Island, is 70 miles west of Juneau and 80 miles north of Sitka. **Elevation:** Sea level. **Transportation:** Scheduled seaplane service from Juneau; charter floatplane service; state ferry service in summer. **Population:** 206.

Visitor Facilities: There are two bar-and-grills. (Rose's Plaza, one of the two, has four rooms to rent.) The Corbins, who run fishing trips on their ketch, the *Demijohn,* have a fishing lodge rental cabin near Pelican. Pelican Cold Storage Company store sells groceries and other supplies and fishing licenses. Marine engine repair is available. Fishing guide services available locally. Transient moorage at the city harbor.

Established in 1938 by Kalle (Charley) Raataikainen, and named for Raataikainen's fish

A waterfront view of the small community of Meyers Chuck. (R.S. Meyer)

packer, *The Pelican,* Pelican relies on commercial fishing and seafood processing. The cold storage plant processes salmon, halibut, crab, herring and black cod, and is the primary year-round employer. Pelican has dubbed itself "closest to the fish," a reference to its close proximity to the rich Fairweather salmon grounds. Nonresident fishermen swell the population during the salmon trolling season, from about June to mid-September, and the king salmon winter season, from October through April.

Local recreation includes kayaking, hiking, fishing, and watching birds and marine mammals. According to a local wag, special events here include the arrival and departure of the state ferry, the tide change, sunny days and a woman in a dress.

PETERSBURG, on the northwest tip of Mitkof Island at the northern end of Wrangell Narrows, lies midway between Juneau and Ketchikan. **Elevation:** Sea level. **Transportation:** Daily scheduled jet service; commuter and charter air service; scheduled state ferry service. **Population:** 3,137.

Visitor Facilities: Complete services and facilities available.

Named for Peter Buschmann, who selected the present townsite for a salmon cannery and sawmill in 1897, Petersburg continues to rely on the fishing and logging industries. Unlike many other Southeast communities, Petersburg has grown steadily harvesting and processing salmon, halibut, shrimp, black cod, roe herring and crab. It is home port to the largest commercial fishing fleet in Southeast.

Often referred to as Alaska's "Little Norway," this picturesque city overlooks Wrangell Narrows, the 23-mile-long channel separating Mitkof and Kupreanof islands. In-city attractions include the Sons of Norway Hall, built in 1912, and Clausen

Top *— Town of Pelican viewed from a nearby mountaintop. (Gail Corbin)*

Left *— Petersburg is often called Alaska's "Little Norway." (Rollo Pool, staff)*

29

Memorial Museum. Three roads lead out of town to fishing spots, campgrounds, hiking trails and salmon and waterfowl viewing areas. The big event of the year is the Little Norway Festival, held on the weekend closest to Norwegian Independence Day (May 17), when residents celebrate the community's heritage with costumes, dancing, contests and a big fish bake.

POINT BAKER, at the northwest tip of Prince of Wales Island, is 50 miles west of Wrangell. **Elevation:** Sea level. **Transportation:** Private boat or charter floatplane. **Population:** 93.

Visitor Facilities: Limited. The Point Baker Trading Post has a bar, restaurant and laundry, and carries groceries, liquor, ice, gas and diesel. Hunting and fishing licenses and rental boats are also available at the trading post. Transient moorage at state floats.

Port Alexander on Baranof Island. (Tom Paul, reprinted from ALASKA GEOGRAPHIC®)

Traditional clothing is worn during Petersburg's Little Norway Festival. (Rollo Pool, staff)

Point Baker was named by Captain George Vancouver in 1793 for the second lieutenant on his ship *Discovery.* Fish buyers operated here from about 1919 through the 1930s. The Forest Service opened the area for homesites. Most of Point Baker's year-round residents are fishermen, and the population increases in summer with visiting fishermen. Halibut and salmon fishing are excellent in the area and residents also hunt for deer. Humpback whales pass by Point Baker and the birdlife here includes eagles and blue herons.

PORT ALEXANDER, on the south end of Baranof Island, is 65 miles south of Sitka and 90 miles west of Wrangell. **Elevation:** 20 feet. **Transportation:** Private boat or charter floatplane. **Population:** 162.

Visitor Facilities: Bed-and-breakfast lodging. Port Alexander Cold Storage has limited groceries, gas and diesel, and fishing and hunting licenses. Public moorage at state floats.

Port Alexander evolved into a year-round fishing community in the 1920s, settled by fishermen trolling the Chatham Strait fishing grounds. The community prospered until the late 1930s, when the decline in salmon and herring stocks and the outbreak of World War II knocked the bottom out of fish buying, packing and processing at Port Alexander. Today, the majority of residents are commercial fishermen and choose to live here for the independent and subsistence lifestyle the area offers.

PORT PROTECTION is located at the northwest tip of Prince of Wales Island near Point Baker, 50 miles west of Wrangell and southwest of Petersburg. **Elevation:** Sea level. **Transportation:** Private boat or charter floatplane. **Population:** 55.

Visitor Facilities: Food and lodging at Wooden Wheel Cove Trading Post, which also carries groceries, some clothing and other supplies, along with gas and diesel. Limited boat repair and boat rentals are available. Fishing and hunting licenses are sold here. Guide services may be arranged through the trading post or inquire locally. Transient moorage at public float.

Left — *Winter at Port Protection. (Joe Upton, reprinted from* ALASKA GEOGRAPHIC®)

Below — *View from Harbor Mountain of Sitka and Sitka Sound. (Rollo Pool, staff)*

Like its neighbor, Point Baker, Port Protection was used as a fish buying station and later settled by fishermen who had long used the cove for shelter from southeast storms. Credit for its "discovery" is given to a man named Johnson, who came ashore in the early 1900s to replace a wooden wheel lost off his boat and gave the spot its first name — Wooden Wheel Cove. In the late 1940s, Laurel "Buckshot" Woolery established a trading post and fish buying station. Much of the land is still leased from the Forest Service, although there are some privately owned parcels. The residents are either fishermen or retirees. Each household has at least one small boat, in addition to fishing vessels, to travel between homes in Port Protection and to Point Baker to pick up mail.

Excellent fishing in the immediate area in summer for salmon, halibut and rockfish. Boaters, kayakers and canoeists can make Port Protection their starting point for circumnavigating Prince of Wales Island. The community's two big local events are Fourth of July and the end of fishing season barbecue.

SITKA is on the west side of Baranof Island, 95 miles southwest of Juneau. **Elevation:** Sea level.

Above — *Fishermen on Starrigavan Bay near Sitka. (Rollo Pool, staff)*

Below — *View of historic downtown Skagway. (Chlaus Lotscher)*

Transportation: Scheduled jet service, commuter and charter flights; state ferry service. **Population:** 7,611.

Visitor Facilities: All services available. Overnight accommodations at the Shee Atika Lodge, Sheffield Sitka and two bed-and-breakfasts.

The site was originally occupied by Tlingit Indians. Alexander Baranof established a fort here in 1799, and by 1806 Sitka was the capital of Russian Alaska. Salmon was the mainstay of the economy from the late 1800s until the 1950s, when their numbers decreased. A pulp mill was established at nearby Silver Bay in 1960. Today, tourism, along with the mill, commercial fishing, cold storage plants and government provide most jobs.

Sitka's Russian and Tlingit past is the major attraction for visitors. Replicas of the old Russian Blockhouse and St. Michael's Cathedral, and the original Russian Bishop's House (built in 1842), are open to the public. The Castle Hill historic site is where Alaska changed hands from Russia to the United States in 1867. Sitka National Historical Park encompasses the Russian Bishop's House and the site of the Tlingit fort burned by the Russians in 1804. The park also has a totem pole collection and museum. Museums in town include the Sheldon Jackson Museum at Sheldon Jackson College and the Isabell Miller Museum in the Centennial Building.

Special events include the annual Sitka Summer Music Festival and the All-Alaska Logging Championships. The music festival, held for three weeks in June, features an international group of professional musicians. The All-Alaska Logging Championships, held the last weekend in June, draws loggers from around Alaska and the Pacific Northwest to compete in contests of logging skills.

Sitka's road system provides access to area hiking trails, campgrounds and fishing spots.

SKAGWAY, at the north end of Taiya Inlet on Lynn Canal, 90 air miles northwest of Juneau, 13 nautical miles from Haines, 100 road miles from the Alaska Highway. **Elevation:** Sea level. **Transportation:** Daily scheduled flights from Juneau and Haines via local commuter services; charter air service; scheduled state ferry service; connected to the Alaska Highway by Klondike Highway 2. **Population:** 761.

Visitor Facilities: As a mainline port on the state ferry system and one of two Southeast communities connected to the Alaska Highway (the other is Haines), Skagway has complete visitor facilities.

The oldest incorporated city in Alaska (incorporated June 6, 1900), Skagway owes its birth to the Klondike gold rush. Thousands of gold seekers arrived to follow the White Pass and Chilkoot trails to the Yukon goldfields. After the gold rush, Skagway continued both as a port and as terminus of the White Pass & Yukon Route railway, which operated between Skagway and Whitehorse, Yukon Territory, from 1900 until 1982.

A six-block area of downtown Skagway is included in Klondike Gold Rush National Historical Park. Park Service rangers lead daily guided walks of downtown in summer, and film and slide shows are offered at the visitor center. The Trail of '98 Museum, owned and operated by the citizens of Skagway, has an interesting collection of gold rush memorabilia. Also included in the historical park is the 33-mile-long Chilkoot Trail, the old gold rush route over the mountains to Lake Bennett, where early gold seekers built boats to take them down the Yukon River to the Klondike. The Chilkoot Trail attracts more than two thousand hardy souls each summer.

TENAKEE SPRINGS is located on the north shore of Tenakee Inlet on the east side of Chichagof Island, 50 miles northeast of Sitka. **Elevation:** Sea level. **Transportation:** Scheduled and charter seaplane service; state ferry service. **Population:** 156.

Visitor Facilities: Overnight accommodations at Tenakee Tavern's Hotel. Food and lodging at Snyder Mercantile Company, which also carries groceries and other supplies. Fishing and hunting

licenses sold locally. Laundry facilities and fuel (marine gas, diesel, propane) are available. Boat mechanic in town. Public moorage at the state floats.

Tenakee's natural hot springs first drew early prospectors and miners, and by 1895 the springs were enlarged to accommodate the increasing number of visitors. Ed Snyder built a general store here in 1899 and a post office was established in 1903. A cannery operated sporadically at Tenakee from 1916 to the 1960s. Some residents still make their living fishing commercially, although most year-round residents are retirees. The community also sees an influx of summer visitors: tourists, commercial fishermen and pleasure boaters, and Juneau and Sitka residents who have summer homes here.

Tenakee's major attractions are its quiet isolation and its hot springs. There is only one street — Tenakee Avenue — which is about two miles long, and two vehicles. Residents walk or use three-wheel motorbikes or bicycles. The bathhouse is located on the waterfront. There is a Forest Service trail that leads east 7.8 miles from Tenakee along the shoreline of Tenakee Inlet to Coffee Cove. The area also offers beachcombing and hunting and fishing.

THORNE BAY, on the east coast of Prince of Wales Island, 47 air miles northwest of Ketchikan, 42 road miles east of Craig. **Elevation:** Sea level. **Transportation:** Scheduled seaplane service from Ketchikan; 60 road miles from Hollis; private boat. **Population:** 392.

Visitor Facilities: There is a bed-and-breakfast

Tenakee Springs. (Rollo Pool, staff)

Logs float in salt water at Thorne Bay. (Rollo Pool, staff)

and a snack bar. Stores and services include a laundromat; auto and boat repair; grocery, liquor, clothing, sporting goods, gift and hardware stores; and fuel supply outlets (marine gas, diesel, propane, unleaded and regular gasoline available). Fishing and hunting licenses available from the Tackle Shack. Several outfitters offering fishing trips operate out of Thorne Bay. Boats may be rented. Limited boat moorage available.

Thorne Bay was incorporated in 1982, making it one of Alaska's newest cities. The settlement began as a logging camp in 1962, when Ketchikan Pulp Company (now Louisiana Pacific) moved its operations from Hollis to Thorne Bay. Camp residents created the community — and gained city status from the state — as private ownership of the land was made possible under the Alaska Statehood Act. Employment here depends mainly on the lumber company and the U.S. Forest Service. The area has good access to hunting and saltwater and freshwater sportfishing.

TOKEEN, on the west coast of El Capitan Island off Sea Otter Sound, 60 miles southwest of Wrangell, 30 miles northwest of Craig, 80 miles northwest of Ketchikan. **Transportation:** Charter seaplane service or private boat. **Population:** 3.

Visitor Facilities: A store here carries some groceries, liquor and other supplies. Limited emergency fuel available includes marine gas, diesel and regular gasoline. Public moorage at float.

Tokeen once had a mink farm and a cold storage plant. It is now privately owned and operated as a store and commercial fishermen's stop. The settlement likely was established by the former residents of Old Tokeen in the late 1930s or early 1940s.

Old Tokeen, located on the northwest end of Marble Island seven miles to the northwest, once had Alaska's largest marble quarry. Nearly $2 million worth of marble was taken out between 1905 and 1932. Tokeen marble was used in the Federal Building in Fairbanks, the Capitol Building in Juneau and the Washington State Capitol in Olympia, Washington. Little remains of the mining operation except piles of waste marble.

WHALE PASS, on the northeast coast of Prince of Wales Island, 64 road miles north of Klawock. **Elevation:** Sea level. **Transportation:** By road, floatplane or private boat. **Population:** 93.

Visitor Facilities: There is a small grocery store and a gas pump.

Whale Pass was the site of a floating logging camp. The camp moved out in the early 1980s, but new residents moved in after a state land sale. The community was connected to the Prince of Wales Island road system in 1985.

WRANGELL, located at the northwest tip of Wrangell Island on Zimovia Strait, 32 miles southeast of Petersburg, 85 miles north of Ketchikan. **Elevation:** Sea level. **Transportation:** Daily scheduled jet service and commuter air service; air charter services; state ferry service. **Population:** 2,376.

Visitor Facilities: There are two motels and all other services are available.

Wrangell is the only Alaskan city to have existed under four nations and three flags — the Stikine Tlingits, the Russians, British and Americans. The Russians built a stockade here in 1834, which became a fort under the British in 1840, then a U.S. military post in 1868. The Stikine River fur trade and later gold brought settlement to Wrangell. Today, the economy is based on logging, fishing, government jobs and tourism.

Wrangell's history is featured at three local museums: the private Our Collections Museum; Chief Shakes Island, in Wrangell Harbor, with its

Children at former Whale Pass floating logging camp wore life jackets at all times. (Walt Matell, reprinted from ALASKA GEOGRAPHIC®)

Boaters take a break at a waterfall in Paradise Cove near Wrangell. (Rollo Pool, staff)

This petroglyph is one of many on beaches around Wrangell. (U.S. Forest Service)

Surf rolls in on the beach near Yakutat. (Rollo Pool, staff)

totem poles and replica tribal house; and Wrangell Museum, housed in the oldest building in Wrangell. Petroglyphs may be seen at Wrangell Museum and from the beach near the ferry terminal, reached by a boardwalk trail.

Many Wrangell area attractions and recreational activities are accessible by boat or plane. The Stikine River Delta north of Wrangell, accessible by boat, is a prime habitat for waterfowl, eagles, moose and bear. Garnet Ledge is 7.5 miles from Wrangell Harbor and may be reached at high tide by small boat. A permit is required to dig garnets at the ledge. Permits available through the Wrangell Museum.

Celebrations and events in Wrangell include the salmon derby, held mid-May to early June; a big Fourth of July celebration; and the Tent City Festival, commemorating Wrangell's gold rush days, which takes place the first weekend in February.

YAKUTAT is located on the Gulf of Alaska coast, 225 miles northwest of Juneau, 220 miles southeast of Cordova. **Elevation:** Sea level. **Transportation:** Daily scheduled jet service; air charter; private boat. **Population:** 453.

Visitor Facilities: Food and lodging at Glacier Bear Lodge and Yakutat Airport Lodge. There are also a cafe, bar and bank. All supplies are available at Yakutat Hardware, Mallott's General Store, Monti Bay Foods and other local businesses. Fishing and hunting licenses may be purchased locally. Fishing guide services are available through local lodges and there are five registered hunting guides. Rental cars and charter aircraft available. Marine gas, diesel, unleaded and regular gasoline are sold locally. Transient moorage at city harbor.

Yakutat Bay is one of the few refuges for vessels along this long, stormy stretch of coast in the Gulf of Alaska. Sea otter pelts brought Russians to the area in the 19th century. Fur traders were followed by gold seekers, who came to work the black sand beaches. Commercial salmon fishing developed in this century and the first cannery was built here in 1904. Today's economy is based primarily on fishing and fish processing.

The Yakutat City School District's information sheet for teacher applicants describes Yakutat's primary attraction as outdoor recreation. "If you enjoy the outdoors, there is plenty for you to do, including cross-country skiing, snowmobiling, hunting, fishing, hiking, biking and berry picking in the late summer and early fall." Cannon Beach has good beachcombing and a picnic area. Hunting and fishing in particular draw visitors. Steelhead fishing is considered among the finest anywhere, and king and silver salmon run in abundance in Yakutat area salt water, rivers and streams May through September. The Situk River, 12 miles south of Yakutat by road, is one of Alaska's top fishing spots.

Some lower 48 travelers flying to Anchorage pick a flight with a Yakutat stop, hoping for a clear day and a clear view from the air of Malaspina Glacier northwest of town.

Attractions

Alaska Chilkat Bald Eagle Preserve

Three bald eagles survey their surroundings from an old cottonwood tree in 48,000-acre Alaska Chilkat Bald Eagle Preserve, created in 1982 to protect the largest known congregation of bald eagles in North America. Up to 3,500 of the big birds come from throughout southeastern Alaska and western Canada to a five-mile stretch of the Chilkat River near Haines from October through January to feed on spawned out chum salmon. (Third Eye Photography, reprinted from ALASKA GEOGRAPHIC®)

Glacier Bay National Park and Preserve

The 3.3-million-acre Glacier Bay National Park and Preserve is located 50 air miles west of Juneau near the northern end of the Alaska Panhandle. It is bordered by Icy Strait and Cross Sound on the south, the Pacific Ocean on the west and Canada on the north. Here are located some of the world's most impressive tidewater glaciers. Other major attractions are the bay itself, whales and other wildlife, the massive Fairweather Range and the vast, unspoiled outer coast.

In Glacier Bay the dynamics of the Pleistocene epoch, which lasted more than a million years, have been condensed into a 7,000-year-long "little ice age," during which there were four glacier advances. The last retreat from the maximum advance took place in 230 years — the fastest recorded retreat anywhere on earth.

When Captain George Vancouver sailed through Icy Strait in 1794, he charted Glacier Bay, at that time only a slight indentation in a 4,000-foot-thick wall of ice that was the terminus of a massive glacier flowing a hundred miles down from the Saint Elias Range. Almost 100 years later when naturalist John Muir built a cabin at Muir Point the terminus of Muir Glacier was just to the north, 35 miles from where Vancouver had seen it. Now the terminus has retreated more than 25 additional miles, leaving a broad bay and a long, narrow inlet.

Glacier Bay is an invaluable outdoor laboratory for scientists seeking to understand the dynamics of glaciers. In one day visitors can travel by boat from the "little ice age" across two centuries of plant succession, seeing how ice-scoured land recovers by stages to support a mature coastal forest.

The park encompasses 16 active tidewater glaciers, including several on the remote, seldom-visited western edge of the park along the Gulf of Alaska and Lituya Bay. Icebergs calved off these glaciers float in the waters of the bay.

Wildlife abounds here. A boat trip into the many fjords offers sightings of humpback whales, killer whales cutting the water with their tall dorsal fins, or hair seals poking their heads up to stare at passing boats. During late spring hundreds of seals haul out on floating ice to give birth to their pups.

Along gravel beaches, brown and black bears and an occasional rare glacier bear (the bluish color phase of the black bear) forage for food. On high rocky ledges mountain goats are often sighted. In the rain forest roam moose, Sitka black-tailed deer, lynx, marten and mink.

More than 225 bird species have been reported in the park. Among the most common are black oystercatchers, cormorants, guillemots, puffins, gulls and terns. Fishing for silver and king salmon, Dolly Varden, cutthroat trout and halibut is excellent in the bay.

Glacier Bay offers many opportunities for exploration by kayak or canoe, as well as motorboats. Portions of the park offer excellent cross-country hiking and backpacking. Many peaks over 10,000 feet high challenge the experienced mountaineer. There are few established trails, but camping and hiking are permitted throughout the park. A campground with 25 sites is located near the lodge and park headquarters at Bartlett Cove.

No roads lead to Glacier Bay. Access is by scheduled or charter air service to the small community of Gustavus, cruise ships and charter boats, private boats and tours via kayak.

Humpback whales cruise Glacier Bay. (C.W. Mason, reprinted from ALASKA® magazine)

Klondike Gold Rush National Historical Park

Right — *Arctic Brotherhood Hall, one of the most photographed buildings in Alaska, has an intricate driftwood facade. The hall, along with other gold rush-era buildings, sits within an eight-block historical district (encompassing most of downtown Skagway) which is part of Klondike Gold Rush National Historical Park. The historical park, established in 1975 by the United States and Canada to commemorate the Klondike gold rush of 1897-98, also includes the Chilkoot and White Pass trails. (Staff)*

Below — *Hikers pause above Deep Lake on the 33-mile-long Chilkoot Trail. Each year, more than 2,000 visitors hike the historic trail, which was the principal route to the Klondike goldfields during the gold rush of 1897-98. (Rob Lesser, reprinted from* The MILEPOST® *)*

Marine Parks

Five of the 12 marine parks established by the state of Alaska as part of an international system of shoreline parks and recreation areas are located in Southeast. This marine park system stretches from near Olympia, Washington, up through British Columbia, Canada, and as far north as Prince William Sound. Most of the Alaska parks have no developed facilities, but they offer sheltered anchorages in scenic locations as well as outdoor recreation opportunities. The Southeast parks are the following:

Chilkat Islands — Located 13 miles south of Haines by boat, directly off the tip of the Chilkat Peninsula.

Sullivan Island — Located on a three-mile-long peninsula at the southern tip of this island in Lynn Canal, approximately 19 miles south of Haines and six miles south of the Chilkat Islands.

St. James Bay — Located on the west side of Lynn Canal 12 miles northwest of Tee Harbor, which is north of Juneau, and approximately 42 miles south of Haines.

Shelter Island — Located six miles west of Tee Harbor and approximately 20 miles northwest of downtown Juneau. The park straddles the north central portion of the island and includes Hand Troller Cove (also called Shelter Cove) on the western side of the island and Halibut Cove on the eastern side.

Oliver Inlet — Located 12 miles south of Juneau on Admiralty Island between Seymour Canal and Stephens Passage. There's a portage route between the inlet and Seymour Canal, as well as a State Parks Division recreation cabin, a five-mile tramway and a registration/information station for Admiralty Island National Monument.

Tongass National Forest

The Tongass National Forest is the largest national forest in the United States, encompassing 16.8 million acres, or more than 73 percent of all the land in southeastern Alaska. The national forest, named for a clan of Tlingit Indians who lived at its southern end, was created in 1907 by President Theodore Roosevelt to protect timber resources, wildlife and fisheries.

Of the total acreage, 5.3 million acres are wilderness lands set aside as Admiralty Island National Monument near Juneau and Misty Fiords National Monument near Ketchikan, as well as 12 wilderness areas: Russell Fiord Wilderness near Yakutat, Endicott River Wilderness near Haines, West Chichagof-Yakobi and South Baranof wildernesses near Sitka, Tracy Arm-Fords Terror Wilderness near Juneau, Petersburg Creek-Duncan Salt Chuck and Tebenkof Bay wildernesses near Petersburg, Stikine-LeConte Wilderness near Wrangell, South Prince of Wales Wilderness on Prince of Wales Island, and the Coronation Island, Warren Island and Maurelle Islands wildernesses off the northwest coast of Prince of Wales Island.

The West Chichagof-Yakobi Wilderness offers a 65-mile-long stretch of rugged Pacific coastline, with exposed offshore islands and rocky highlands protecting quiet bays, inlets and lagoons. The area is wonderful for boaters and kayakers, who may explore the picturesque ruins of early day mining camps.

Tracy Arm-Fords Terror Wilderness features Tracy and Endicott arms, deep, narrow and iceberg-dotted fjords that extend more than 30 miles into the heavily glaciated Coast Mountain Range. Fords Terror, off of Endicott Arm, has sheer rock walls enclosing a narrow entrance into a small fjord, named for a crew member of a naval vessel who rowed in at slack tide in 1889 and was caught in turbulent, iceberg-laden currents for six "terrifying" hours when the tide changed.

The powerful Stikine River dominates the Stikine-LeConte Wilderness. The river valley is narrow, surrounded by steep, rugged peaks, many of them glaciated. Its delta is 17 miles wide, formed from numerous slow-moving, silt-laden channels. The lower Stikine has the second largest gathering of bald eagles in southeastern Alaska each April when the birds gather to feast on smelt runs. Another attraction is LeConte Glacier — southernmost glacier in North America to empty directly into salt water.

The Tongass National Forest lies west of the U.S.-Canada border, stretching from Ketchikan north to Cross Sound and up the eastern side of Lynn Canal. Excluded from the national forest are Glacier Bay National Park and the general area around Haines and Skagway. Another section of Tongass National Forest surrounds Yakutat. Like all national forests, Tongass is managed as a working forest, with logging and mining activities taking place along with recreational pursuits and fishery management.

To the south, the forests are primarily western hemlock and Sitka spruce, with scattered red cedar and Alaska yellow cedar. Farther north, the percentage of hemlock increases and mountain hemlock becomes more abundant. Red cedar extends only to the northern shore of Frederick Sound and Alaska yellow cedar often is found only as a small tree in swamps or muskeg. Other

Admiralty Island National Monument

Located about 15 miles west of Juneau, Admiralty Island National Monument encompasses 937,396 acres, or 90 percent of Admiralty Island. The island is bounded on the east and north by Stephens Passage, on the west by Chatham Strait and on the south by Frederick Sound.

The predominantly Tlingit Indian village of Angoon lies at the mouth of Mitchell Bay on the west side of Admiralty Island, adjacent to the wilderness. Excluded from the monument are mining interests at the north end of the island and east of Angoon.

Admiralty has many giant brown bears — the reason the Indians referred to the island as "The Fortress of Bears." Outstanding areas include Seymour Canal, which supports one of the largest concentrations of bald eagles in southeastern Alaska, scenic Mitchell Bay and the Admiralty Lakes Recreational Area. A 25-mile trail system links the eight major lakes on the island as part of the Cross-Admiralty Canoe Trail, a series of lakes, streams and portages across the island from Mole Harbor on the east to Mitchell Bay on the west.

Tideflats on the west coast of Admiralty Island shine in the sunlight. (George Wuerthner)

Trees form an interesting pattern on a nearly vertical slope in Misty Fiords National Monument. (R. Romei, U.S. Forest Service)

Misty Fiords National Monument

Misty Fiords National Monument is located at the southern end of the national forest, extending northward from Dixon Entrance to beyond the Unuk River. It abuts Canada on the east and south. Misty Fiords encompasses 2.3 million acres (of which only 142,757 acres is nonwilderness), making it the largest wilderness in Alaska's national forests and the second largest in the nation. In the nonwilderness portion at Quartz Hill, U.S. Borax and Chemical Corp. is mining a deposit of molybdenum estimated to be one of the largest in the world.

Taking its name from the almost constant precipitation characteristic of the area, Misty Fiords is covered with thick forests on nearly vertical slopes. Dramatic waterfalls plunge into the salt water through narrow clefts or course over great rounded granite shoulders, fed by lakes and streams which absorb the annual rainfall of more than 14 feet. The major waterway cutting through the monument, Behm Canal, is more than 100 miles long and extraordinary among natural canals for its length and depth.

This monument offers magnificent scenery. Inlets, bays, arms and coves — some long and narrow, some short and broad — are variations on the fjords for which the area is named. The highlands are dotted with thousands of lakes, large and small, and innumerable streams. The Walker Cove-Rudyerd Bay Scenic Area, with its vertical granite cliffs topped by snowy peaks, has been protected for many years and is now part of the monument.

common species are red alder, black cottonwood and lodgepole pine.

Beneath the towering conifers grow young evergreens and shrubs such as devil's club, blueberry and huckleberry. Moss and ferns cover the ground, and lichens drape many trees. The dense forest is broken by muskeg bogs, glacial outwash plains and marshlands in river valleys and deltas. Wildflowers splash color against a variated green background.

Camping is permitted anywhere in the national forest except day-use areas or where a sign specifically prohibits it. No permits or fees are required for wilderness camping; fees are charged for some of the developed campgrounds. The Forest Service maintains some 150 public recreation cabins in Southeast which are available for a nominal fee by advance reservation. Many hiking trails also are maintained throughout the national forest.

Alaska Maritime National Wildlife Refuge

Black oystercatcher (below left) is one of 21 species of birds that breed on St. Lazaria Island, part of the Alaska Maritime National Wildlife Refuge and one of the largest seabird colonies in Southeast. The 65-acre island (below right) is located at the entrance to Sitka Sound, approximately 15 miles southwest of Sitka. Millions of birds breed here, including tufted puffins, rhinoceros auklets and ancient murrelets. The island is believed to have the world's largest concentration of storm petrels — nearly half a million. Since seabirds are sensitive to disturbance, the Fish and Wildlife Service requires permits to land on the island. Forrester Island and the Hazy Islands are included in the Alaska Maritime National Wildlife Refuge.

(Photo left: Matt Donohoe, reprinted from ALASKA GEOGRAPHIC®; photo right: Staff)

Mendenhall Wetlands State Game Refuge

The 3,600-acre Mendenhall Wetlands State Game Refuge, located along the coastline north of Juneau, provides excellent opportunities for viewing migrating birds, including geese, ducks, swans and shorebirds. This is one of the few areas in the state where visitors may see redheads, ring-necked ducks, and blue-winged and cinnamon teal. The refuge encompasses estuaries created by numerous streams which flow into Gastineau Channel. During the year the wetlands host more than 140 species of birds, nearly a dozen species of mammals, eight fish species and other marine life.

Spring bird migrations peak in April and May; by June most of the waterfowl and shorebirds have moved on to breeding grounds farther north. Relatively few species of birds nest on the Mendenhall Refuge, but it remains important through the summer as a feeding station. After the breeding season, birds traveling south to wintering grounds stop at the refuge. Shorebirds arrive in late July, waterfowl begin arriving in late August and September. Species of waterfowl and shorebirds include mallards, pintails, green-winged teal, northern shovelers, American wigeons, and several species of sandpipers.

The most visible waterfowl on the refuge are the Vancouver Canada geese, 400 to 600 of which form a resident population that over-winters on open water near the mouth of the Mendenhall River and some creeks. Other geese found on the refuge include cackling Canada geese, lesser Canada geese, white-fronted geese and snow geese.

Mammals that may be seen include harbor seals, Sitka black-tailed deer, black bears, muskrats, land otters, mink, short-tailed weasels, snowshoe hares, porcupines, little brown bats and long-tailed voles.

Recreational activities include hiking, wildlife viewing and photography, boating, fishing, sightseeing and waterfowl hunting in season. The refuge is accessible from several points on the Juneau and Douglas Island road systems.

Southeast's Rivers

Southeastern Alaska is not known for its rivers, but there are a few which offer recreationists excellent float trips by raft or white-water kayak adventures. They are:

Alsek-Tatshenshini rivers — These two spectacular rivers join together in Canada and flow (as the Alsek) to the Gulf of Alaska at Dry Bay, about 50 miles east of Yakutat and 110 miles northwest of Gustavus. The river flows in part through Glacier Bay National Park.

Chickamin-LeDuc-South Fork rivers — This river system, which offers excellent scenery, is located 45 miles northeast of Ketchikan within Misty Fiords National Monument. The Chickamin River heads at Chickamin Glacier and flows southwest 40 miles to Behm Canal. The LeDuc heads at a glacier in British Columbia and flows southwest 30 miles to the Chickamin. The South Fork Chickamin River heads at a glacier and flows west 18 miles to the Chickamin.

Chilkat-Klehini-Tsirku rivers — The 42-mile-long Klehini and the 25-mile-long Tsirku are tributaries to the Chilkat River, which enters salt water near Haines. These are swift rivers, but have no white water. The Chilkat and Tsirku rivers flow through the Chilkat Bald Eagle Preserve.

Stikine River — The Stikine, a national wild and scenic river, has headwaters inside British Columbia and flows 400 miles — through two provincial parks and the Coast Range — to salt water near Wrangell. The lower 130 miles from Telegraph Creek, British Columbia, to Alaska tidewater and the upper portions of the Stikine are used by many canoeists, kayakers and rafters. A 60-mile section above Telegraph Creek flows through the Grand Canyon of the Stikine and is considered unnavigable and dangerous.

Taku River — This silty river heads in Canada and flows southwest 54 miles into Taku Inlet, 20 miles northeast of Juneau.

Unuk River — This river heads in Canada on the east side of Mount Stoeckl and flows southwest 28 miles to the head of Burroughs Bay, 50 miles northeast of Ketchikan. It is located within Misty Fiords National Monument.

Kayakers paddle across the mirror-smooth surface of Weird Bay. (Division of Tourism)

Rafters tackle challenging Tsirku River. (Bart Henderson, reprinted from ALASKA GEOGRAPHIC®)

Sea Kayaking

Southeastern Alaska's sheltered waterways and open coast draw sea kayakers from all over the world. Kayakers can visit tidewater glaciers and natural hot springs, meeting whales and sea otters along the way.

Among the places popular with sea kayakers are Glacier Bay National Park and Preserve, Tracy Arm-Fords Terror Wilderness, Pelican to Sitka through West Chichagof-Yakobi Wilderness, Misty Fiords National Monument and Hoonah to Tenakee Springs.

A sea kayak with a spray cover (or a closed-deck canoe) is well suited to exploring the labyrinth of channels and fjords. Kayaks can slip through channels where the water is just inches deep at high tide. They can take refuge on tiny islands when the weather kicks up, or tie up to public docks in town. The boats can be carried (at no charge) aboard Alaska state ferries. Operators of some sightseeing vessels offer dropoff service for kayakers, and folding boats can be flown into remote spots.

Sportfishing

Southeast offers a variety of fishing experiences from pristine wilderness lakes and streams to ocean trolling. Access to most sportfishing in this area is by private or charter boat from most communities or by small planes — usually chartered in the larger communities such as Juneau, Ketchikan, Petersburg, Sitka and Wrangell.

A variety of species are available depending on where the angler drops a line. Salmon are the most popular sport fish in Southeast; during the summer several communities sponsor derbies that offer prizes for the largest salmon caught.

Southeast's sheltered marine waters are perhaps the best place in Alaska to fish for king salmon, the most prized species in the state. These fish range from 10 to 50 pounds, which is trophy size, and can attain 90 to 100 pounds. Kings are present all year. The best period for the biggest fish, however, is from mid-April to mid-June when mature fish are moving through. "Feeders" or smaller kings up to 25 pounds are available throughout the remainder of the year.

Left — *Wildlife viewing on Manzanita Lake. (Rollo Pool, staff)*

Above — *A catch of prized king salmon cools on ice. (Staff, reprinted from* ALASKA GEOGRAPHIC®)

Silver (coho) salmon are available from July through September; best month is August. Silvers average 12 pounds, but can exceed 20 pounds.

Fishing for pink salmon is good during July and August. These salmon average three or four pounds, but occasionally attain 10 pounds.

Chum salmon are available in Southeast waters from July to September. They range from two to 15 pounds, but commercially caught chums have weighed in at 35 pounds. Red salmon are available in June and July. These are small salmon, commonly weighing two to seven pounds (trophy size is anything over 10 pounds).

Other fish encountered in this region are halibut, which can tip the scales at over 300 pounds; rainbow trout and steelhead, which may weigh 10 pounds and occasionally reach 20 pounds; Dolly Varden, which usually weigh one to three pounds (world record is 8.07 pounds); cutthroat trout, which range from one to three pounds, but occasionally reach seven pounds; Arctic grayling up to 20 pounds; and brook trout from one to five pounds. An isolated population of northern pike is found in the Pike Lakes system near Yakutat.

Basket Bay

Scenic Basket Bay is located on Chichagof Island on the west side of Chatham Strait northwest of Angoon, eight miles south of the mouth of Tenakee Inlet.

This is a good spot for sightseeing or fishing. Lots of silver salmon enter this bay in August. At the mouth of Kook Creek, a large stream that enters the bay through a limestone cliff, is a flat that extends about 400 yards into the head of the bay. The stream goes underground three times between the bay and Kook Lake, which has fishing for cutthroat and Dolly Varden trout.

There is an old, unmaintained trail between Basket Bay and Kook Lake.

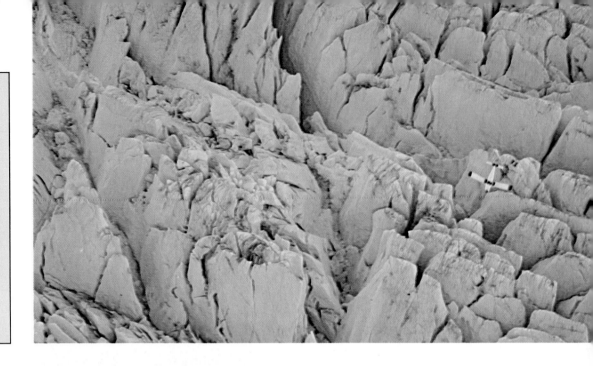

Goddard Hot Springs

Above — *Popular with Sitka area residents are the two cedar bathhouses owned by the city of Sitka at Goddard Hot Springs, on Hot Springs Bay off of Sitka Sound, 16 miles south of Sitka. In the mid-1800s there were three cottages at Goddard for invalids from Sitka. By the 1920s a three-story hotel had been built. The hotel later served as a Pioneers' Home, but was torn down in the 1940s. (Ernest Manewell, reprinted from ALASKA GEOGRAPHIC®)*

Juneau Icefield

The 15-mile-by-70-mile Juneau Icefield is the world's largest glacial accumulation outside of Greenland and Antarctica. Located in the Coast Mountains 25 miles north of Juneau, the ice cap covers 1,500 square miles, extending over the border into Canada and north nearly to Skagway. The glaciers are born in high mountains that rise out of the sea to more than 13,000 feet within a few miles of the coast. The ice field's annual snowfall of more than 100 feet accumulates over the years until its weight compacts it into ice, which then deforms and begins to flow down the valleys to the sea. When the rate of ice buildup is greater than the amount lost annually to melting or calving of icebergs at the terminus, the glacier will advance. If the reverse happens and the ice melts faster than new ice accumulates, the glacier will retreat.

Each summer since 1946, scientists have been studying the ice field, searching for secrets about weather patterns, the Ice Age and about the plants and wildlife that survive some of the world's worst weather.

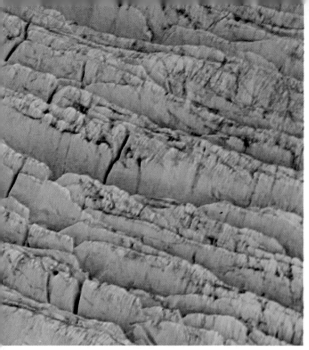

Above — *Small aircraft over Mendenhall Glacier. (Mike Affleck, reprinted from ALASKA® magazine)*

Right — *Helicopter tour lands on Juneau ice cap for photos. (Rollo Pool, staff)*

More than 30 glaciers, including the most visited glacier in Alaska — the Mendenhall, located only 13 miles from downtown Juneau — begin in this ice field. The Mendenhall Glacier is about 12 miles long and 1.5 miles across at its face. It is retreating slowly, fewer than 100 feet per year, and has melted back more than two miles in the last 200 years.

One glacier that is definitely advancing is the Taku Glacier on the north side of Taku Inlet, 13 miles southeast of Juneau. Extending about 30 miles, this glacier is the largest from the Juneau Icefield. If it continues advancing, perhaps one day there will be icebergs floating in Juneau Harbor as were common in the 1890s. Today, the bergs melt before they reach Juneau.

The best way to see Juneau Icefield is via charter flightseeing on a clear or high-overcast day. Air charters and helicopter tours of the ice field are available in Juneau.

Lighthouses

Southeastern Alaska is the location of 12 historic lighthouses that are part of a chain of navigational beacons operated by the U.S. Coast Guard. These are familiar and picturesque sights to those who travel the Inside Passage. Originally all had a lighthouse keeper — sometimes a family — but none are staffed today. From south to north:

Tree Point Light Station was constructed in 1904 and is the first light seafarers sight when traveling to Alaska from the south. It is located on a point extending to the southwest from the east shore of Revillagigedo Channel and marks the entrance to the channel near the U.S.-Canada border.

Mary Island Light Station was built in 1903 and is the second lighthouse encountered by mariners entering Alaska's Inside Passage from the south. It is located on a five-mile-long island between Felice Strait and Revillagigedo Channel, 30 miles southeast of Ketchikan.

Guard Island Light Station, about eight miles from downtown Ketchikan, was built in 1904 to mark the easterly entrance to Tongass Narrows.

Lincoln Rock Light Station, located on the westerly end of Clarence Strait adjacent to Etolin Island, was completed in 1903.

Cape Decision Light Station at the south tip of Kuiu Island between Sumner and Chatham straits, 26 miles southeast of Port Alexander, was completed in 1932 — the last lighthouse built in Alaska.

Five Finger Islands Light Station was one of the earliest lighthouses in Alaska, beginning operation in 1902, and also the last manned lighthouse in the state, being automated in 1984. It marks the south entrance to Stephens Passage, 67 miles east of Sitka and 45 miles northwest of Petersburg.

Fairway Island Light Station was built in 1904 just inside the easterly entrance to Peril Strait, 15 miles west of Angoon.

Cape Spencer Light Station, located at the entrance to Cross Sound, 30 miles west of Gustavus and 45 miles northwest of Hoonah, was first lighted in 1913 with a small, unwatched acetylene beacon. It was replaced in 1925 with a 200-mile range radio beacon, the first in Alaska. Unmanned since 1974, it is now on the National Register of Historic Places.

Point Retreat Light Station was built in 1904 on the northerly tip of the Mansfield Peninsula on Admiralty Island, 20 miles northwest of Juneau.

Sentinel Island Light Station was one of the earliest lighthouses in Alaska, beginning operation in 1902. Located on a small island 25 miles northwest of Juneau, it marks the entrance to Lynn Canal.

Point Sherman Light Station was built in 1904 on the east shore of Lynn Canal, 46 miles northwest of Juneau.

Eldred Rock Light Station was the last major station commissioned in Alaska during the surge of lighthouse construction from 1902-06. This octagonal lighthouse, located in Lynn Canal, 55 miles northwest of Juneau and 20 miles southeast of Haines, was completed in 1906.

Five Finger Islands lighthouse.
(U.S. Coast Guard)

New Eddystone Rock

Below — *Spectacular New Eddystone Rock, a popular subject for photographers, is located east of Revillagigedo Island in East Behm Canal, 35 miles northeast of Ketchikan in Misty Fiords National Monument. The 234-foot shaft of rock, called a "stack" by geologists, was named in 1793 by Captain George Vancouver of the Royal Navy because of its resemblance to the lighthouse rock off Plymouth, England. (Rollo Pool, staff)*

Pack Creek

Right — *Bear with salmon at Pack Creek, on the east side of Admiralty Island within Admiralty Island National Monument, about 28 miles south of Juneau. Observation platforms at Pack Creek provide excellent views of bears fishing for spawning salmon during the summer and fall runs. Access is by floatplane or boat. Primitive camping only is available. (John S. Crawford, reprinted from Wolves, Bears and Bighorns)*

Trocadero Soda Springs

Trocadero Soda Springs are located on the west coast of Prince of Wales Island about 12 miles southeast of Craig.

The seldom-visited carbonated "soda" springs are reached by walking about a mile up an unnamed creek that flows into a small inlet on the south shore of Trocadero Bay. The springs form two giant golden steps — banks of yellow tufa, or sediment, formed by the constant runoff from the springs. The area around the bubbling, hissing springs features yellow and red lunar like mounds and craters.

The highly carbonated water is described as having "a sharp, pleasant taste." Although water from other carbonated springs in Southeast has been bottled and sold in the past, Trocadero water has never been commercially marketed.

SOUTHCENTRAL GULF COAST

The Southcentral/Gulf Coast region curves 650 miles north and west from Icy Bay in southeastern Alaska, encompassing Kodiak Island, the Kenai Peninsula, Cook Inlet and Prince William Sound.

Southcentral's mainland has a roller coaster topography of high mountains and broad river valleys. On the east, the Copper, Chitina and Matanuska rivers are hemmed in by the Chugach, Wrangell and Talkeetna mountains and the Alaska Range. On the west, the Susitna River empties into the muddy upper reaches of Cook Inlet, a 220-mile-long body of water between the Kenai Mountains and Aleutian Range. The other major indentation in the mainland is Prince William Sound, a 15,000-square-mile maze of water, ice and islands. The Kodiak Archipelago extends southwest from the Kenai Peninsula, protecting the western flank of the mainland, to some extent, from Gulf of Alaska storms. At 3,588 square miles, Kodiak ranks as the state's largest island.

The region's climate is primarily maritime —

Dog mushing in the Caribou Hills on the Kenai Peninsula. (© Chlaus Lotscher)

rain and fog — with mild temperature fluctuations. Nearer the mountains, temperature changes are greater and the climate generally harsher. In Anchorage, January temperatures average 13°F and July temperatures average 57°F. Shielded by the Chugach and Kenai mountains from the gulf's moisture-laden clouds, Anchorage averages 15 inches of precipitation annually. On the coast side, however, Whittier's annual average precipitation is 174 inches.

The varied terrain and climate support a wide assortment of plants and wildlife. The moisture-demanding vegetation of Southeast continues along the coast to the Kenai Peninsula and Kodiak Island. Sitka spruce and western hemlock dominate coastal forests. Inland, birch, alder and aspen dominate. At higher elevations, forests give way to subalpine brush, fields of wildflowers, berries and alpine meadows. Major river valleys have stands of black cottonwood. Chugach National Forest, created in 1907, encompasses 5.8 million acres of Southcentral's forests.

Variety also characterizes the animals of Southcentral. Brown/grizzly bears, the only large mammal native to Kodiak Island, are equally at home in portions of the Matanuska and Susitna

Tidal flats of Kachemak Bay are home to sandhill cranes. (© Chlaus Lotscher)

Left — A rainbow and cotton grass frame a small lake on the Kenai. (©Chlaus Lotscher)

Below — Dall sheep rams in the Alaska Range. (George Wuerthner)

valleys and on the flats of western Cook Inlet. Sitka black-tailed deer, mountain goats and Dall sheep have been introduced to Kodiak and elk to nearby Afognak Island. Mountain goats roam the sheer cliffs of the Chugach and Wrangell mountains. Moose thrive on the Kenai Peninsula and occur throughout the rest of Southcentral, except on islands of Prince William Sound and the Kodiak group. Dall sheep are found in the Talkeetna, Wrangell and Chugach mountains, on the slopes of the Alaska Range and on inland peaks of the Kenai Mountains. Sitka black-tailed deer and black and brown/grizzly bears inhabit the coastal forests of Prince William Sound. Wolves roam the Kenai Peninsula, the Nelchina basin, the Copper River valley, the Eagle River valley near Anchorage and the rolling country northwest of Cook Inlet.

Smaller mammals include lynx, pine martens, weasels, beavers, muskrats, mink, red foxes, land otters, porcupines, wolverines, snowshoe hares, shrews, voles and lemmings. Southcentral has congregations of bald and golden eagles, hawks and falcons and an overwhelming number of shorebirds and waterfowl. The world's population of dusky Canada geese summers on the Copper River flats, and rare trumpeter swans nest on the Kenai Peninsula and near the Copper River.

Lake Clark National
Park and Preserve
■Mt. Redoubt

*Lake
Clark*

▲Mt. Iliamna

Iliamna Lake

*Kukaklek
Lake*

Kamishak Bay

Katmai National
Park and Preserve

▲Mt. Douglas

▲Fourpeaked
Mountain

▲Mt. Kaguyak

▲Mt. Kukak
▲Mt. Denison

Mt. Trident▲
t. Mageik▲ ▲Mt. Katmai

▲ Mt. Martin

charof
tional
ildlife
efuge

Shelikof Strait

Port Lions■
Uganik Bay■   Ouzinkie■   ■Pleasant Harbor
Kodiak■
■Kodiak
■Woody Island

National
Karluk■   ■Larsen Bay
Kodiak Island
Wildlife
Old Harbor■
Refuge
Sitkalidak Island

Akhiok■

Sitkinak Strait
Tugidak Island   *Sitkinak Island*
Trinity Islands

*Prince
William
Sound*

Chugach
National Forest

Hinchinbrook
Island

■Chenega
Bay

■Katalla

Cape Hinchinbrook
Light Station

*Montegue
Island*

Kayak Island

Cape St. Elias
Light Station

Kenai National
Wildlife Refuge

■Seward

*Harding
Icefield*

Kenai Fjords
National Park

Blying Sound

▲Middleton Island

■Homer
Kachemak Bay
State Park   ■Halibut Cove

Seldovia■

Tutka Bay■

English Bay■ ■Port Graham

▲Augustine Island
▲Augustine Volcano

Chugach Islands

Gulf of Alaska

Barren Islands

Shuyak Island

■Port William

Afognak Island   Marmot Island

Southcentral/
Gulf Coast

Location

Cartography by David A. Shott

N

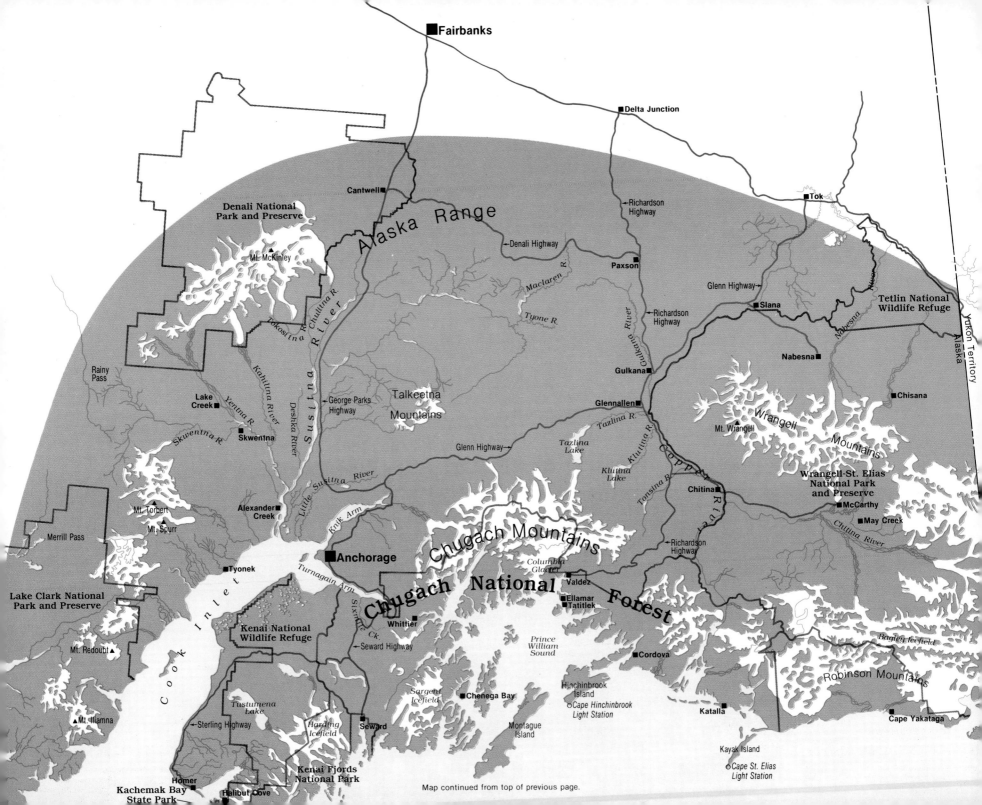

Fairbanks

Delta Junction

Tok

Denali National
Park and Preserve

Cantwell

Alaska Range

Richardson
Highway

Denali Highway

Paxson

Mt. McKinley

Maclaren R.

Glenn Highway

Tetlin National
Wildlife Refuge

Tyone R.

Slana

Richardson
Highway

Rainy
Pass

Gulkana River

Nabesna

Nabesna River

Yukon Territory

Alaska

Gulkana

Lake
Creek

Tokositna R.

Chulitna R.

Susitna River

George Parks
Highway

Talkeetna
Mountains

Glennallen

Chisana

Mt. Wrangell

Wrangell

Kahiltna River

Yentna R.

Skwentna

Mountains

Skwentna R.

Deshka River

Tazlina R.

Tazlina
Lake

Klutina R.

Copper River

Glenn Highway

Wrangell-St. Elias
National Park
and Preserve

Klutina
Lake

McCarthy

Alexander
Creek

Little Susitna River

Susitna River

Tonsina R.

Chitina

May Creek

Mt. Torbert

Knik Arm

Chitina River

Merrill Pass

Mt. Spurr

Chugach Mountains

Chugach Mountains

Columbia
Glacier

Richardson
Highway

Anchorage

Tyonek

Turnagain Arm

Chugach National

Forest

Valdez

Lake Clark National
Park and Preserve

Sixmile Ck.

Ellamar
Tatitlek

Bagley Icefield

Whittier

Kenai National
Wildlife Refuge

Seward Highway

Prince
William
Sound

Cordova

Mt. Redoubt

Robinson Mountains

Sargent
Icefield

Cook Inlet

Chenega Bay

Hinchinbrook
Island

Tustumena
Lake

Cape Hinchinbrook
Light Station

Mt. Iliamna

Sterling Highway

Katalla

Cape Yakataga

Harding
Icefield

Seward

Montague
Island

Kayak Island

Homer

Cape St. Elias
Light Station

Kenai Fjords
National Park

Map continued from top of previous page.

Kachemak Bay
State Park

Halibut Cove

Below — *Horseback riders explore Fox River Flats in the Kachemak Bay area.*

Right — *Augustine Volcano in quieter days; she erupted in April 1986. (©Photos by Chlaus Lotscher)*

Rich Gulf Coast waters support crabs, shrimp and clams. Salmon, herring, cod, Dolly Varden and cutthroat trout abound and provide food for harbor and Dall porpoises, sea lions, sea otters and killer whales. Largest marine mammals in the area are the baleen whales — humpbacks, fins and minkes.

The human population of Southcentral is widely and variously dispersed. Aside from a few people living at Cape Yakataga, the Gulf Coast from Icy Bay to the Copper River Delta is relatively uninhabited, accessible only by plane or private boat.

At Hinchinbrook Entrance, the gulf merges with Prince William Sound, home of major salmon, crab and shrimp fisheries. Cordova is the primary fishing port for the eastern sound, processing crab, salmon, razor clams, halibut and herring. In the western sound, the small community of Whittier is the hub of small boat traffic and port for the state ferries connecting the major Prince William Sound communities with the Kenai Peninsula and Kodiak Island.

The major population center in Southcentral — and in Alaska — is Anchorage. Hub of the state's commerce, transportation and communications, Anchorage is located on a narrow plain at the foot of the Chugach Mountains. The city is bounded by Knik Arm and Turnagain Arm, offshoots of Cook Inlet.

Southcentral is a land of contrasts. A land of cities, but also of those rare spots that afford splendid isolation for the wanderer. Hoarfrost thickly coats each twig in winter, but shallow lakes beckon summer swimmers. Rimmed by mountains and washed by the sea, Southcentral offers the most rugged of outdoor experiences, yet a friendlier wilderness can be touched just out the back door of many a cozy home.

The Communities

AKHIOK is located on the south side of Kodiak Island, 80 miles southwest of Kodiak and 340 miles southwest of Anchorage. **Elevation:** 50 feet.

53

Transportation: Boat; scheduled or charter air service from Kodiak. Population: 107.

Visitor Facilities: Arrangements may be made to stay in private homes. Limited groceries may be purchased at Ayakulik Inc. General Store in town or during the May-September fishing season at the Columbia-Wards Fisheries Lazy Bay cannery store five miles south of the village. Marine gas, diesel, regular gasoline available.

The community originally was a sea otter hunting settlement. Today, commercial fishing forms the basis of its economy. Many of the residents are commercial fishermen. Other employers include the cannery, school, health services, the city and occasional construction jobs. Almost all of Akhiok's residents depend on subsistence fishing and hunting for various food sources. Species harvested include salmon, crab, shrimp, scallop, clam, duck, seal, deer, rabbit and bear.

Akhiok is located adjacent to the Kodiak National Wildlife Refuge. The community's Russian Orthodox church, Protection of the Theotokos Chapel, which was built around 1900 on the site of an earlier structure, is on the National Register of Historic Places.

ALEXANDER CREEK, near the mouth of Alexander Creek in the Susitna River delta, is 27 miles northwest of Anchorage. **Transportation:** Boats; charter floatplane service from Anchorage. **Population:** 17.

Visitor Facilities: Food and lodging at Gabbert's Fish Camp. Marine engine and boat repair, hunting and fishing licenses, gas, moorage, guide service and rental boats and motors available from Gabbert's, which also operates a river taxi service.

Alexander Creek is an unincorporated community located near the former site of a small Indian village reported by U.S. Geological Survey geologist George Eldridge in 1898.

Some area residents are commercial fishermen; others are retired. The Gabbert family runs the sportfishing lodge. Fishing is excellent for king salmon from May 20 to July 6; silver, pink, red and chum salmon from July 16 to September; rainbow trout in May and September; and grayling from July to September. Hunting in the area is for moose, black bear and ducks.

Cape House Lodge at Cape Yakataga. (Patti Gilbert, reprinted from ALASKA GEOGRAPHIC®*)*

CAPE YAKATAGA is located on the Gulf of Alaska, 35 miles west of Icy Bay, 140 miles southeast of Cordova and 265 miles southeast of Anchorage. **Elevation:** 12 feet. **Transportation:** Scheduled or charter air service from Cordova. **Population:** 4 to 8.

Visitor Facilities: Food and lodging at Cape House Lodge by advance reservation.

Yakataga is said to mean "canoe road" because of two reefs forming a canoe passage to the village. The settlement was started about the turn of the century by placer miners. Besides the Cape House Lodge operation, residents today mine and trap for a living. Activities in the area include beach-combing and hunting for moose, mountain goat, black bear and brown bear, according to Patti Gilbert, manager of the lodge.

CHENEGA BAY is located at Crab Bay on

Akhiok on Alitak Bay, Kodiak Island. (Chlaus Lotscher, reprinted from ALASKA GEOGRAPHIC®*)*

Evans Island, 50 miles southeast of Seward. **Transportation:** Boat or charter floatplane from Seward. **Population:** 70.

Visitor Facilities: Two rooms with cooking facilities available in the community building. Laundry facilities. Limited supplies at Chenega Bay Co-op. Fishing and hunting licenses may be purchased locally. Marine gas, diesel and regular gasoline available. Moorage at community dock.

The original community of Chenega was destroyed during the 1964 earthquake. Relocated to Chenega Bay, the new community was dedicated in 1984, and consists of 21 homes, an office building, school and community store. The primary occupations in Chenega Bay are fishing and other seasonal employment.

Chenega Bay is built on the site of the former Crab Bay herring saltery. At nearby Sawmill Bay are the ruins of Port Ashton, another abandoned herring saltery, which is accessible by boat, floatplane or by foot along the beach at low tide.

The Port San Juan Hatchery, operated by the Prince William Sound Aquaculture Association, is located about two miles across Sawmill Bay by boat from Chenega Bay. The hatchery, which is open to visitors, grows pink and chum salmon and reportedly is one of the largest of its kind in the world in terms of number of fry released.

La Touche Island, site of an abandoned copper mining community, is located about four miles from Chenega Bay across Elrington Passage. There are a few homes and a private airstrip on the island.

Recreational activities at Chenega Bay include bottle collecting, rockhounding, beachcombing, hiking or backpacking. Cross-country skiing is good in winter. Whales and sea lions may be seen nearby. Bird watching is possible year-round. Fishing in nearby waters is good in season for salmon, trout, halibut and rockfish. Hunting is primarily for deer and black bear on Evans and neighboring islands.

Some lands near Chenega Bay are owned by the local village corporation. Contact them for information on land use.

CHISANA is located in the Wrangell Mountains

Chenega Bay on Evans Island. (Dave Wigglesworth, reprinted from ALASKA GEOGRAPHIC®)

on the Chisana River, 30 miles southeast of Nabesna and about 60 miles south of Northway. **Elevation:** 3,170 feet. **Transportation:** Charter air service from Northway, Glennallen or Tok. **Population:** 6 to 20.

Visitor Facilities: Food and lodging by advance reservation at Wrangell R Ranch and Pioneer Outfitters lodges. There are no other facilities.

This community, located within Wrangell-St. Elias National Park and Preserve, was settled during the Chisana gold rush of 1913. The gold rush was short-lived and Chisana quickly became a ghost town. It now serves as the base of operations for a few hunting guides, recreationists and small-scale gold miners.

Anthony Dimond, Alaska's territorial delegate to Congress from 1932-45, was the town's U.S. Commissioner. His courtroom, cabin and the women's log jail, are still standing.

Hunting, horseback trips, hiking and history are the primary visitor attractions.

CORDOVA, on Orca Inlet on the southeast shore of Prince William Sound, 147 miles southeast of Anchorage. **Transportation:** Daily jet service from Anchorage; scheduled state ferry service from Valdez, Whittier and Seward. **Population:** 2,108.

Visitor Facilities: There are two hotels, two motels, six restaurants, laundromats, banks and a variety of shopping facilities. This is a major Prince William Sound community and all visitor facilities are available.

Modern-day Cordova owes its origins to Michael J. Heney, builder of the Copper River & Northwestern Railway. The town was the railroad

terminus and ocean shipping port for copper ore from the Kennecott mines in the Wrangell Mountains. The railroad and the town prospered until 1938 when the mine was closed. Today, the Prince William Sound fishery and fish processing plants form the economic base of the community.

Cordova has a museum, library and public swimming pool. There is skiing from December to May on 3,500-foot Eyak Mountain, which has a chair lift and rope tows. Celebrations during the year include the Silver Salmon Derby from mid-August to the first of September and the Iceworm Festival in February. Highlight of this event is the 100-foot-long "iceworm" that winds its way through the streets of Cordova.

ELLAMAR is located on the east shore of Virgin Bay on Prince William Sound, 180 miles southeast of Anchorage, 40 miles northwest of Cordova and 24 miles southwest of Valdez. **Transportation:** Boat; charter floatplane service from Anchorage, Valdez or Cordova; scheduled service to Tatitlek (two miles south of Ellamar). **Population:** About 10 year-round.

Visitor Facilities: None.

Located on the old Tatitlek townsite. The Native village was moved by the Ellamar Mining Company after copper was discovered at the site in 1897. By 1902 Ellamar was a bustling town, but its heyday wasn't to last. Mines throughout the Sound started closing in 1919 and by the end of the 1920s Ellamar Mining was gone. The town was revitalized for a time by two short-lived cannery operations.

Ellamar is in the process of being redeveloped as a summer and weekend recreational community by Ellamar Properties Inc. of Anchorage, which acquired most of the available land and has platted a subdivision of 143 recreational lots and 14 commercial lots.

Year-round residents include a scrimshaw artist, a pilot, a welder and retirees.

Recreational activities in the area include fishing for salmon and halibut, boating, hunting, cross-country skiing and photography. Whales, sea otters and sea lions frequent the area. Behind Ellamar, 3,051-foot Ellamar Mountain offers views of waterfalls. Columbia Glacier is 12 miles to the northwest.

ENGLISH BAY is located at the south entrance to Port Graham on the Kenai Peninsula, 10 miles southwest of Seldovia. **Transportation:** Boat; scheduled and charter air service from Homer. **Population:** 172.

English Bay village may have been originally a Russian post called Alexandrovsk, meaning "Alexander." It was later called Odinochka, meaning "a person living in solitude."

This Native community is unincorporated. Its Russian Orthodox church, built about 1930 to replace the original 1870 structure, is a national historic site.

HALIBUT COVE is located on the south shore of Kachemak Bay, six miles southeast of Homer and 125 miles south of Anchorage. **Elevation:** 10 feet. **Transportation:** Boat; private ferry service from Homer. **Population:** 52.

Visitor Facilities: Accommodations available at Quiet Time Lodge, Halibut Cove Bed and Breakfast and Cove Cabins. Meals at The Saltry restaurant. Guide services available. Boats available for charter; public moorage available.

Between 1911 and 1928 Halibut Cove had 42 herring salteries and a population of about 1,000. From 1928 to 1975 the population stayed around 40, most of whom were fishermen. Since 1975 the community has steadily grown and now has a summer population of about 160, including several commercial artists and many fishermen. Octopus ink paintings, oil paintings, fish prints, pottery, batiks and silkscreen prints may be seen at several art galleries.

Bird watching in the area is excellent and there

View of English Bay, located at the south entrance to Port Graham. (Will Thompson)

Scenic Halibut Cove on Kachemak Bay is home to several artists. (Marion Beck)

are good hiking trails. Kachemak Bay is one of Alaska's most popular spots for halibut fishing, with catches often weighing 100 to 200 pounds. Halibut up to 350 pounds are fished from June through September. Inquire locally or in Homer about fishing guides.

KARLUK is on the west coast of Kodiak Island, 75 air miles from Kodiak. **Elevation:** 137 feet. **Transportation:** Boat, scheduled and charter air service from Kodiak. **Population:** 90.

Visitor Facilities: Accommodations available in summer at Karluk Lodge, a private fishing lodge located across Karluk Lagoon from the village. Limited groceries and supplies available at a small store operated by the tribal council. Fishing and hunting licenses and guide services available at Karluk Lodge.

Russian hunters established a trading post in Karluk in 1786. Between 1790 and 1850 many tanneries, salteries and canneries were established in the area. In 1800, Karluk was renowned for having the largest salmon cannery in the world and the river was known as the greatest red salmon stream in the world, according to a community profile issued by the state.

A post office was established in 1892. In the early 1900s, canneries were constructed by the Alaska Packers Association. Overfishing of the area forced the canneries to close in the 1930s. The buildings today stand vacant and deteriorating.

Karluk is located adjacent to the Kodiak National Wildlife Refuge. The community's Ascension of Our Lord Russian Orthodox chapel, built in 1888, is a national historic site.

Fishing is the primary source of livelihood for Karluk residents. Almost all residents depend on fishing and hunting as a food source.

Visitors should be aware that land along the Karluk River as well as the riverbed is owned by Koniag Inc., and the village corporations of Karluk and Larsen Bay. A daily user fee is charged for fishing or camping on the Karluk River.

KODIAK is located at the north end of Chiniak Bay near the eastern tip of Kodiak Island. **Transportation:** Commercial jet service from Anchorage or Seattle; scheduled state ferry service

Fishing supports most residents of Karluk. (Kathy Hunter, reprinted from ALASKA GEOGRAPHIC®)

from Seward and Homer. **Population:** 6,069.

Visitor Facilities: There are several hotels and motels in Kodiak. There also are about 17 restaurants, as well as general merchandise and sporting goods stores and gift shops. There are three state campgrounds accessible by road from town. There are several remote fly-in hunting and fishing lodges in the Kodiak area and recreation cabins are available on Kodiak National Wildlife Refuge. Air charter services in Kodiak offer flightseeing trips and fly-in hunting and fishing trips. Charter boats are available for fishing and hunting trips, sightseeing and photography. There are five car rental agencies, an airport bus service, taxi cabs and a year-round van touring service.

Kodiak Island, home of the oldest permanent European settlement in Alaska, is about 100 miles long. It is the largest island in Alaska, with an area of 3,670 square miles. Kodiak was Russian Alaska's first capital city, until the capital was moved to Sitka in 1804.

Kodiak is the third largest commercial fishing port in the U.S. Some 2,000 commercial fishing vessels use the harbor each year, delivering salmon, shrimp, herring, halibut and whitefish, plus king, tanner and Dungeness crab to the 15 seafood processing companies in Kodiak. These canneries are small, functional processing plants; no tours are available during operation.

Kodiak also is an important cargo port and transshipment center. Container ships stop here to transfer goods to smaller vessels bound for the Aleutians, the Alaska Peninsula and other destinations.

Attractions in Kodiak include Alaska's only outdoor theater production, *Cry of the Wild Ram,* the story of the first Russian-American colony in Alaska. The play is presented each August in the Frank Brink Amphitheater on Monashka Bay. Fort Abercrombie, one of the first secret radar installations in Alaska, is now a state park and a national historic landmark.

Special events include the Kodiak Crab Festival, a week-long celebration in May; the state fair and rodeo held in August; and St. Herman's Day August 9, honoring Father Herman, the first saint of the Russian Orthodox Church in North America, who was canonized in Kodiak in 1970.

One of the original clerics who established the oldest parish in Alaska, Father Herman's church is on the National Register of Historic Places and is open afternoons in summer. Also open to the public is the St. Innocent Veniaminov Research Institute Museum.

LAKE CREEK, on the Yentna River, is 70 miles northwest of Anchorage. **Transportation:** Boat; charter floatplane service. **Population:** 20 year-round.

Visitor Facilities: Food and lodging by advance reservation at Riversong Lodge, Lake Creek Lodge, McDougall Lodge and Wilderness Place Lodge. A few grocery items, camera film and sporting goods may be purchased at the lodges. Raw furs may be purchased from local trappers. Fishing and hunting licenses available at lodges. Boats may be rented. Guide services, marine engine repair services, fuel (marine gas, diesel, regular) and moorage available.

At the turn of the century, a trading post was established across the Yentna River from Lake

Kodiak is a major community. (Jon Nickles, reprinted from ALASKA GEOGRAPHIC®)

Creek to serve the trappers and gold miners in the area. Ruined cabins remain, as does the hulk of a paddle-wheeled steamboat once used for transportation.

Today, five families live year-round in the area. Residents guide fishermen and hunters and provide lodging for recreationists.

In summer there is excellent fishing for five species of salmon, some up to 65 pounds, as well as for trout and grayling. The hunting season is in September for moose, bear and ducks. Lake Creek, a clear stream that flows about 50 miles south from near Mount McKinley through scenic countryside, provides white-water excitement for river floaters, as well as good fishing.

Carl Dixon of Riversong Lodge writes: "In winter things quiet down some. It provides us with close times with the family and neighbors for reading, visiting, skiing, snow machining. We travel to Skwentna 15 miles for mail and some children attend school there via snow machine. In winter, the moose come right in the yard. We must protect our plum trees! In February, we act as a checkpoint for the Iditaski Cross Country race for skiers. It is the longest cross-country race in the world at 335 kilometers."

The willow ptarmigan is the state bird. (Helen Rhode, reprinted from ALASKA GEOGRAPHIC®)

LARSEN BAY is located on the northwest coast of Kodiak Island, 62 miles southwest of Kodiak. **Elevation:** 20 feet. **Transportation:** Boat; scheduled and charter air service from Kodiak. **Population:** 215.

Visitor Facilities: Arrangements may be made for accommodations in private homes. Groceries and supplies available at Larsen Bay Community Store or Larsen's Mercantile. Fishing and hunting licenses may be purchased locally. Private boats may be rented and charter aircraft is available. Marine gas, diesel, propane and regular gasoline available.

Larsen Bay was named for Peter Larsen, an Unga Island furrier, hunter and guide. The Native name for the town is Uyak. The area is thought to have been inhabited for 2,000 years by the Aleut people. In certain sections of the community, hundreds of artifacts have been unearthed. In the early 1800s

Tom Spersted at his May Creek cabin. (Barry Santana, reprinted from ALASKA GEOGRAPHIC®)

there was a tannery in Uyak Bay. The Alaska Packers Association built a cannery in the village of Larsen Bay in 1911. The cannery is now owned by Kodiak Island Seafoods Inc.

Commercial fishing is the main source of income today. There are some jobs locally with the city and tribal council. Residents also depend on subsistence hunting and fishing.

The main attraction for visitors is the Karluk River, which is located two to three miles from the head of Larsen Bay. This river is known for its excellent king salmon, silver salmon and steelhead fishing. Raft trips from Karluk Lake to Karluk Lagoon also are popular. Visitors should be aware, however, that land along the Karluk River as well as the riverbed is owned by Koniag Inc., and the village corporations of Karluk and Larsen Bay. A daily user fee is charged for fishing or camping on the Karluk River.

Hunting in the area is good for Sitka black-tailed deer. Other wildlife includes Kodiak brown bear, fox, rabbit, ermine, otter, seals, whales, sea lion

and porpoise. Bird watchers may see eagles, gulls, petrels, kittiwakes, mallards, green-winged teals, widgeons, pintails, lesser Canada geese, puffins, loons, cormorants and more.

MAY CREEK, on the Nizina River, is 12 miles from McCarthy and 65 miles from Chitina. **Elevation:** 1,650 feet. **Transportation:** Mail plane from Gulkana; charter air service. **Population:** Less than 12.

Visitor Facilities: None.

The May Creek area had a roadhouse during the early 1900s gold rush when the Nizina District was booming. The May Creek airstrip was developed by the Alaska Road Commission in territorial days and was used by the entire region from McCarthy to Dan Creek before local strips were built. May Creek is located within Wrangell-St. Elias National Park and Preserve.

Area residents rely primarily on subsistence hunting and gathering, although there is some gold panning.

The biggest attraction in the area for visitors,

according to Judith Miller, is "the superb hiking, beautiful scenery and great roads and trails remaining from the early mining days. It's easy to get around following the old trails, though many areas are fairly wet. There are many beaver dams and swampy areas across or near the roads, consequently the best mode of transportation is by foot. However, the rich swamp areas result in abundant wildlife and waterfowl. It is not a particularly rich moose habitat, but black and grizzly bears are abundant. Beavers and other water animals are commonly seen. Trumpeter swans migrate to this area every summer and nest in the lakes. The hiking opportunities are a complete spectrum of easy rambling meadowlike areas to sheer steep rock pitches and high mountain and glacier landscapes."

OLD HARBOR is on the southeast shore of Kodiak Island, 54 miles from Kodiak. **Elevation:** 20 feet. **Transportation:** Boat; scheduled and charter air service from Kodiak. **Population:** 405.

Visitor Facilities: Arrangements may be made for accommodations in private homes. Some groceries and supplies carried at two local stores. Guide service available. It may be possible to charter private boats. Diesel and gas and moorage available.

The village of Old Harbor was established at Three Saints Harbor, site of the first Russian settlement in Alaska a century earlier, in 1884. The Old Harbor post office was established in 1931. The town was nearly destroyed by a tidal wave from the 1964 Good Friday earthquake, but has since been rebuilt.

Described by one resident as an "old fishing village," many of Old Harbor's residents are commercial fishermen. Most residents also depend on subsistence activities. Seafood harvested for subsistence uses include salmon, halibut, cod, Dolly Varden, crab, herring, shrimp, scallops, clams and seal.

Old Harbor is a second-class city, incorporated in 1966. It is located adjacent to the Kodiak National Wildlife Refuge.

OUZINKIE is located on the west coast of Spruce Island, 10 miles north of the city of Kodiak.

View of Old Harbor village from the cemetery. (©Chlaus Lotscher)

Elevation: 55 feet. **Transportation:** Boat; scheduled or charter air service from Kodiak. **Population:** 240.

Visitor Facilities: Arrangements may be made to stay in private homes. Groceries available at Ouzinkie Community Store. Marine gas, diesel and regular gasoline available.

Originally settled as a retirement community for the Russian-American Company, the Royal Packing Company constructed the first cannery at Ouzinkie in 1889. The fishing industry flourished over the years, with new canneries replacing those that were destroyed by fire.

Ouzinkie's economic base continues to be primarily commercial fishing, although since 1976 — when the last cannery burned down — there have been no local fish processing facilities, and Ouzinkie fishermen have had to utilize those in Kodiak in addition to floating processors. There

are a few other jobs locally with the store, city government, clinic, and schools. Most residents also depend on subsistence fishing and hunting.

The Russian Orthodox Nativity of Our Lord Chapel, built in 1906, is a national historic site.

PLEASANT HARBOR is located on Spruce Island, three miles west of Ouzinkie and 12 miles north of Kodiak. **Transportation:** Boat; charter air service to Ouzinkie airstrip or floatplane service to Pleasant Harbor. **Population:** 26.

Visitor Facilities: Food and lodging at Pleasant Harbor Lodge. Laundry available. Marine engine and boat repair services available. Moorage available.

The community of Pleasant Harbor was founded in 1923 when Chris Opheim homesteaded a piece of land which included Sunny Cove and Pleasant Harbor. He and his family operated a cod saltery in Sunny Cove. Son Ed Opheim inherited the

homestead and in 1947 moved his family to Pleasant Harbor where the family earned a living by salting and smoking salmon. Ed Opheim later built and operated a sawmill.

The tidal wave generated by the 1964 Good Friday earthquake washed away both the old house at Sunny Cove and Ed and Anna's Pleasant Harbor home. The Opheims have since rebuilt on higher ground. The family has been selling homesites and there are now 13 homes in the community.

Most residents earn their living by fishing. Others take seasonal jobs in Kodiak and a few work for the lodge.

Attractions include Monks Lagoon, about an hour's walk from Pleasant Harbor, where Saint Herman lived and worked during the early days of Russian America. It is now a Russian Orthodox sanctuary. The chapel built over Saint Herman's grave is a national historic site. The monks at New Valaam Monastery in Pleasant Harbor will share

with visitors their knowledge of the history of the church in Alaska.

Ed Opheim Sr. on Spruce Island: "My years of living here these past 63 years have been years of enjoyment. There are always things to do. One of our favorite doings is going after beach wood to Monks Lagoon and taking time to beachcomb on low tide and then load our skiffs with different woods for our heating stoves. And to watch the salmon head up Monks Lagoon fish streams to the lakes inland. One of my favorite things to watch in years past was to see the sun come out of the ocean in the early mornings. To climb Mount Herman on a breezy day with the sky full of high fluffy clouds and wildflowers at different levels is an experience not soon forgotten. In the fall of the year I have watched the storm come in at east cape with mountain seas breaking against the broken shoreline.

"Living here with our grown sons that now have children of their own, these young people have

the chance to do and see what we have seen and done these many past years. Anna and I are most fortunate to live here on Spruce Island."

PORT GRAHAM is located on the Kenai Peninsula, eight miles southwest of Seldovia, 27 miles south of Homer and 150 miles south of Anchorage. **Elevation:** 93 feet. **Transportation:** Boat; scheduled and charter air service from Homer. **Population:** 174.

Visitor Facilities: Food and lodging at a boarding house. Laundromat available. Groceries, clothing and other supplies available at Port Graham General Store or Port Graham Variety. Fishing and hunting licenses may be purchased locally. Marine gas, diesel and regular gasoline available.

Port Graham village grew around a cannery and wharf first reported by the U.S. Geological Survey in 1909. Most of the residents work in the fishing industry and related businesses. The Columbia-Wards cannery operates in spring and summer.

According to the president of the Port Graham Corporation, "The whole area around our village is good for sightseeing. There are places to fish for halibut, red salmon, trout, silvers." Visitors should be aware that the Port Graham Corporation has instituted a permit system for recreational use of its lands in the Rocky Bay and Windy Bay areas.

PORT LIONS is located on the north coast of Kodiak Island, 21 miles from Kodiak. **Elevation:** 52 feet. **Transportation:** Boat; scheduled and charter air service from Kodiak; scheduled state ferry service from Homer and Seward via Kodiak. **Population:** 301.

Visitor Facilities: Accommodations at Settler's Cove Inn and Lions Den Chalet. Meals at both lodges and at Driftwood Cafe. Groceries and supplies at Port Lions General Store Inc. and Port Lions Community Store. Fishing and hunting licenses available from the city of Port Lions. Boats and off-road vehicles may be rented. Guide services, marine engine repair, diesel and gas and moorage available.

Port Lions was founded in 1964 by Lions International, the Bureau of Indian Affairs and the Public Health Service for the residents of Afognak, whose homes were destroyed by tidal waves in the aftermath of the Good Friday earthquake.

For many years, Port Lions was the site of the large Wakefield Cannery on Peregrebni Point. The cannery burned down in March 1975. Floating

Above — Causeway connects Port Lions to city dock. (Jon Nickles, reprinted from ALASKA GEOGRAPHIC®)

Below — Old one-line cannery at Port William ceased operations in the 1970s. (Nina Faust, reprinted from ALASKA GEOGRAPHIC®)

crab processors have operated here in recent years.

The economy of Port Lions is based primarily on commercial fishing and related businesses. There are a few other jobs with the lodges, cafe, stores, boat harbor, oil company, school, city and health clinic. All residents depend to some extent on subsistence activities for food.

Snowmobile riding and boating are very popular in Port Lions. The surrounding area also offers good hunting and fishing, and an abundance of wildlife for the photographer.

PORT WILLIAM is located on the south shore of Shuyak Island, 65 miles north of Kodiak. **Transportation:** Boat; scheduled and charter

floatplane service. **Population:** 9.

Visitor Facilities: None.

Port William originally was a cannery. For years it was the only ice and cold storage plant in the Kodiak area. Now privately owned, the cannery facilities are no longer operating. Residents of Port William are commercial fishermen.

Most of Shuyak Island is a wilderness. The northern end of the island is the new Shuyak Island State Park, while a section along the east side has been proposed for a state game sanctuary. The middle of the island is Kodiak Island Borough lands.

There is fishing for Dolly Varden in the spring, and for silver and pink salmon in the fall. There are many birds, including bald eagles and puffins. Poor grade jade and jasper can be found on some beaches. There is hunting for deer, bear and elk (on Afognak Island just to the south). Other wildlife includes sea lions (on the Latax Rocks to the north), sea otters, land otters, beavers and whales.

SELDOVIA is located on the Kenai Peninsula, 20 miles south of Homer and 130 miles south of Anchorage. **Transportation:** Boat; scheduled air service from Anchorage via Homer; air charter service from Homer or Anchorage; scheduled state ferry service from Homer or Kodiak. **Population:** 435.

Visitor Facilities: Accommodations at Boardwalk Hotel, Seldovia Lodge, Seldovia Rowing Club (bed-and-breakfast), and High Tide Originals (bed-and-breakfast). Meals at lodging facilities (except Boardwalk Hotel) and at four restaurants.

There are several local stores carrying groceries, supplies, gifts, and arts and crafts. Fishing and hunting licenses available from the city clerk or local sport shop. Marine engine, boat and auto repair services available. Rental transportation includes a car and skiffs from the Boardwalk Hotel; aircraft (through Homer); and bicycles from two rental shops. All types of fuel and public moorage are available.

Quiet waters reflect buildings along Seldovia Slough. (Jerrianne Lowther, staff)

Seldovia, first settled by the Russians around 1800, is one of the oldest settlements in the Cook Inlet area. About eight miles south of the city is a coal mine which was used by early Russian settlers. It is now on the National Register of Historic Places. St. Nicholas Russian Orthodox Chapel, built around 1890 and restored in 1981, is a national historic site.

Sea otter hunters first came to the area in the 1890s and trading posts were opened. The abundance of herring in the area promoted the building of several processing plants in 1922, but this boom was short-lived. The first salmon cannery was built about 1910, and after World War I more than 50 fox farms were established in the bays and coves of the peninsula. Today the main industries are fishing and tourism.

The community has a spectacular view — on clear days — of Kachemak Bay and Cook Inlet. Mounts Augustine, Iliamna, Redoubt and Spurr, all active volcanoes, can be seen.

The area has much wildlife. Birds include bald eagles, ravens, crows and many species of ducks, gulls and songbirds. Sea otters are abundant in nearby waters. King, tanner and Dungeness crab, butter clams, halibut and salmon are plentiful.

Salmonberries, blueberries, huckleberries, currants and other berries abound in late summer and early fall.

Popular activities are photography, hiking, snowmobiling, ice skating, cross-country skiing, beachcombing and picnicking.

SKWENTNA is located on the Skwentna River, 62 miles north of Tyonek and 70 miles northwest of Anchorage. **Elevation:** 148 feet. **Transportation:** Boat; daily commuter service or air charter service from Anchorage. **Population:** About 20.

Visitor Facilities: Food and lodging year-round at Skwentna Roadhouse. Laundry facilities available. No grocery store; supplies are obtained from Anchorage. Skwentna Roadhouse is a dealer for snow machines, boats, outboard motors, all-terrain vehicles, generators and parts. Fishing and hunting licenses available at Skwentna Roadhouse. Hunting guide services through local registered guides; guided fishing trips and hunting drop-offs

The Iditarod Trail was first used as a mail route in 1910. (Staff, reprinted from ALASKA GEOGRAPHIC®)

---

through Skwentna Roadhouse. Snow machines, off-road vehicles and boats may be rented. Snow machine, marine engine, boat and aircraft repair services available. Fuel available: Marine gas, diesel, unleaded and regular gasoline. Moorage facilities available.

Skwentna was started in 1923 when Max and Belle Shellabarger homesteaded here and started a guide service, and later a flying service and weather station. After World War II, the Army built the airstrip and maintained a small post for a short time. The FAA maintained the airstrip until the early 1970s, when it was abandoned. The community grew up around the airstrip, which the state began maintaining in 1981. As residents point out, calling Skwentna a "town" is misleading. It has a runway, school, roadhouse and post office, which act as the hub for about 200 people living in the Yentna Valley. Recent state land sales have brought more people into the area.

Most area residents make their living in Anchorage, on the North Slope or through their own fishing lodges. As one resident puts it: "There is no work and not everybody can live off of trapping as people will think they can when they show up."

There are several fishing lodges in the area, including Salmon-Run, Lake Creek, Riversong, Tala-View, Shell Lake and McDougall lodges. The Yentna Valley offers good salmon and rainbow fishing, as well as Dolly Varden, grayling, whitefish and pike. The Yentna and Skwentna river drainages are also a popular area with jet boats out of Susitna Landing and float trips may be arranged through the Skwentna Roadhouse.

The area gets heavy snows in winter and is a popular spot for weekend snowmobilers and cross-country skiers. Skwentna is an official checkpoint on the annual Iditarod Sled Dog Race in March, as well as a gas stop for the Anchorage-to-Nome Gold Rush Classic snow machine race in February. It also is the turn-around point for the 200-mile Iditaski cross-country ski race, which starts in Knik, as well as several 200-mile sled dog races.

Hunting is good for moose, grizzly and black bear along area rivers. Dall sheep and caribou are available on fly-out hunts. There also is hunting in the area for grouse and ptarmigan in late winter.

TATITLEK is located on Prince William Sound, two miles southeast of Ellamar, 25 miles southwest of Valdez, 40 miles northwest of Cordova and 120 miles southeast of Anchorage. **Transportation:** Boat; scheduled and charter air service from Valdez. **Population:** 105.

Visitor Facilities: Accommodations and meals at a boarding house operated by Tatitlek Village IRA Council or arrangements may be made to stay at private homes. Laundry facilities available. Groceries available at Aurora's Pop Shop and Bob's. The sale and importation of alcoholic beverages is prohibited. Fishing and hunting licenses may be purchased locally. Air charter service available locally; boats may be available for rental. Diesel and moorage available.

Sitting in the shadow of 3,858-foot Copper Mountain, the dominent feature of Tatitlek is the blue-domed Russian Orthodox church. Residents make their living primarily by fishing.

Tatitlek and Copper Mountain. (Nancy Simmerman, reprinted from ALASKA GEOGRAPHIC®)

Bird watching and wildlife viewing opportunities in the area are good. Seabirds, bald eagles, sea otters, bears and mountain goats are frequently seen.

TUTKA BAY is located nine miles south of Homer. **Transportation:** 45-minute boat ride or 10-minute floatplane or helicopter trip from Homer. **Population:** About 30 year-round.

Visitor Facilities: Accommodations and meals at Tutka Bay Lodge. There are no other visitor facilities.

This tiny community is scattered about in coves,

Digging butter and steamer clams at Tutka Bay. (Nelda J. Osgood)

bights and lagoons of Tutka Bay. Much of the bay is within Kachemak Bay State Park and there is a state fish hatchery in Tutka Lagoon.

Residents earn their living by boat building, fishing, working for the Alaska Department of Fish and Game and producing cottage crafts.

Tutka Bay has secluded bays, virgin forests and tidepools teeming with marine life. Wildlife includes orca and minke whales, sea lion, sea otter, land otter, black bear, seal, porpoise, bald eagle and a wide variety of birds, including puffin, cormorant, mallard, oldsquaw, pintail, merganser, bufflehead, goldeneye, loon and common murre.

There is fishing for salmon, halibut, Dolly Varden, shrimp and crab; clamming; photography; beachcombing; hiking; hunting for bear and ducks; and viewing prehistoric petroglyphs and archaeological sites.

TYONEK is located on the northwest shore of Cook Inlet, 43 miles southwest of Anchorage. **Elevation:** 80 feet. **Transportation:** Boat; scheduled and charter air service from Anchorage. **Population:** 302.

Visitor Facilities: Guest house accommodations may be arranged through the Native village of Tyonek. There is a snack bar and groceries are available at RNL Grocery. The sale and importation of alcoholic beverages is prohibited. Fishing and hunting licenses and guide services available locally. Regular gasoline available.

Tyonek was the American Alaska Commercial Company's major outpost in upper Cook Inlet in the late 1800s, replacing an earlier Russian-American Company post. With the discovery of gold at Resurrection Creek in the 1880s, Tyonek became a major disembarking point for goods and people. The population of Tyonek decreased when Anchorage was founded but it still is the main settlement on the western shore of Cook Inlet.

Employment opportunities at Tyonek are limited. Many residents are commercial fishermen and there are jobs with the school, store, post

Tutka Bay Lodge guest house in winter. (Nelda J. Osgood)

Tyonek on Cook Inlet. (Steve McCutcheon, reprinted from ALASKA GEOGRAPHIC®)

Whittier on Passage Canal. (Third Eye Photography, reprinted from ALASKA GEOGRAPHIC®)

office, village administration and other government agencies. The village also has benefited from the sale of oil and gas rights on reservation land.

Tyonek residents continue to follow a subsistence lifestyle resembling that of their ancestors. They fish for king, pink and red salmon, hooligan, rainbow trout, Dolly Varden and whitefish. Hunting is for moose, ducks, geese, spruce hens, porcupine, beluga whales and seals. Berries are gathered in late summer and early fall.

Visiting sportfishermen should note that much of the land along the Chuitna River is owned by the Tyonek Native Corporation and fishermen must have a guide from Tyonek. Land on the north side of the Chuitna River mouth is public land.

UGANIK BAY is located on the northwest side of Kodiak Island, 40 miles west of Kodiak. **Elevation:** 50 feet. **Transportation:** Boat; scheduled and charter floatplane service from Kodiak. **Population:** 15.

Visitor Facilities: None. Limited groceries and supplies available at cannery store. Guide service available. Marine gas and regular gasoline available.

West Point in Uganik Bay was the location of an Eskimo village in the 1800s. Today, there are a few homes at West Point and one in Mush Bay in the east arm of Uganik Bay. Fishing is the only industry. There were four canneries operating in the bay in the 1920s. Today only one salmon cannery, owned by Kodiak Alaskan Seafoods Inc., operates during July and August.

Uganik Bay is located within the Kodiak Island National Wildlife Refuge. Steelhead, rainbow and silver salmon are available at Lake Uganik. Most visitors to the area are deer or bear hunters who fly in with air charter operators from Kodiak.

WHITTIER is located on the Kenai Peninsula at the head of Passage Canal on Prince William Sound, 75 miles southeast of Anchorage. **Elevation:** 30 feet. **Transportation:** Scheduled air service from Anchorage; Alaska Railroad shuttle from

Portage; scheduled state ferry service from Valdez and Cordova. **Population:** 268.

Visitor Facilities: Accommodations and meals at Anchor Inn and Sportsman's Inn. There are several other restaurants in town, two bars, gift shops, laundry facilities, a grocery and a general merchandise store. Marine supplies and charter boats and tours are available. Marine engine, boat and auto repair services available. A list of guides, outfitters and charter services is available from the city office. Marine gas, diesel, unleaded and regular gasoline available.

Named after the poet John Greenleaf Whittier, Whittier was created by the U.S. government during World War II as a supply port. The 14-story Begich Towers, used by the Army for housing, now houses more than half of Whittier's population. The Buckner Building, completed in 1953 and once the largest building in Alaska, was also used to house Army personnel. Whittier Manor, built in the early 1950s by private developers as rental units for civilian employees and soldiers, became a condominium in 1964.

Since military and government activities ceased, the economy of Whittier rests largely on the fishing industry, tourism and the port.

Whittier is the jump-off point for travel across Prince William Sound. In summer, travelers arrive either by ferry or on the railroad shuttle from Portage on the Seward Highway. Recreational activities in the area including hiking, scuba diving, fishing, sailing and other water sports. Wildlife in the area includes whales, porpoises, sea lions and sea otters. Just across Passage Canal is Kittiwake Rookery, largest of its kind in the world.

WOODY ISLAND is located three miles east of Kodiak. **Transportation:** Private boat; charter floatplane service. **Population:** 1 to 4 in winter; 1 to 6 in summer.

Visitor Facilities: None.

The island was named by the Russian explorer Urey Theodorovich Lisianski in 1804. Woody Island figured in the early history of Alaska as a boat-building center and a port from which the Russian-American Ice Co. shipped ice to the California coast in the early and middle 1880s. It is believed the first horses in Alaska were brought to Woody Island in 1867. The first road built in Alaska — 2.7 miles long — was built around this island.

One of Woody Island's longtime residents is Yule Chaffin, author of a book on the area.

Attractions

Caines Head State Recreation Area

Caines Head State Recreation Area is located on Caines Head, a headland that juts into the west side of Resurrection Bay eight miles south of Seward. The Harding Icefield, Bear Glacier and numerous islands in the bay can be seen from high ground within the recreation area.

This undeveloped, 5,961-acre park has several World War II ammunition storage bunkers and gun emplacements that guarded the entrance to Resurrection Bay. Although there are no facilities at the park, there is a ranger in residence and its shore is used frequently by boaters.

Tidewater glaciers on College Fjord in Prince William Sound. (Staff)

Chugach National Forest

Among national forests, the Chugach ranks second in size only to the Tongass National Forest in southeastern Alaska. The Chugach totals 5.8 million acres — about the size of the state of New Hampshire. It is a beautiful land of majestic mountains, free-flowing streams, frigid mountain lakes and productive wetlands. It encompasses three geographic regions: the northeastern Kenai Peninsula, the arc of Prince William Sound and the Copper River Delta/Bering River area east of Cordova. Special features of the Chugach are Kayak Island, site of the first documented landing of Europeans in Alaska; Columbia Glacier, one of the largest tidewater glaciers in the world; Portage Glacier, one of the most visited recreational facilities in Alaska; and the wetland of the Copper River Delta, which serves as nesting, staging and feeding habitat for millions of birds each year.

The diverse lands and waters of the Chugach provide habitat for a wide variety of birds, mammals and fish. Black and brown bears inhabit almost all of the Chugach, foraging on open tundra slopes and in intertidal zones. In late summer bears may be seen feeding on spawned-out salmon along streams and rivers. Black bear occur in most areas of the Chugach, with the exception of some of the islands. Brown bears are found along the eastern shore of Prince William Sound and on the Copper River Delta and are occasionally seen on the Kenai Peninsula.

Record-size moose — some with antler spreads of more than six feet — inhabit the Kenai Peninsula; moose also have been transplanted to the Copper River Delta. Sitka black-tailed deer have been transplanted to many islands in Prince William Sound and caribou have been transplanted to the Kenai Peninsula. Dall sheep can be seen on mountainsides of the Kenai Peninsula; mountain goats are found on steep hillsides along Prince William Sound, the Copper River Delta and occasionally above Portage Valley. Smaller mammals include lynx, coyotes, red foxes, wolverines, wolves, porcupines, red squirrels, beavers, land otters, parka squirrels, pikas and hoary marmots.

Visitors to Prince William Sound may see Dall porpoises, harbor seals, sea otters, sea lions, killer and humpback whales.

More than 214 species of birds have been recorded on the Chugach. Seabirds, such as black-legged kittiwakes, nest in sea-cliff colonies by the thousands. Ptarmigan scurry over alpine tundra, bald eagles perch on shoreline snags and tangled rain forest undergrowth hosts Steller's jays.

Saltwater fish include halibut, red snapper and five species of salmon. Razor clams can be dug near Cordova and shrimp and three species of crab may be harvested. Lakes on the Kenai Peninsula contain landlocked Dolly Varden and many larger lakes and streams are migratory routes for Dolly Varden, rainbow trout and salmon. Other freshwater fish include arctic grayling, hooligan, burbot, lake trout and cutthroat trout.

The Chugach has popular summer and winter recreation areas that are easily accessible from Anchorage and other area communities.

There are 16 campgrounds. Three dozen public-use cabins also are available for a nominal fee by advance reservation.

Some 200 miles of hiking trails lead to back-country cabins, ski areas and popular fishing spots. Major hiking trails include the popular 38-mile Resurrection Pass Trail, a scenic National Recreation Trail that follows a route originally established in the late 1800s by miners along gold-bearing Resurrection Creek and travels through 2,600-foot-high Resurrection Pass; the 10-mile Devils Pass Trail, which joins the Resurrection Pass Trail at 2,400-foot-high Devils Pass; the Crow Pass Trail, a 27-mile-long alpine trail that also passes through Chugach State Park; the Johnson Pass Trail, a 23-mile route that follows a portion of the historic Iditarod Trail, which once extended from Seward to Nome; the 21-mile Russian Lakes Trail, which provides access to good trout and salmon fishing; and Lost Lake Trail, which extends seven miles to alpine country with spectacular views.

The Summit Lake/Manitoba Mountain area offers cross-country skiing, alpine mountaineering, snowshoeing and snowmobile recreation opportunities. Turnagain Pass, 60 miles southeast of Anchorage, also is open for winter use.

Chugach State Park

Hikers enjoy a spectacular view of Anchorage, Knik and Turnagain arms and the Alaska Range from Chugach State Park, which at nearly 495,000 acres is one of the nation's largest state parks. This mountainous park on the doorstep of Alaska's largest city offers an excellent wilderness experience, summer or winter. The abundant wildlife ranges from the popular bald eagles and whales to the less popular mosquitoes (27 varieties). Favorite hikes include the Old Johnson Trail, a historic settler's route above Turnagain Arm; the alpine tundra trails of Arctic Valley; the Old Iditarod Trail over Crow Pass; the Eklutna Lake region; and the Hillside Trail system. Other activities are camping, boating, hunting and fishing. This park is widely used during the winter; large sections above tree line provide easy traveling by skis, dog sled, snowshoes and snowmobile. (Betty Sederquist, reprinted from ALASKA GEOGRAPHIC®)

Denali State Park

Boaters enjoy the peaceful waters of Byers Lake, location of Byers Lake campground, the main recreational development in 324,420-acre Denali State Park. The state park, which straddles the main highway between Anchorage and Fairbanks, offers spectacular views of Mount McKinley and surrounding peaks and glaciers in Denali National Park to the north. Features of this park include wildlife undisturbed by infrequent contact with man, a summer explosion of tundra plant life and constantly shifting channels of wide glacier-fed streams. The park offers backcountry camping, outstanding cross-country skiing, and a variety of hiking experiences including the easy five-mile Byers Lake Trail around Byers Lake; the scenic seven-mile Cascade Trail from the Byers Lake Trail to a Curry Ridge viewpoint; and a longer alpine hiking route. (Staff, reprinted from The MILEPOST®)

Kachemak Bay State Park and State Wilderness Park

Located across Kachemak Bay from Homer, this is one of the largest and most majestic parks in the state system. Kachemak Bay State Park encompasses 120,000 acres; the adjoining wilderness park, 280,000 acres. This largely undeveloped park offers wilderness experiences combining ocean, forest, mountains and glaciers, as well as varied weather and wildlife. The waters of Kachemak Bay, reputedly among the most productive in the world, teem with marine life. Highlights include Grewingk Glacier, Poot Peak, Gull Island, China Poot Bay, Humpy Creek, Halibut Cove Lagoon and Tutka Lagoon hatchery.

This park offers excellent opportunities for observation and study of wildlife that includes seabirds, seals, sea otters, whales, eagles and bears. Park visitors have many opportunities

for boating, beachcombing, camping, hiking and mountain climbing. Once above tree line, climbers and skiers will find glaciers and snowfields stretching for miles. Hunting and fishing is permitted.

(Photo above left: © Chlaus Lotscher; above right: Jeff Johnson)

73

Kenai Fjords National Park

The approximately 580,000 acres of Kenai Fjords National Park encompass a coastal mountain-fjord system on the southeastern side of the Kenai Peninsula. Highlight of the park is the 300-square-mile Harding Icefield — one of four major ice caps in the United States — almost a mile above the Gulf of Alaska. It is believed to be a remnant of the last ice age — 10,000 years ago — when ice masses covered half of Alaska. The ice field's skyline is marked by *nunataks*, the peaks of mountains which have their lower slopes buried by thousands of feet of ice. Moist marine air blowing in from the Gulf of Alaska dumps 400 to 600 inches of snow on the ice field each year. The pull of gravity and weight of the overlying snow causes the ice to spread to all points on the compass until it is shaped into glaciers that flow downward, carving the landscape into spectacular shapes. There are 34 major glaciers that radiate from the ice field, among them, tidewater glaciers that calve directly into salt water. The park was named after the long valleys that once were filled with glacial ice and are now deep, seawater-filled fjords.

Bald eagles nest in spruce and hemlock treetops along the shoreline and mountain goats inhabit rocky slopes. Moose, black and brown bears, wolves and Dall sheep wander the park. Raucous Steller sea lions live on rocky islands at the entrance to Aialik and Nuka bays; centuries of hauling out have worn the granite rocks smooth. Harbor seals can be seen resting on icebergs. Killer whales, Dall porpoises and sea otters, as well as minke and humpback whales also are seen. Thousands of seabirds, including horned and tufted puffins, auklets, petrels, common murres and black-legged kittiwakes rear their young on steep cliffs.

Dolly Varden and king, silver, red, chum and pink salmon spawn in the park's streams. Shrimp, crab and other shellfish are found off the coast. Sportfishing for salmon and bottom fish is popular in Resurrection Bay and to some degree in Aialik Bay.

The only overnight facility in the park is a Park Service cabin in Aialik Bay, which is available for a nominal fee by advance reservation. Camping is permitted in the park without fee or permit.

There is access from the Seward Highway to the Exit Glacier ranger station, from which a trail leads to the ice field, but most of the park is accessible only by boat or amphibious plane. Boat tours and flightseeing trips are available in Seward or Homer.

The Exit Glacier area is open to winter visitors for skiing, snowshoeing, snowmobiling and dog mushing. Other popular recreational activities in the park are boating, fishing, wildlife viewing, kayaking the fjords, backpacking and bird watching.

Above — *Spectacular topography of Kenai Fjords National Park. (National Park Service)*

Right — *Black-legged kittiwakes and chicks. (David Wm. Miller, reprinted from ALASKA GEOGRAPHIC®)*

Marine Parks

The state of Alaska has established 12 marine parks as part of an international system of shoreline parks and recreation areas stretching from near Olympia, Washington, up through British Columbia, Canada, and as far north as Prince William Sound. Eventually there may be more than 150 of these parks, each a one-day boat trip from the other. Most of these parks have no developed facilities, but they do offer sheltered anchorages. The seven marine parks located in Prince William Sound are the following:

Surprise Cove — Located at the entrance to Cochrane Bay approximately 15 miles east of Whittier along a major route for pleasure boats between Whittier and western Prince William Sound.

Zeigler Cove — Located on the northern shore of the entrance to Pigot Bay on the west side of Port Wells, approximately 14 miles east of Whittier.

Bettles Bay — Located on the western shoreline of Port Wells, approximately 20 miles from Whittier.

South Esther Island — Located at the confluence of Wells Passage and Port Wells in upper Prince William Sound, approximately 20 miles due east of Whittier.

Horseshoe Bay — Located on Latouche Island in southwestern Prince William Sound, approximately halfway between Seward and Whittier. The old gold mining town of Latouche is two miles to the northeast.

Sawmill Bay — Located on the north shore of Port Valdez, approximately 14 miles west and south of Valdez.

Shoup Bay — Located on the north shore of Port Valdez, 7.5 miles west of Valdez. During the 1964 earthquake, an undersea slide created a 170-foot-high wave here (listed in the *Guinness Book of World Records*). Reportedly the bay emptied and refilled three times.

Shuyak Island State Park

Kayakers approach a pod of sea otters off Shuyak Island, northernmost sizable island of the Kodiak archipelago. Shuyak Island State Park, one of the newest in the state park system, covers 11,000 acres on the northern end of Shuyak Island and includes a number of smaller islands, rocks, passages and lagoons that offer safe cruising by canoe or kayak. The volcanic peaks of the Alaska Peninsula across 30-mile-wide Shelikof Strait can be seen on clear days. Sea otters are abundant and there are relatively high numbers of bald eagles and seabirds. Hiking is good on open tundra areas. Flowers are everywhere in spring and summer. Two shelter cabins may be reserved; wilderness camping is permitted. The park is easily reached by charter plane from either Kodiak or Homer. (Gary Dobos, reprinted from ALASKA GEOGRAPHIC®)

Wrangell-St. Elias National Park and Preserve

Located northwest of Yakutat and northeast of Cordova and Valdez, Wrangell-St. Elias is the largest unit in the national park system, encompassing 13.2 million acres of superlative scenery, abundant wildlife and fascinating history. Wrangell-St. Elias and adjacent Kluane National Park in Canada encompass the largest area of parkland in North America. This is North America's "mountain kingdom." The Wrangell, St. Elias and Chugach mountain ranges converge, forming a mountain wilderness unsurpassed in North America and comparable to all other major mountain groups in the world. The region contains the largest concentration of peaks exceeding 14,500 feet in North America; the park includes nine of the 16 highest peaks in the United States. Mount St. Elias, at 18,008 feet, is the second tallest peak in the United States; Mount Logan, across the border in Kluane park, soars to a height of 19,850 feet, second only to Mount McKinley in North American summits.

This park has been shaped by fire as well as ice. Mount Wrangell (14,163 feet) erupted as recently as 1930. Others considered to be active are Mount Sanford (16,237 feet) and Mount Drum (12,010

Clusters, or cushions, of moss campion can reach two feet in diameter. (© Chlaus Lotscher)

Mount Drum, elevation 12,010 feet, in the Wrangell Mountains. (George Wuerthner)

feet). On the western flank of Mount Drum are three large thermal springs known as mud volcanoes.

The area also contains the largest concentration of glaciers on the continent. One of these, Malaspina Glacier, is North America's largest piedmont glacier, a type formed when two or more glaciers flow from a confined valley to form a broad fan-shaped ice mass at the base of mountains. Malaspina Glacier, a national natural landmark, covers about 1,500 square miles — more area than the state of Rhode Island. Hubbard Glacier, which flows out of the St. Elias Mountains into Disenchantment Bay, is one of the largest and most active glaciers in North America, traveling as much as 32 feet per day.

Chitistone and Nizina canyons "far exceed the scale of Yosemite Valley in California" and include an even greater variety of geological wonders, says the Park Service. There is a spectacular 300-foot waterfall in the upper Chitistone Canyon and the

lower canyon has sheer walls rising 4,000 feet above the river.

Wrangell-St. Elias contains many prehistoric and historic sites: ancient Eskimo and Indian villages and camps, as well as sites of Russian fur trading posts, gold rush relics, and early industrial complexes such as the Kennecott Mine, the most famous and richest copper mine in Alaska until market conditions led to its abandonment in 1938. Mining continues today at Dan Creek, Rex Creek, Upper Kotsina and Nabesna.

Diverse habitats support varied wildlife. On higher slopes range Dall sheep and mountain goats — the sheep in the Wrangell Mountains and northern slopes of the Chugach Range, the goats in the coastal mountains. Caribou from three herds forage on park lands. Moose browse throughout the lowlands and river bottoms and two herds of introduced bison range along the Copper River and Chitina River. Brown and black bears share lower elevations with wolves, wolverines, coyotes, red foxes and a variety of small furbearers.

Marine mammals which can be observed in Yakutat Bay, where the park touches the sea, include seals, sea lions, sea otters, and two species of dolphin, as well as killer whales.

Grayling, lingcod and trout thrive in lakes adjacent to the Chitina River valley and on the northern slopes of the Wrangells, while the Copper River supports a major salmon run.

Recreation in Wrangell-St. Elias includes hunting, fishing, mountaineering, backpacking, photography, cross-country skiing, rafting/kayaking and wildlife observation. Rustic accommodations are available at privately operated lodges, cabins and camps scattered throughout the park and preserve. There are no designated campgrounds. No permits are necessary for camping or backpacking.

Wrangell-St. Elias is accessible by the unpaved, 65-mile-long Chitina-McCarthy Road which extends up the Chitina River valley to the Kennicott River just west of McCarthy. Access to the northern section of the park is from Slana along a 43-mile unpaved road to the mining community of Nabesna. All other access is by boat or air.

Alaska Maritime National Wildlife Refuge

The 3.5 million acres of this wildlife refuge encompass more than 2,400 parcels of land on islands, islets, rocks, spires, reefs and headlands of Alaska coastal waters from the Chukchi Sea to southeastern Alaska.

Many islands of southcentral Alaska are part of this refuge. Accessible by charter boat from Seward are Barwell Island, 20 miles southeast of Seward, the Chiswell Islands, 35 miles southwest of Seward, Nuka Island, 36 miles east-southeast of Seldovia, and the Pye Islands, east of Nuka Island and 30 miles west of the Chiswells. On the west side of Cook Inlet, Chisik and Duck islands, 55 miles southwest of Kenai, can be reached by charter boat from Kenai or Homer. The Barren Islands, located between the Kenai Peninsula and the Kodiak Island group, are accessible by boat or air charter from Homer.

Visitors who boat near the islands may easily view seabirds and marine mammals, but in order to protect the wildlife, permits are required to land on any of these islands.

It is estimated that nearly 60 percent of the 105,000 nesting seabirds on the south side of the Kenai Peninsula use the 200 islands of the Chiswell group. What is believed to be the largest seabird colony in Cook Inlet — some 80,000 birds, mostly black-legged kittiwakes and common murres — occupies 5,700-acre Chisik Island and tiny Duck Island nearby. Other birds common throughout this area are puffins, parakeet and rhinoceros auklets, fork-tailed storm petrels and cormorants.

The Chiswells and the Pye Island group harbor Steller sea lion rookeries. Other marine mammals that may be seen are sea otters, seals, porpoises and several species of whales. Land mammals in some areas include black bears and land otters.

The female Steller sea lions seen below display aggressive posturing along the ledges of an island in the Chiswells, a haul-out area for some 2,000 Steller sea lions. (David Wm. Miller, reprinted from ALASKA GEOGRAPHIC®)

Kenai National Wildlife Refuge

This refuge originally was established in 1941 as the Kenai National Moose Range to protect habitat of these huge animals. In 1980 the refuge was renamed and expanded to encompass 1.97 million acres — 1.35 million of which are wilderness lands. Kenai Refuge is bounded on the northeast by Chugach National Forest, on the southeast by Kenai Fjords National Park and on the south by Kachemak Bay State Park.

The refuge covers much of the total land area of the Kenai Peninsula and includes some of each type of Alaskan habitat: tundra, mountains, wetlands and forests.

Moose are abundant in the Cook Inlet area. (Helen Rhode, reprinted from ALASKA GEOGRAPHIC®)

Numerous lakes in the northern lowland region combine to form the only nationally designated trails in the Alaska refuge system: the Swanson River and Swan Lake canoe trails, enjoyed annually by many hundreds of visitors. One special feature is a portion of the Harding Icefield to the southeast. Others are the Tustumena-Skiland benchlands, a unique ecological area of mountain and glacial formations, Dall sheep and mountain goat ranges and brown bear and timberline moose habitat; the Kenai River and its tributaries, which provide vital spawning and rearing habitat for millions of salmon; the Chickaloon watershed and estuary, the major waterfowl and shorebird staging area on the peninsula; and the Skilak Loop area, a road-accessible region with abundant wildlife and scenic vistas.

The Kenai River king salmon fishery is world renowned. The river supports the largest genetic strain of king salmon anywhere, according to the Fish and Wildlife Service. The world record sport-caught king salmon, weighing 97.25 pounds, was caught here in 1985. Other fish occurring in refuge waters include red, pink and silver salmon, lake trout, Dolly Varden, rainbow trout, steelhead, kokanee, grayling and char.

The refuge has 15 road-accessible public campgrounds. Backcountry camping varies from fly-in and boat-in locations to sites accessible only by trail. There are more than 200 miles of trails on the refuge, several of which provide access to alpine benchland open to off-trail hiking.

The two popular canoe trails provide excellent opportunities to see many kinds of wildlife in their natural habitat. Cow moose visit this area to give birth to one or two calves in late May or early June. Many species of songbirds, shorebirds and waterfowl nest along the lake shores, marshlands and surrounding forests. Beaver inhabit many lakes and streams.

The 80-mile Swanson River Canoe Trail links more than 40 lakes with 46 miles of the Swanson River. The 60-mile Swan Lake Canoe Trail — separate from and south of the Swanson River Trail — connects 30 lakes with forks of the Moose River. Either trail can be traveled in less than a week.

Kodiak National Wildlife Refuge

This refuge encompasses about 1.8 million acres on Kodiak, Uganik, Afognak and Ban islands — all part of the Kodiak Archipelago. The city of Kodiak, accessible by commercial jet and the Alaska Marine Highway system, is some 250 air miles from Anchorage and about 21 miles northeast of the refuge boundary. The refuge is larger than the state of Delaware, but because of the convoluted coastline, no place on the island is more than 15 miles from the sea.

The refuge's varied landscapes include glacially carved valleys, tundra uplands, lakes, wetlands, sand and gravel beaches, salt flats, meadows and rugged mountains to 4,000 feet. Spruce forests dominate the northern part of Kodiak Island and all of Afognak Island. In the interior of the refuge sedges and fireweed up to six feet high are often mixed with salmonberry, blueberry and rose bushes. Dense thickets of willow, alder and elderberry abound. Devil's club, with thorns that

Kodiak brown bear roams unchallenged. (Gerry Atwell, reprinted from ALASKA GEOGRAPHIC®)

Backpacker hikes cross-country in Kodiak National Wildlife Refuge.
(George Wuerthner)

can penetrate leather, grow up to six feet high in the woods and on the slopes. The heathland in the southwest portion of the refuge is covered with hummocks — small knolls of grass and soil that make walking difficult.

This refuge was originally established in 1941 to protect the habitat of the huge Kodiak brown bears and other wildlife. The bears remain the refuge's most well-known feature, attracting visitors from all over the world. The refuge supports the highest density of brown bears in the world. The three largest brown bears ever taken and 33 of the 50 largest in the Boone and Crockett North American records are from Kodiak Island. Females weigh about 650 pounds; males up to 1,500 pounds.

The refuge is roadless and reached most easily by chartered floatplane or boat from the city of Kodiak. Wilderness camping is allowed throughout the refuge without advance reservations, permits or fees. There are nine public-use cabins available for a nominal fee by advance reservation. The predominant recreational activities are hunting, fishing and trapping. Other activities include hiking, wildlife viewing and photography, beachcombing, berry picking and clamming.

Bald eagles are common at the refuge. (Gerry Atwell, reprinted from ALASKA GEOGRAPHIC®)

McNeil River State Game Sanctuary

The McNeil River State Game Sanctuary and the large numbers of brown bears that congregate to feast on spawning chum salmon attract photographers from all over the world. Nowhere else can there be seen groups of up to 20 wild brown bears or 60 or so individual bears coming and going.

McNeil River is located approximately 200 air miles southwest of Anchorage and 100 air miles west of Homer. The river drains into Kamishak Bay in the shadow of Augustine Island, an active volcano with a history of violent eruptions, the most recent in April 1986. McNeil River is bordered to the south by Katmai National Park and Preserve.

The greatest number of bears are seen at McNeil River falls, about one mile up from the river mouth. In order to reduce disturbance of the bears and minimize the risk of human-bear encounters, the Alaska Department of Fish and Game allows visitors to the sanctuary by permit only during the peak season July 1 through August 25. (Larry Aumiller, reprinted from ALASKA GEOGRAPHIC®)

Tetlin National Wildlife Refuge

This 700,000-acre refuge is the most easterly in Alaska. It is bordered on the north by the Alaska Highway, on the east by Canada, on the south by Wrangell-St. Elias National Park and Preserve and on the west by the Tetlin Reserve (formerly the Tetlin Indian Reservation).

Tetlin Refuge is a showcase of geographic and ecological features created by wildfires, permafrost and fluctuating river channels. The refuge features an undulating plain broken by hills, forests, ponds, lakes and extensive marshes. The glacial Chisana and Nabesna rivers dominate the wetlands as they meander across before joining to form the Tanana River. Parabolic sand dunes, formed of windblown glacial flour, are found southeast of Northway and at Big John Hill.

These varied habitats are home to an equally diverse group of animals. The refuge also is a stopover for migrating birds and its wetlands provide important summer breeding habitat for waterfowl. (Jo Keller, U.S. Fish and Wildlife Service, reprinted from ALASKA GEOGRAPHIC®)

Southcentral Rivers

The Southcentral/Gulf Coast region has many rivers that offer a wide variety of wilderness and boating experiences. Some of the more popular rivers are:

Chitina River — A silty glacial river located in the Chugach Mountains in Wrangell-St. Elias National Park and Preserve. This river heads at Chitina Glacier and flows west-northwest 112 miles to the Copper River, 1.2 miles east of Chitina, 66 miles northeast of Valdez.

Chulitna and Tokositna rivers — The Chulitna, located along the George Parks Highway north of Talkeetna, is described as "a glacier river of consequence." It runs partially through Denali State Park. The Middle Fork is clear water, generally shallow and rocky. The East Fork is clear, too, but fast (four to five miles per hour). Below the West Fork confluence, the Chulitna is even faster. The Tokositna River is described as one of the most scenic, yet easy to run rivers in the area. It has glaciers along its course and Mount McKinley towers above it. The Tokositna can be reached in a few minutes by air charter from Talkeetna to Home Lake. Its flow is moderately swift, but it presents no special obstacles down to its confluence with the Chulitna River.

Copper River — This major glacial river heads on the north side of the Wrangell Mountains and flows south 250 miles through a gap in the Chugach Mountains to the Gulf of Alaska, just east of Cordova. Although the Richardson and Glenn highways parallel the river, they are rarely within sight or sound. This braided river passes through

Broad and braided Susitna River. (Sepp Weber, reprinted from ALASKA® *magazine)*

true wilderness country and features silty, but always swift water.

Gulkana River — A river trip of nearly 300 miles is possible by using this wild and scenic river. Boaters may paddle and portage through the Tangle Lakes Canoe Trail, then float the Middle Fork Gulkana to the Gulkana River, which joins the Copper River for the final leg to the Gulf of Alaska.

Kahiltna River — This river heads at Kahiltna Glacier, 35 miles northeast of Talkeetna between Mount Foraker and Mount Hunter in the Alaska Range, and flows southeast to the Yentna River, 53 miles northwest of Anchorage.

Karluk River — This river heads in Karluk Lake on the west coast of Kodiak Island and flows north and west 24 miles through Karluk Lagoon to Shelikof Strait at the village of Karluk.

Kenai River — This river heads at Kenai Lake on the Kenai Peninsula and flows west 75 miles to Cook Inlet at Kenai. Much of this river is located on the Kenai National Wildlife Refuge. It features an exciting white-water canyon for the experienced paddler.

Klutina River — This river heads at Klutina Glacier in the Chugach Mountains and flows 63 miles northeast to the Copper River at Copper Center on the Richardson Highway, 66 miles northeast of Valdez.

Lake Creek — This clear-water stream heads in Chelatna Lake and flows southeast 56 river miles to the Yentna River. This river offers spectacular views of the Alaska Range and Mount McKinley to the northeast, and excellent fishing for Dolly Varden, grayling and rainbow trout.

Little Susitna River — The "Little Su" heads at Mint Glacier in the Talkeetna Mountains and flows southwest 110 miles to Cook Inlet, 13 miles west of Anchorage.

Maclaren River — This river heads at Maclaren Glacier in the Clearwater Mountains and flows southwest 55 miles to the Susitna River.

Nabesna River — This river heads at Nabesna Glacier and flows northeast to join with the Chisana River to form the Tanana River near Northway Junction on the Alaska Highway. The river begins in Wrangell-St. Elias National Park and Preserve and flows through Tetlin National Wildlife Refuge.

Skwentna River — This river heads at South Twin Glacier below Mount Spurr and flows north and east 100 miles to the Yentna River near the settlement of Skwentna, 70 miles northwest of Anchorage. The Skwentna is considered one of the most difficult and remote, but spectacular wilderness rivers in Alaska, recommended only for expert paddlers who are experienced in wilderness travel. It has many difficult rapids and steep-walled canyons.

Susitna River — This large river heads at Susitna Glacier in the Alaska Range and flows southwest 260 miles to Cook Inlet, 24 miles west of Anchorage. This river's Tanaina Indian name, said to mean "sandy river," first appeared in 1847 on a Russian chart.

Talachulitna River — This river heads on Beluga Mountain and flows south and northwest to the Skwentna River, 14 miles upriver from the settlement of Skwentna, which is 70 miles northwest of Anchorage. The upper reaches of Talachulitna Creek, which drains Judd Lake, may be shallow and have logjams.

Tazlina, Nelchina and Little Nelchina rivers — These rivers offer a variety of water conditions and trip alternatives. The Tazlina River drains Tazlina Lake and flows east 30 miles to the Copper River, seven miles southeast of Glennallen and about 140 miles east of Anchorage. The Nelchina River heads at Nelchina Glacier and flows north and southeast 28 miles into Tazlina Lake. The Little Nelchina is a 48-mile-long tributary to the Nelchina.

Tyone River — This river heads at Tyone Lake and flows northwest 30 miles to the Susitna River, 68 miles northwest of Gulkana. This trip combines lake paddling with an easy river journey. About half the distance is across three adjoining lakes: Louise, Susitna and Tyone.

Yentna River — This river is formed by its East and West forks and flows southeast 75 miles to the Susitna River, 30 miles northwest of Anchorage. This flat-water glacial river winds in graceful sweeps through the basin south of Mount McKinley.

Southcentral Sportfishing

Southcentral and the Gulf Coast offer a wide range of fishing experiences, from lakes and streams to ocean trolling. A variety of species are available, depending on where the angler drops a line.

King salmon, the most prized species in Alaska, are found throughout this region. These fish often reach 30 pounds and more and can attain 90 to 100 pounds. The best catches of kings in Prince William Sound are made near Valdez and Cordova

Charter-boat fishermen out of Homer go after pink salmon. (© Chlaus Lotscher)

in late winter and early spring and near Whittier in early summer. Saltwater fishing for kings is available in lower Cook Inlet from mid-May through late July. On Kodiak Island, kings start arriving in the Karluk River in early June.

Silver salmon arrive in Prince William Sound in late July and remain through mid-September; they also occur in rivers in the Cordova area in the fall. These flashy fighters can be found in waters off the lower Kenai Peninsula in July and August; and in rivers draining into upper Cook Inlet from mid-July to September. Silvers can be taken from Kodiak Island waters in late August and early September. Silver salmon range from eight to 20 pounds, and can attain 25 pounds.

Fishing for pink salmon is excellent in Prince William Sound from mid-June through mid-August. In the Cook Inlet area, fishing for pinks

ranges from poor to fair from mid-July through mid-August. In waters of the Kenai Peninsula, fishing for pinks is best from mid-July to mid-August. These small salmon, which average three or four pounds, but occasionally attain 10 pounds, start arriving in Kodiak waters in late June.

Chum salmon, which commonly weigh about 10 pounds, but occasionally reach 30 pounds, are available in Prince William Sound during July and August and often are caught while fishing for silvers or pinks. These fish are scattered sparingly throughout Cook Inlet streams from mid-July through mid-August and they usually arrive in Kodiak waters in late July and early August.

Ruby-fleshed red salmon are much prized for food; they commonly weigh six to 10 pounds, although they occasionally weigh up to 15 pounds. In some rivers they apparently will not hit a lure, but there is excellent fly-fishing for reds in the Gulkana and Klutina rivers in the Copper River area in late June and July, in the Russian River on the Kenai Peninsula from early June to late August and in the Kenai River from mid-July through early August. Reds also are available in several rivers in the Kodiak area from June to the first of September.

Other fish encountered in this region are halibut that can tip the scales at 300 pounds; rainbow trout, which may weigh 10 pounds and occasionally reach 20 pounds; char and Dolly Varden, which usually weigh one to three pounds, but occasionally reach the nine- to 12-pound mark;

lake trout can reach 30 pounds; grayling; burbot (also called lush or lingcod) average two to five pounds, but can attain 20 pounds.

There is easy access to good sportfishing in the Southcentral/Gulf Coast region by car, but the majority of the best fishing locations are reached only by plane or boat. Many communities have charter operators that offer fishing trips or simply transportation to fishing spots.

Columbia Glacier

A floatplane taxis in front of Columbia Glacier, star attraction of Prince William Sound and one of the largest tidewater glaciers on the Alaska coast. The glacier covers more than 440 square miles. Its terminus measures more than six miles across and 164 to 262 feet above sea level. It is expected to recede 22 miles in the next 20 to 50 years, leaving behind a deep fjord. Scientists are studying its retreat and increased iceberg production, which could pose a hazard to oil tankers from Valdez. Plankton-rich waters attract great numbers of fish, which in turn attract bald eagles, kittiwakes, gulls and harbor seals. The glacier can be viewed from the state ferries; boat and flightseeing tours are available in Whittier, Valdez and Cordova. (Staff, reprinted from The MILEPOST® *)*

Copper River Delta

Right — *The 400-square-mile delta of this major glacier-fed river is noted for its spectacular waterfowl and shorebird migrations each spring and, to a lesser extent, each fall. The Copper River Delta, part of Chugach National Forest, protects one of the larger known concentrations of nesting trumpeter swans in North America. The total population of dusky Canada geese on the delta, the only nesting area of this subspecies, ranges from 7,500 to 13,500. Nesting waterfowl are joined in spring and fall by thousands of migrating shorebirds.*

Hundreds of thousands of pintail ducks migrate through in the spring and many remain to breed and nest. Other species found in the delta are white-fronted geese, snow geese, teal, wigeons, shovellers, scaup and goldeneyes. Many thousands of sandhill cranes stop to rest and feed on the flats on their way North to nest. Flocks of western and dunlin sandpipers arrive in late April and early May.

Access to the delta is by floatplane or boat from Cordova or by the Copper River Highway. (Jerriane Lowther, staff)

Kayak Island

Left — *Driftwood litters the desolate shore of Kayak Island, site of the first documented landing by Europeans on North America's northwest coast. Naturalist Georg Wilhelm Steller and other members of an expedition led by Captain Commander Vitus Bering landed on the west shore of Kayak Island on July 20, 1741. No trace of the landing remains today, but the site is on the National Register of Historic Places. The remote, narrow island, located 62 miles southeast of Cordova, offers excellent opportunities for beachcombing, hiking, camping, photography, berry picking, fishing, hunting and exploring. (U.S. Forest Service)*

Katalla

Although a ghost town today, Katalla once was an oil and coal boom town and may be again one day. Located 50 miles southeast of Cordova, the old town is near one of the first oil strikes in Alaska, made in 1896, and the state's first oil well, drilled in 1902. The town was established about 1903 as a supply point for the oil field. The Bering River coalfields about 15 miles to the northeast once were connected to Katalla by a railroad.

The town's population may have been as high as 10,000 during the boom year of 1907. Around 1910, the government restricted coal mining and other mineral development in Alaska and Katalla lost much of its population practically overnight. A small refinery built in 1911 produced gasoline and heating oil for the area market until part of the plant burned in 1933 and the entire operation was abandoned. A number of old buildings still stand at Katalla and the remains of the old refinery can be seen, along with the old wells and rusting steam engines.

Much of the wilderness surrounding Katalla is part of the Chugach National Forest. However, new exploration is under way on private land at the old refinery site. Additional development is planned at the coalfields and other areas. A road connecting Katalla with the Copper River Highway and Cordova is proposed and if ever built could bring new life to the old boom town.

Cape St. Elias towers over the historic lighthouse at the southern tip of Kayak Island. (Gil Mull, reprinted from ALASKA GEOGRAPHIC®)

Lighthouses

Alaska's Gulf Coast harbors two historic lighthouses that are part of a chain of navigational beacons operated by the U.S. Coast Guard.

Cape St. Elias Light Station is located on the southernmost tip of Kayak Island on Cape St. Elias. The cape was named by Captain Commander Vitus Bering on July 20, 1741, for the saint whose day it was according to the Russian Orthodox Church calendar. The 1,665-foot-high cape is an unmistakable landmark for mariners; the waters to the south were regarded as "one of the most dangerous points along the entire coast." Construction of the lighthouse was completed on September 16, 1916. At one time there were three lighthouse keepers in residence; the light was automated in 1974. It is listed on the National Register of Historic Places and is considered the best existing 1916 example of a major Alaska lighthouse.

Cape Hinchinbrook Light Station marks Hinchinbrook Entrance, main gateway to Prince William Sound from the east. Cape Hinchinbrook, named on May 12, 1778, by the English explorer Captain James Cook for Viscount Hinchinbroke, is on the south tip of Hinchinbrook Island, 35 miles southwest of Cordova. Construction of the station was completed in 1910; it was automated in 1974.

ALASKA PENINSULA
ALEUTIANS

The Alaska Peninsula curves southwest about 500 miles from Naknek Lake to the first of the more than 124 Aleutian Islands. The Aleutian Chain then extends south and west more than a thousand miles. The region also includes the Pribilof Islands in the Bering Sea. This is primarily a mountainous country; only on the Bering Sea side of the peninsula does the terrain flatten out.

The island links of the Aleutian Chain form a slender divider between two of the world's wildest bodies of water, the stormy North Pacific and the equally turbulent Bering Sea. Five major island groups — the Near, Rat, Andreanof, Fox, and Krenitzin islands — make up the Aleutians, which bridge the expanse between North America and Asia.

These islands actually are the peaks of an arc of submerged volcanoes that is approximately 1,400 miles long and 20 to 60 miles wide, rising as high as 9,372 feet above sea level (Shishaldin Volcano on Unimak Island) and 32,472 feet above the ocean floor. On the Pacific side the chain is

Pavlof Volcano, elevation 8,905 feet, in the Aleutian Range. (Lorelei Mack)

bordered by the Aleutian Trench, an extraordinary trough more than 2,000 miles long, 50 to 100 miles wide, with a maximum depth of 25,000 feet. This is where continental plates meet and dive beneath the earth's crust. To the north the relatively shallow Bering Sea slopes downward, forming the world's largest known underwater valley, some 249 miles long, with a maximum depth of 10,677 feet.

The Aleutians are the longest archipelago of small islands in the world and contain the greatest number of active volcanoes in the United States. At least 26 of the chain's 57 volcanoes have erupted since 1760. Eruptions, earthquakes and tsunamis remain a common threat in the region.

Aleutian weather has a well-earned reputation as the worst in the world. Storm fronts generally move from west to east here, but often climatic conditions on the Pacific side differ vastly from those on the Bering side, placing the islands in the middle of a continual weather conflict. Measurable precipitation occurs more than 200 days each year, with an annual average of 33.44 inches at Cold Bay on the Alaska Peninsula and 28.85 inches at Shemya in the extreme western Aleutians. On a more positive note, Aleutian temperatures are milder than elsewhere in Alaska due to their

The common murre nests in colonies along coastal sea cliffs and islands. (Dan O. Dunaway)

Arctic foxes were introduced to the Aleutians during the fox-farming era from 1880-1930. (R.H. Day, reprinted from ALASKA GEOGRAPHIC®)

southerly position and the tempering effect of the surrounding waters. At Shemya temperatures range from 39° to 53°F in summer and from 28° to 39°F in winter. The island gets 57 inches of snow. At Dutch Harbor, near the mainland, temperatures range from 40° to 60°F in summer and from 27° to 37°F in winter. Annual snowfall there is 81 inches. There is little or no permafrost.

The Aleutian Islands are treeless except for a few scattered stands of spruce transplanted to sheltered locations. In summer the islands become an emerald grassland studded with a variety of wildflowers.

More than 230 species of birds have been recorded in the region. Marine mammals — whales, sea otters, fur seals, sea lions, harbor seals, elephant seals and walruses—are attracted by the churning seas which support rich food supplies of plankton, fish and shellfish.

Unimak Island, closest to the mainland, is the natural western limit for caribou, brown/grizzly bears, wolves, wolverines, ground squirrels and weasels. Nearly all Aleutian land mammals west of Unimak were introduced by man: foxes, horses, cattle, sheep, caribou and reindeer. Norway rats arrived aboard sailing ships in the mid-1800s; the Rat Islands were named for them.

Nearly the entire Aleutian Chain is included in the Alaska Maritime National Wildlife Refuge, but only a few hardy bird-watchers visit this remote area. The Alaska Peninsula's parks and refuges are less remote and two (Katmai and Izembek) are accessible by road from nearby communities. The Alaska Peninsula has been a major big game hunting area for many years, especially for brown/grizzly bears.

Aleuts, the first inhabitants of the chain, still live there, predominantly at Atka, Nikolski, Unalaska, Akutan, False Pass, and St. Paul and St. George in the Pribilofs.

Military bases, first established on these remote islands during World War II, remain today on Adak and Shemya islands and at Cold Bay and King Salmon on the Alaska Peninsula. The Coast Guard has loran stations on Attu and St. Paul islands.

Fishing and seafood processing are the principal

Alaska Peninsula/ Aleutian Islands

N

Location

Cartography by David A. Shott

Katmai National Park and Preserve

Mt. Douglas ▲
Fourpeaked Mountain

Naknek
King Salmon
South Naknek
Lake Camp
Naknek Lake
Grosvenor Lake
Mt. Kaguyak ▲
Brooks Camp
Mt. Denison ▲
Mt. Kukak ▲
Mt. Griggs ▲
Mt. Novarupta ▲ ▲ Mt. Katmai
Mt. Trident ▲
Mt. Mageik ▲

Egegik

King Salmon River

Mt. Martin ▲

Becharof Lake

Becharof National Wildlife Refuge

Mt. Peulik ▲

Pilot Point

Ugashik

Alaska

Mt. Chiginagak ▲

Shelikof Strait

Kodiak Island

St. Paul Island

Alaska Maritime National Wildlife Refuge

Saint Paul

St. George Island
Saint George

Pribilof Islands

Port Heiden
Mt. Aniakchak ▲
Aniakchak

Aniakchak National Monument

Aniakchak Bay

Bristol Bay

Peninsula

Chignik Bay

Chignik Lagoon
Chignik
Chignik Lake

Mt. Veniaminof ▲

Ivanof Bay
Perryville

Nelson Lagoon

National

Wildlife

Mt. Dana ▲

Pavlof Sister ▲
Amak Island

Izembek National Wildlife Refuge

Pavlof Volcano ▲

Sand Point

Unga Island

Alaska Maritime National Wildlife Refuge

Refuge

Cold Bay
Belkofski
Frosty Peak ▲
King Cove

Unimak Island

Roundtop Mountain ▲
False Pass

Shumagin Islands

Cape Sarichef Light Station
Mt. Fisher ▲
Shishaldin Volcano ▲
Isanotski Peaks ▲
Pogromni Volcano ▲
▲ Mt. Westdahl

Scotch Cap Light Station

Map continues at top of next page.

Akutan Island

Akun Island

Mt. Akutan ▲ ■ Akutan

Krenitzin Islands

Mt. Bogoslof

Makushin Volcano ▲

■ Dutch Harbor
■ Unalaska

Unalaska Island

Mt. Okmok ▲

Ūmnak Island

Fox

Islands of Four Mountains

Pass

Mt. Vsevidof ▲

Mt. Kagamil ▲ ●Kagamil Island

Anangula Island

Island

Refuge

Mt. Carlisle ▲

Samalga

■ Nikolski

Mt. Cleveland ▲

Chagulak Island

Mt. Yunaska ▲

Herbert Island

Mt. Amukta ▲

Yunaska Island

Mt. Seguam ▲

Amukta Island

Mt. Korovin ▲ ▲ Mt. Sarichef

Mt. Kliuchef ▲

Seguam Island

Mt. Koniuji ▲

Atka Island

▲ ■ Atka

Great Sitkin Island

Seguam Pass

Great Sitkin Volcano ▲

Amlia Island

A l a s k a   M a r i t i m e   N a t i o n a l   W i l d l i f e   R e f u g e

Map continues below right.

Attu ■

Attu Island

Shemya Island

Mt. Moffett ▲

Mt. Bobrof ▲ ▲ Mt. Kanaga

■ Adak

Semichi Islands

Shemya ■

Buldir Volcano

Tanaga Volcano

Agattu Island

Near Islands

Buldir Island

Kiska Volcano ▲

Segula Island

Little Sitkin Island

Mt. Cerberus ▲

Gareloi Island

Mt. Gareloi ▲

Kanaga Island

Adak Island

Kiska Island

Rat Island

Little Sitkin Volcano

Semisopochnoi Island

Andreanof Islands

Ogliuga Island

Skagul Island

Tanaga Island

Rat

Amchitka Pass

Unalga Island

Islands

Amchitka Island

Amtignak Island

Ulak Island

A l a s k a   M a r i t i m e   N a t i o n a l   W i l d l i f e   R e f u g e

economic activities in the region, with Unalaska and Akutan ranking among the top 20 U.S. ports in value of commercial landings. The catch is mainly king crab, but tanner crab (marketed as snow crab) also is important and the bottom fish catch is increasing. There also is fishing for salmon, halibut, cod, herring and shrimp. In the Pribilofs, fur seals are harvested.

Transportation to the Aleutians is infrequent and expensive. Rough flying weather and extraordinary operational costs due to small populations combine to give Reeve Aleutian Airways the distinction of flying the most expensive air miles in America. Freight service by sea is irregular. The Alaska Marine Highway system makes four trips a year between Seward and Dutch Harbor, with stops at Chignik, Sand Point, King Cove and Cold Bay.

The Communities

ADAK, located on Adak Island in the Aleutian Chain, 1,200 miles southwest of Anchorage. **Elevation:** 20 feet. **Transportation:** Military or scheduled airline from Anchorage. **Population:** Approximately 4,000.

Visitor Facilities: Approval for entry to the island must be obtained in advance from the Commanding Officer. Accommodations at Navy lodge or private homes. Restaurant, laundromat and banking services available. A McDonald's restaurant is to be established here. All supplies carried by Navy commissary and exchange. Fishing and hunting licenses are available. Auto and marine engine repair and gas are available.

This U.S. Navy base is the westernmost city in the United States and Alaska's largest naval base. Military installations on Adak allowed U.S. forces to mount a successful offensive against the Japanese-held islands of Kiska and Attu during World War II.

The civilian population is limited to teachers, construction workers, U.S. Fish and Wildlife Service personnel and civil service workers. School

superintendent Bradley A. Raphel says the weather is so unpredictable here that all four seasons can be experienced in one day. "The only attractions tourists may be interested in would be the old Quonset huts left intact from World War II. There is also a small museum which houses World War II memorabilia. Salmon fishing is plentiful. Watching eagles guard the island while being teased by the ravens is an interesting way to pass the time of day." There's also swimming, racquetball, bowling and indoor tennis.

AKUTAN is on the east coast of Akutan Island, 17 miles east of Unalaska, 750 miles southwest of Anchorage. **Transportation:** Boats; scheduled and charter amphibious aircraft from Cold Bay or Dutch Harbor. **Population:** 107.

Visitor Facilities: Accommodations available at The Bayview Plaza, owned by the Akutan Corp. There is a laundromat. Groceries and other supplies may be purchased at McGlashan Store. Arts and crafts include fox traps and carvings.

Above — Military housing at Adak (pop. 4,000), the largest community in the Chain. (Staff, reprinted from ALASKA GEOGRAPHIC®)

Below — A boardwalk connects homes at Akutan on Akutan Island. (Bureau of Land Management)

Repair services for marine engines and boats may be available. Arrangements may be made to rent boats. Gas, diesel and boat moorage are available.

The village was established in 1878 as a fur storage and trading port by the Western Fur and Trading Co. The company's first resident agent Hugh McGlashan helped establish a commercial cod fishing and processing business, and people from nearby villages moved to Akutan. The U.S. government evacuated Akutan residents to the Ketchikan area during World War II.

"We work on processing boats, fishing boats or in town," according to one resident. Akutan Corp. president Tom McGlashan points out that hunting and fishing are done for subsistence. "At times we can walk a short distance and cast with a fishing pole. Other times we need a skiff. Almost every family owns a skiff, so it is not difficult to travel in search of food." Game includes seal, wild cattle, ducks and geese. Fish include salmon, pogies, black bass, cod, herring, halibut, flounder and trout. Clams, sea urchins and "bidarkies" or chitons are also gathered for food.

An Aleutian storm front heads into Atka. (Staff, reprinted from ALASKA GEOGRAPHIC®)

Alexander Nevsky Chapel, a Russian Orthodox church built in 1918, to replace an 1878 structure, is listed on the National Register of Historic Places.

ATKA is located on Atka Island near the end of the Aleutian Chain, 90 miles east of Adak, 1,100 miles southwest of Anchorage. **Elevation: 40 feet. Transportation:** Boat; scheduled and charter aircraft from Cold Bay. **Population: 80.**

Visitor Facilities: Atka Village Council rents two rooms with kitchen facilities. Laundromat available. Groceries and other supplies are available from Atka Native Store. Grass baskets are crafted here. Fishing and hunting licenses available. Autos may be rented. Fuel available includes marine gas, diesel and regular gasoline.

Atka is the most western and most isolated Native village on the Aleutian Chain. The community has persisted through the decades despite a lack of local jobs. After the end of sea otter hunting in the late 1800s, Atka had no cash economy, although there was a fox farming boom in the 1920s. The economy today is based primarily on subsistence hunting and fishing and wages earned from seasonal employment in the crab and salmon fisheries elsewhere in the Aleutians. The village is located within the Alaska Maritime National Wildlife Refuge. Fish include halibut, salmon, black cod, Pacific Ocean perch and king crab. Game includes reindeer (introduced in 1914), foxes, seals and sea lions.

ATTU, on Attu Island in the Aleutian Chain, is 1,700 miles west of Anchorage and 500 miles east of the USSR mainland. **Elevation: 60 feet. Transportation:** Air charter or U.S. Coast Guard aircraft. **Population: 24.**

Visitor Facilities: None.

The treeless island of Attu is farthest west of the Aleutian Chain and westernmost of the Near Islands. The entire island is part of the Alaska Maritime National Wildlife Refuge. A Coast Guard loran station is located at Massacre Bay on the southeast coast of the island. A granite memorial here honors American soldiers who fought and died in the Aleutians during World War II. Attu was the site of a brutal 19-day battle during May 1943 between American forces and Japanese

entrenched on the island. Much evidence of the battle still remains on the east end of the island. The Attu battlefield and old Army and Navy airfields have been named national historic landmarks. Listed on the National Register of Historic Places is the wreckage of a P-38 fighter aircraft on the east bank of the Temnac River.

BELKOFSKI, located on the east end of the Alaska Peninsula, about 12 miles southeast of King Cove. **Transportation:** Boat or seaplane from King Cove. **Population: 12.**

Visitor Facilities: None. Belkofski's original settlers were Russians, who arrived in 1823 to harvest sea otters. Belkofski flourished until the near extinction of the sea otter forced residents to seek subsistence elsewhere.

Belkofski residents travel to King Cove, the

Chignik Lagoon lies nestled on the south shore of the Alaska Peninsula. (Jack Dodge)

available. All types of fuel and moorage available.

Chignik, also called Chignik Bay, is an Aleut village established as a fishing village and cannery in the second half of the 19th century.

Most people in Chignik depend on subsistence hunting and fishing, but commercial fishing for salmon and crab provides seasonal employment. Salmon are caught from spring until early winter and cod, black bass and halibut are caught year-round. Other fish caught are rainbow trout and Dolly Varden. Dungeness, king and tanner crab, clams and octopus also are harvested. Game includes, moose, caribou, ptarmigan, ducks and geese.

The village is located within the 3.5 million acre Alaska Peninsula National Wildlife Refuge.

CHIGNIK LAGOON, on the south shore of the Alaska Peninsula, five miles west of Chignik. **Elevation:** 50 feet. **Transportation:** Boat; charter plane from King Salmon, Dillingham or Kodiak. **Population:** Winter, 60; summer, 1,100.

Visitor Facilities: Limited. A restaurant operates in summer only. Groceries and other supplies may be purchased at Columbia Ward Fisheries cannery store 2.5 miles across the lagoon. Limited fishing gear available at tackle shop. Hunting and fishing licenses are available and there is a local guide. Marine engine and boat repair at cannery in summer only. The cannery also carries gas and diesel.

Chignik Lagoon took its name from its proximity to Chignik. The area was originally populated by Kaniagmuit Eskimos. After the Russian occupation, the intermarriage of the Kaniags and Aleuts produced the Koniags who now reside in Chignik Lagoon. It developed as a fishing village and now serves, along with Chignik, as a regional fishing center.

Like neighboring Chignik, subsistence hunting and fishing are the mainstay of the local economy, with commercial fishing providing seasonal employment. In the fall, residents pick blueberries, cranberries, raspberries and salmonberries.

Veniaminoff Volcano, which last erupted in 1983, dominates the horizon to the west. Wildflowers abound along the beaches and there is fossil hunting along the north side of the lagoon. The nearby valley provides hiking opportunities (watch for brown bears). Many eagles can be observed nesting and hunting in the area. There is beach recreation along Ocean Spit, which protects the lagoon from the open sea.

CHIGNIK LAKE on the Alaska Peninsula is located 15 miles southwest of Chignik and 265 miles southwest of Kodiak. **Transportation:** Scheduled air service from Anchorage. **Population:** 153.

Visitor Facilities: None. This fishing village was established in the 1950s. Most residents move to a fish camp in summer near the village of Chignik Lagoon. Some people also work in the Chignik Bay cannery.

COLD BAY is located 40 miles from the extreme westerly tip of the Alaska Peninsula, 630 miles southwest of Anchorage and 180 miles from Unalaska. **Elevation:** 100 feet. **Transportation:** Boat; scheduled airline or charter service from

Pribilofs or to Sand Point for work. The Holy Resurrection Russian Orthodox Church here, on the national register, was built in the 1880s.

CHIGNIK, on the south shore of the Alaska Peninsula at the head of Anchorage Bay, is 450 miles southwest of Anchorage. **Elevation:** 30 feet. **Transportation:** Boat; scheduled airline and air charter from King Salmon; limited state ferry service from Kodiak. **Population:** 120.

Visitor Facilities: Accommodations may be arranged in private homes or the canneries. Meals at Meta's Restaurant. Supplies may be purchased at the general store, variety store, Chignik Pride Store, This-N-That Supply, the bakery and two hardware stores. Hunting and fishing licenses available. Rental transportation includes boats and charter aircraft. Marine engine, boat and car repair

Cold Bay is a transportation and communications hub for the region. (Lorelei Mack)

Anchorage; limited state ferry service in summer. Population: 250.

Visitor Facilities: Hotel accommodations available through Pauloff Services Inc. or Flying Tigers. There is a restaurant and a laundromat. Limited groceries and supplies at the Flying Tigers store. Fishing and hunting licenses and fishing guide services are available. Aircraft mechanic, truck rental and gas and diesel available.

After the onset of World War II, a large airbase was built at Cold Bay; the landscape still bears the mark of bulldozed roads and decaying quonset huts. The airstrip is the third longest in Alaska and the airport now serves as the transportation and communications hub for the entire Aleutians/Pribilof Islands region. Nearly all adult residents are employed in the operation and maintenance of the airport and related services.

Cold Bay is the gateway to Izembek National Wildlife Refuge and the southwestern portion of the Alaska Peninsula National Wildlife Refuge. Izembek refuge attracts 142 species of birds, but was established in 1960 primarily to benefit the black brant, which are attracted by the eelgrass beds at Izembek Lagoon.

The west side of Izembek Lagoon also is the site of the 1902 wreck of the three-masted schooner *Courtney Ford*. A good example of 19th century commercial ships, it is also the oldest intact hull in the state.

There is good fishing in the area for Dolly Varden, salmon, arctic char, Pacific cod, flounder and halibut.

EGEGIK, on the northwest coast of the Alaska Peninsula, is 38 miles southwest of Naknek, 70 miles south of Dillingham and 340 miles west of Anchorage. Elevation: 50 feet. Transportation:

Boat; scheduled and charter plane. **Population:** 75 in winter; up to 1,000 in summer.

Visitor Facilities: Accommodations at private homes or Becharof Lodge. Meals at lodge or at restaurant in town during summer. Laundromat available. Groceries and supplies may be purchased at Egegik Trading Co., Egegik Enterprises or Egegik Seafoods (cannery store). Fishing and hunting licenses are available; guide services through Becharof Lodge. Marine engine and boat repair in summer. Marine gas, diesel, propane and regular gasoline available.

Originally a fish camp, the town developed in the early 1900s around a cannery that was built at the river's mouth. The economy today is based on commercial fishing. Several canneries in the area provide employment from May to August. Residents supplement their income with subsistence hunting and fishing.

Becharof National Wildlife Refuge is accessible by plane or skiff up the Egegik River. There is sportfishing for salmon and trout and hunting for caribou and bear. Local residents also jokingly refer to the local sport of "mud-mucking," meaning driving the terrible roads.

FALSE PASS is located on the east end of Unimak Island, about one mile from the end of the Alaska Peninsula, 35 miles southwest of Cold

Bay. **Elevation:** 20 feet. **Transportation:** Boat; scheduled and charter airline from Cold Bay. **Population:** 75.

Visitor Facilities: Limited accommodations available through Peter Pan Seafoods. The cannery store is open year-round. Fishing and hunting licenses are available. Boats and charter aircraft rented. Fuel available includes marine gas, diesel, propane and regular gasoline. Moorage facilities available.

The name False Pass was derived from the fact that the Bering Sea side of Isanotski Strait, which connects the Bering Sea to the Gulf of Alaska, is extremely shallow and cannot accommodate large vessels. False Pass originated with the establishment of a cannery in 1918 by P.E. Harris Co. (now Peter Pan Seafoods and owned by the Bristol Bay Native Corp.).

The economy of False Pass has always been tied to salmon fishing and processing. It suffered a blow during the winter of 1980-81 when the cannery and central power facility burned down. Despite the loss, the village is thriving. Most crab and salmon boats passing through the strait continue to stop at False Pass to take on water and visit the store.

The village is located within the Alaska Maritime National Wildlife Refuge. Bears are often seen near

Left — Commercial fishing and area canneries support residents of Egegik. (Staff, reprinted from ALASKA GEOGRAPHIC®)

Right — Fishing boats at False Pass. (Rick Furniss, reprinted from ALASKA GEOGRAPHIC®)

the village. During migrations, spectacular concentrations of waterfowl rest and feed in the freshwater and saltwater wetlands, lagoons and shoals bordering the Bering Sea side of the pass. Shorebirds frequent the beaches, tidal flats and shallow areas. Harbor seals are abundant; sea lions also are present; an occasional walrus also is observed. The once-rare sea otter is re-establishing itself in the area.

IVANOF BAY is at the northeast end of Kupreanof Peninsula, 230 miles southwest of King Salmon, 510 miles southwest of Anchorage. **Transportation:** Charter plane from Sand Point. **Population:** 45.

Visitor Facilities: None. Groceries may be purchased at the Ivanof Bay General Store.

The bay on which this predominantly Aleut village is located was named by Lieutenant Dall of the U.S. Coast and Geodetic Survey in 1880. The village occupies the site of a former salmon cannery.

Almost all residents of Ivanof Bay fish for a living. Most families move to cabins in Chignik for the summer salmon fishing season. A few residents work for the store, school and village, and most of the men run traplines in the winter for mink, otter, red fox, wolverine, ermine and lynx. Subsistence hunting and fishing also play a big role in the economy of Ivanof Bay.

KING COVE is located on the Pacific side of the Alaska Peninsula, 18 miles southeast of Cold Bay, 630 miles southwest of Anchorage. **Transportation:** Boat; scheduled and charter aircraft from Cold Bay or Sand Point. **Population:** 521.

Visitor Facilities: Accommodations at Fleets Inn, owned by King Cove Corp. There is a restaurant and a laundromat is available at the hotel for guests. Groceries and other supplies are carried by Peter Pan Seafoods Co. Store and at John Gould & Sons. Fishing and hunting licenses available. Auto repair services available. Arrangements may be made to rent autos. Fuel available includes marine gas, diesel, propane and regular gasoline. Moorage facilities available.

One of the larger communities in the Aleutian region, King Cove was founded in 1911 when Pacific American Fisheries built a salmon cannery. Although the cannery burned down in 1976, it was immediately rebuilt and is now the largest cannery operation under one roof in Alaska.

King Cove is located within the Alaska Peninsula National Wildlife Refuge. The Alaska Peninsula has long been a major big game hunting area, especially for the huge brown/grizzly bears. According to one resident, the King Cove area is not a paradise for fishermen or hunters, but there's "enough to keep local people busy."

KING SALMON is located on the Alaska Peninsula on the bank of the Naknek River, 15 miles east of Naknek and 290 miles southwest of Anchorage. **Elevation:** 50 feet. **Transportation:** Scheduled airline from Anchorage. **Population:** 545.

Visitor Facilities: Accommodations at King-Ko Inn and Ponderosa Inn. There are two restaurants and a bank. Groceries and other supplies may be purchased at Waterfront Sports Center and King Salmon Commercial. Arts and crafts include carved ivory, baskets and masks. Fishing and hunting licenses and guide services are available. Major repair services for marine engines, boats and aircraft. Rental transportation includes autos in summer and charter aircraft. Boats are also available locally. Marine and regular gas and moorage available.

At the onset of World War II an Air Force base was constructed that continues today as the major military installation in western Alaska. In 1949 the U.S. Army Corps of Engineers built the road connecting King Salmon to Naknek; a post office was established in King Salmon the same year. The community has continued to develop as a government, transportation and service center.

According to John Frederberg of Waterfront Sports Center, "The influx of hunters and fishermen has definitely shown pressure on hunting and fishing, but the Bristol Bay area is still overall one of the best areas in the world. General

Snow dusts the boats at King Cove harbor. (Lorelei Mack)

fun activities are limited to summer and fall outdoor sports. Cabin fever ranks high in winter time. Local school and community activities help greatly. A great place to visit, a good place to live for the right kind of people."

King Salmon is the gateway to several large lakes (Naknek, Iliamna, Becharof, Ugashik) and to Katmai National Park and Preserve. A 10-mile unimproved road leads from King Salmon to the park's western boundary and there are floatplane connections from King Salmon to Brooks River Lodge, ranger station and public campground on Naknek Lake. There are two other lodges in the park. Independent travelers must make their own arrangements for visiting Katmai, including air service to King Salmon and Brooks Camp.

NAKNEK is located on the Alaska Peninsula on the bank of the Naknek River near its mouth, 15 miles west of King Salmon, 56 miles southeast of Dillingham, 300 miles southwest of Anchorage. **Elevation:** 50 feet. **Transportation:** Boat;

scheduled airline and air taxi. **Population:** 318.

Visitor Facilities: Accommodations at Naknek Hotel or Red Dog Inn. There are two restaurants, a laundry and bank. Alaska Commerical Co. and Naknek Trading Co. carry groceries and other supplies. Arts and crafts available for purchase include carved ivory, baskets and masks. Fishing and hunting licenses and guide services are available. Major repair services for marine engines, boats, autos and aircraft. Rental transportation includes autos, boats and aircraft. Fuel available includes marine gas, diesel and regular gasoline. Moorage facilities available.

Naknek is the seat of the 500-square-mile Bristol Bay Borough, a second-class borough incorporated in 1962. The region was settled over 6,000 years ago by Yup'ik Eskimos and Athabascan Indians. The Russians built a fort near the village and fur trappers inhabited the area for some time prior to the U.S. purchase of Alaska. By 1883 the first salmon cannery opened in Bristol Bay and in 1890

the first cannery opened on the Naknek River. By 1900 there were approximately 12 canneries in Bristol Bay.

The community has developed as a major center for commercial fishing and processing. There are nine salmon processors on the Naknek side of the river and the area bustles during the summer when people arrive to fish and work in the canneries. The borough government also is a significant source of employment. Many residents also depend on subsistence hunting and fishing.

Hunting, fishing, camping and photography provide most of the outdoor recreation for borough residents. The Naknek River is famous for its

Beached skiffs at Nelson Lagoon hold hundreds of glass floats. (Robert Gill Jr., reprinted from ALASKA GEOGRAPHIC®)

excellent sportfishing and caribou and bear hunting are popular. There are scores of excellent fishing streams throughout the region.

The Russian Orthodox St. John the Baptist Chapel in Naknek, reportedly constructed in 1886, is on the National Register of Historic Places.

NELSON LAGOON is located on a narrow spit 30 miles west of Port Moller, 550 miles southwest of Anchorage. **Transportation:** Air charter from Cold Bay or Sand Point. **Population:** 62.

The community derived its name from the lagoon, which was named in 1882 for Edward William Nelson of the U.S. Signal Corps, an explorer in the Yukon delta region between 1877 and 1920. The area was settled in 1906 when a salmon saltery was built here. A cannery operated between 1915 and 1917, but there has been no local plant since. For many years Nelson Lagoon was a

seasonal camp, but families began to settle here and a school was established in 1965.

Commercial fishing is the basis for the local economy. Subsistence hunting and fishing is done for caribou, foxes, wolverines, mink, geese and seals.

NIKOLSKI, on Nikolski Bay on the southwest end of Umnak Island, is 116 miles from Dutch Harbor, 880 miles southwest of Anchorage. **Elevation:** 73 feet. **Transportation:** Scheduled or charter flights from Dutch Harbor. **Population:** 57.

Nikolski was actively involved in sea otter hunting during the Russian period. A sheep ranch that is still operating today was established in Nikolski in 1926 as part of the Aleutian Livestock Co.

During World War II, Nikolski residents were evacuated to the Ketchikan area until 1944. In the

mid-1950s the Air Force built a White Alice site which was later operated by RCA Alascom. It was abandoned in 1977.

Most residents work outside the village at crab canneries and processing ships during the fall season, fishing in the summer or at seasonal jobs in Cold Bay or St. Paul. Subsistence hunting and fishing are also important. Dolly Varden and halibut are caught in the bay. Residents also hunt ducks and seals. Octopus, fish and sea urchins can be gathered from the reef.

Ananiuliak (Anangula) Island on the north side of Nikolski Bay is the site of the earliest presently documented evidence of human habitation in the Aleutian Islands. Radiocarbon dating indicates occupation as far back as 8,000 years.

The Chaluka site in the village of Nikolski exhibits 4,000 years of virtually continuous occupation and is listed on the National Register of Historic Places. Also on the register is Nikolski's St. Nicholas Russian Orthodox Church, which was built in 1930.

PERRYVILLE is on the south coast of the Alaska Peninsula, 215 miles southwest of Dillingham and 285 miles south of Kodiak. **Elevation:** 25 feet. **Transportation:** Scheduled airline or air charter from Dillingham and King Salmon. **Population:** 107.

Visitor Facilities: Limited accommodations at the Perryville Motel. The Perryville Commercial Store carries some supplies.

After the 1912 eruption of Mount Katmai, a revenue cutter commanded by Captain K.W. Perry rescued the people of Katmai and moved them to a new location down the coast, where they established a village named in honor of the captain.

In the February 1984 issue of *earthlines/ tidelines*, a Perryville student gave her impressions of her home: "Perryville is located on the Pacific Ocean which gives you the feeling you are living on a deserted island. Then there are the tundra flats, the rolling hills and the mountains in the background. The tundra is like walking on a mattress and the wide variety of berries keep your stomach from growling on a summer walk. They

Nikolski village on Umnak Island. (Staff, reprinted from ALASKA GEOGRAPHIC®)

loons rest in the area in the spring and fall; some stay to nest and molt. Ugashik Bay and the Ugashik, Dog Salmon and King Salmon rivers are important bald eagle feeding areas.

PORT HEIDEN, on the Alaska Peninsula, 150 miles from King Salmon, 435 miles southwest of Anchorage. **Transportation:** Boat; scheduled airline from King Salmon. **Population:** 94.

Visitor Facilities: Accommodations at Reeve Aleutian Airway boarding house. Meals at lodging facility. Fox's General Store and Jack's New Meshik Mall carry groceries and other supplies, and carved ivory crafts may be purchased locally. Fishing and hunting licenses and guide services are available. Arrangements may be made with private owners to rent autos or boats; charter aircraft available.

Port Heiden (pop. 94) on the Alaska Peninsula. (Staff, reprinted from ALASKA GEOGRAPHIC®)

also provide a winter supply of food for the families of the village.

"School is the main attraction during the year with sports, holiday celebrations and special events. Everyone becomes involved and enjoys the feeling of friendship and family. Hunting, fishing, gathering wood and other daily chores keep us busy. And for relaxation we can watch satellite television, take a cruise on our Honda, walk the beach or take a steam bath. Of course, life in Perryville has its downfalls and its totally boring days. But then doesn't every place you live? I think Perryville is a beautiful unique home."

PILOT POINT, on the north coast of the Alaska Peninsula, seven miles northwest of Ugashik, 90 miles south of King Salmon, 380 miles southwest of Anchorage. **Transportation:** Scheduled and charter air service from King Salmon. **Population:** 66.

Visitor Facilities: Lodging at two cabins owned by Aleck Griechen. Groceries and supplies sold at

Pilot Point Trading Co. Fishing and hunting licenses and gas and diesel are available.

This predominantly Aleut village, which had a fish saltery in 1900, originally was known as Pilot Station, named for the Ugashik River pilots who took boats up the river to a larger cannery at Ugashik. The saltery developed into a large cannery, which closed in 1958 because of deterioration of the harbor. In 1933 a post office was established and the name of the village changed to Pilot Point.

Residents depend on commercial salmon fishing (kings, reds, chums, pinks and silvers) for the majority of their cash income.

Record-sized grayling have been taken from the Ugashik Lakes. Other sportfishing is for salmon and trout. Hunting is for moose (scarce), caribou and brown bear. The Kvichak River is a major migration corridor for the sandhill crane and whistling swans that nest near the village. White-fronted and emperor geese, Canada geese and

Fuel available includes marine gas, diesel and regular gasoline.

Port Heiden was founded by Village Public Safety Officer Elliott Reid's grandfather, who came to the area in the 1920s from Norway and married a Native woman.

Port Heiden is the gateway to the 514,000-acre Aniakchak National Monument and Preserve. Access is by floatplane from Port Heiden or King Salmon to Surprise Lake inside the caldera. By foot, it's 10 miles from Port Heiden to the park boundary

Remote and unique St. George depends on the seal industry which has long dominated the Pribilofs. (Division of Tourism)

During World War II the entire population of the Pribilofs was evacuated to an abandoned cannery and mining camp at Funter Bay.

Although the fur seal industry has dominated the economy of the Pribilofs in the past, it is now supplemented by a growing fisheries industry and tourism. Subsistence activities mostly consist of fur seal harvesting for consumption and fishing, especially for halibut.

St. George Island has perhaps the largest seabird colony in the northern hemisphere; 2.5 million seabirds nest on the cliffs each summer. In addition an estimated 250,000 seals congregate in six rookeries on the island. Because of scientific research on the island, camping is not permitted. However the St. George Tanaq Corp. offers guided tour programs in the summer, which include transportation, lodging and meals. Travelers should leave itineraries loose in case weather delays flights and keep baggage to a minimum.

ST. PAUL, located on the southern tip of St. Paul Island, northernmost of the Pribilof Island group. **Elevation:** 20 feet. **Transportation:** Ship; scheduled and charter air service from Anchorage via Cold Bay or Dutch Harbor. **Population:** 595.

Visitor Facilities: Lodging may be arranged through the Tanadgusix Corp. Accommodations at King Eider Hotel. There are four restaurants, laundry facilities, and the Aleut Community Store carries most supplies. Arts and crafts such as ivory jewelry and fur seal garments are sold at four local gift shops. Fishing and hunting licenses available. Repair services available for marine engines, boats and autos. Off-road vehicles available for rent. Fuel available includes diesel, propane, unleaded and regular gasoline.

St. Paul shares both its history and economy with St. George. The fur seal industry has long dominated the economy of the Pribilofs, although both the fisheries industry and tourism are increasingly important.

The million northern fur seals which gather on the shores of the Pribilof Islands in summer can be observed from two blinds; access is by permit or with a tour group.

The island is treeless but covered with various

via a very difficult trail. Aniakchak last erupted in 1931. The Aniakchak River, designated as a wild and scenic river, flows from Surprise Lake to the Pacific Ocean.

ST. GEORGE, located on the northeast shore of St. George Island, 780 miles southwest of Anchorage. **Transportation:** Scheduled airline from Anchorage via St. Paul. **Population:** 158.

Visitor Facilities: Food and lodging at the historic 10-room St. George Hotel. There is a laundromat, and groceries and other supplies are available at St. George Tanaq Store or St. George Community Canteen. Arts and crafts include seal pelts, model baidarkas (skin boats), model seals, and baskets. Tour guide services available in summer through St. George Tanaq Corp. Repair services for marine engines, boats and autos. Arrangements can be made to rent private autos. Fuel available includes marine gas, diesel, propane, unleaded and regular gasoline. Moorage facilities available.

Russian fur hunters brought Aleuts from Unalaska and Atka and founded St. George and St. Paul in 1786. From 1867 to 1909, the U.S. government contracted private companies to harvest seals. After 1910, the government conducted the seal harvesting operation and the Pribilof Islanders were treated as wards of the government. It was not until 1983 that the Pribilof people were given full control of their islands.

The community of St. Paul (pop. 595), which shares its history and economy with St. George. (Division of Tourism)

grasses, sedges and a large variety of wildflowers. The uplands around St. Paul have a diverse population of songbirds, white and blue foxes and about 500 reindeer, descendents of four bucks and 21 does introduced in 1911.

Tourists are encouraged to visit Black Diamond Hill, where they may find shiny crystals of augite. Crystals of olivine and rutile found on the island may reach semiprecious gem size and quality.

SAND POINT, located on the north coast of Popof Island in the Shumagin Islands off the south coast of the Alaska Peninsula. **Transportation:** Scheduled air service from Anchorage; charter air service; state ferry service in summer. **Population:** 870.

Visitor Facilities: Accommodations at Anchor Inn Motel. There are a cafe and laundry facilities. Supplies available at Aleutian Commercial Co. Fishing and hunting licenses and guide services are available. Some repair services available for boats. Moorage facilities available.

One of the most prosperous and modern Aleut villages, Sand Point has a cannery and a locally-owned fishing fleet for crab and salmon. The community was founded by the Russians in the 1870s. The town became a supply center for the surrounding area after a cod fishing station was built by the McCollam Fishing and Trading Co. In 1946, the first cold storage plant in Alaska was built.

Sand Point's St. Nicholas Russian Orthodox Church, constructed in 1936, is on the National Register of Historic Places.

SHEMYA, on Shemya Island at the west end of the Aleutian Chain, is 1,500 miles southwest of Anchorage. **Transportation:** U.S. Air Force plane. **Population:** 500 to 1,200.

Visitor Facilities: Military transient lodging and dining facilities only.

Runways were constructed on Shemya by the U.S. Army in 1943 for the island to be used as a secret air base for bombing runs on Japan. The first bombing mission flown from Shemya was on March 16, 1944; the last on August 13, 1945.

Largest in the Semichi Islands group, Shemya measures 4.5 miles long by 2.3 miles wide. The island is controlled by the U.S. Air Force, which conducts classified operations at Shemya Air Force Base. Visitors must be on official military business.

Black volcanic sand on the island inspired Shemya's nickname of "The Black Pearl of the Aleutians." The island also is referred to as "The Rock" because of its steep cliffs and rocky terrain.

SOUTH NAKNEK is located on the Naknek River, two miles south of Naknek, 15 miles west of King Salmon and 300 miles southwest of Anchorage. **Transportation:** Scheduled airline and air taxi. **Population:** 145.

Visitor Facilities: There is a combined store, snackbar and bar. Fishing and hunting licenses and guide services are available.

South Naknek, located just across the river from Naknek, is part of the Bristol Bay Borough. It was

settled after the turn of the century as a result of salmon cannery development.

Commercial fishing and salmon processing are the mainstays of South Naknek's economy. Three of the five canneries that line the south bank of the Naknek River are in operation and recruit 400 to 500 people from outside the village for the brief summer salmon season. About 75 percent of South Naknek's residents depend on subsistence hunting and fishing for food.

South Naknek's Russian Orthodox Elevation of the Holy Cross Church, built in the early 1900s, is listed on the National Register of Historic Places.

UGASHIK is on the east bank of the Ugashik River on the Alaska Peninsula, eight miles from Pilot Point, 90 miles south of King Salmon and 370 miles southwest of Anchorage. **Transportation:** Boat; scheduled and charter air service from King Salmon. **Population:** 17.

Visitor Facilities: None. Commercial fishing and subsistence hunting and fishing support this small village.

A large Eskimo village was reported here in 1880, but the 1919 flu epidemic decimated the population.

UNALASKA/DUTCH HARBOR. Unalaska is located on the northern end of Unalaska Island, 800 miles southwest of Anchorage; Dutch Harbor is located just across from Unalaska on the east coast of Amaknak Island. **Elevation:** 20 feet. **Transportation:** Boat; scheduled and charter airline from Anchorage; state ferry in summer. **Population:** 1,922 year-round, 3,000 in summer.

Visitor Facilities: Accommodations at Unisea Inn in Dutch Harbor, Carl's Hotel in Unalaska, and the bunkhouses at Sea Alaska Products cannery or Universal Seafoods cannery. There are two restaurants, a delicatessen, a laundromat with showers and sauna, and a bank. Stores here are Alaska Commercial Co., Carl's Mercantile, Aleutian Mercantile and Nicky's Place Book Store. Arts and crafts include Aleut grass baskets, wood block prints, paintings, and wood and ivory carvings. Fishing and hunting licenses may be purchased locally. Most major repair service and all types of fuel are available. Rental boats and trucks and charter aircraft and helicopters are available. Moorage facilities available.

Ounalashka, or Unalaska, was the headquarters of the Russian-American Company and a key port for the sea otter fur trade in the 1700s. After the U.S. purchased Alaska, the North American Commercial Co. became manager of the seal harvest in the Pribilofs and built a station at Dutch Harbor. Unalaska became a major stop for ships heading to and from the Nome goldfields in the early part of this century. Army and Navy installations were built at Unalaska and Dutch Harbor in World War II. At the entrance of the airport is a memorial to those who lost their lives in the Aleutians in World War II. The Dutch Harbor Naval Base and Fort Mears on Amaknak Island have been designated national historic landmarks.

Unalaska is the major civilian port west of Kodiak and north of Hawaii and is the gateway to the Bering Sea region. It is one of the most productive seafood processing ports in the United States. There are five large canneries here.

There are two local attractions on the National Register of Historic Places. They are the Russian Orthodox Church of the Holy Ascension in Unalaska, which was built in 1825, and the Sitka Spruce Plantation in Dutch Harbor, where six trees planted by the Russians in 1805 still survive.

Hiking in the area is easy and there is no need for trails. There are no bears on Unalaska Island, however, hikers should watch out for cliffs, dress appropriately and be prepared for the weather to change for the worse.

Unalaska's Russian heritage is reflected in its church. (Dan O. Dunaway)

Attractions

Aniakchak National Monument and Preserve

This 580,000-acre monument and preserve is located on the Alaska Peninsula 10 miles east of Port Heiden and 150 miles southwest of King Salmon. Its centerpiece is the six-mile-wide, 2,000-foot deep Aniakchak caldera, which was created by the collapse of a 7,000-foot volcano some 3,500 years ago. Later activity built a 2,200-foot cone, Vent Mountain, inside the caldera.

The caldera remained hidden from the outside world until 1922, when a government geologist noticed that the taller peaks in the area formed a circle on the map he was making. Even today, few people have seen the crater and fewer still have walked upon its floor.

It is believed that the caldera at one time contained a deep lake — similar to Oregon's Crater Lake — since some of the lava flows within appear to have taken place under water. Eventually the lake waters began to spill over at a low place in the caldera wall and over time the fast-flowing Aniakchak River has created a spectacular 1,500-foot-deep breach in the wall called The Gates. The wild and scenic Aniakchak River heads in emerald-hued Surprise Lake inside the caldera, which is fed by hot springs, and flows 32 miles southeastward to the Pacific Ocean.

Aniakchak last erupted in 1931, scouring the caldera of vegetation. Today, the lava flows, cinder cones and explosion pits chronicle a history of volcanic activity, as well as the beginnings of revegetation bringing life to the barren landscape.

Aniakchak is difficult to reach and has "notoriously bad weather," says the National Park Service. Violent windstorms in the caldera — even when the weather is calm outside — can make camping there difficult.

Access is primarily by scheduled air service to Port Heiden or King Salmon, where a floatplane can be chartered to Surprise Lake. There are no facilities in the caldera; there is a shelter cabin at the mouth of the Aniakchak River.

Recreation includes hiking the virtually untouched volcanic wilderness, camping, fishing, photography, natural history study, rafting the Aniakchak River, and beach walking.

Aniakchak crater is headwaters of the Aniakchak River. (Bureau of Land Management)

Katmai National Park and Preserve

The original Katmai National Monument at the top of the Alaska Peninsula was created in 1918 to preserve the volcanic wonders of the Valley of 10,000 Smokes formed by a cataclysmic eruption just six years earlier. In later years, the thousands of fumaroles dwindled to a few active vents and the park was enlarged several times to its present four million acres.

The June 6, 1912, eruption of Novarupta Volcano, in which Mount Katmai also collapsed, was one of the most violent ever recorded. It darkened the sky over much of the Northern Hemisphere for several days. Novarupta spewed seven cubic miles of incandescent ash and pumice, which buried the 30-square-mile Ukak River valley as much as 700 feet deep. The valley remains one of the prime attractions of the park, richly colored in shades of yellow, red and tan and dissected by river gorges up to 100 feet deep, but only five to

Left — *The Lethe River cuts through the ashen landscape of Katmai National Park. (© Chlaus Lotscher)*

Above — *Brown bears, like this one in the Brooks River, are plentiful throughout the park. (George Wuerthner)*

Below — *Fisherman shows off a rainbow caught from Rock Creek. (George Wuerthner)*

10 feet wide. Mount Katmai's crater now contains a lake.

Katmai also boasts scenic lakes, rivers, glaciers, waterfalls and a coastline of plunging cliffs and islets. The park is a sanctuary for the largest unhunted population of coastal brown bears in the world and has some of the best sportfishing in southwestern Alaska, particularly for trophy-sized rainbow trout.

Other wildlife includes moose, river otters, marten, weasels, mink, lynx, muskrats, beavers and an occasional caribou. Seals, sea lions, sea otters and beluga and gray whales are found in the coastal waters of Shelikof Strait. Fishing is excellent for Dolly Varden, grayling and lake trout and five species of salmon run in the rivers. A variety of birds, including bald eagles, osprey, ptarmigan, spruce grouse, swans and game ducks, can be readily observed.

From King Salmon, which has daily jet service, access to the park is by scheduled or charter floatplane service. Katmai also is accessible by a 10-mile road from King Salmon to Lake Camp on the western side of Naknek Lake, where there is a boat dock and ramp.

There are several commercial lodges and camps within Katmai, as well as a public campground at Brooks Camp, summer headquarters for the Park Service. Backcountry camping is allowed anywhere by permit.

Recreation in Katmai includes backpacking, canoeing, kayaking, sportfishing, photography and wildlife observation. The Grosvenor and Savonoski rivers and a series of large lakes connected by portage form a circular waterway of almost 100 miles for canoeists and kayakers. The wild and scenic Alagnak and Nonvianuk rivers provide a good float trip to the Kvichak River and Bristol Bay. From Brooks Camp there are trails to viewpoints and a bear observation platform. A 23-mile dirt road leads from Brooks Camp to the Valley of 10,000 Smokes.

Alaska Maritime National Wildlife Refuge

Most of the approximately 3.5 million acres of the Alaska Maritime National Wildlife Refuge are in the Aleutian Islands Unit. This refuge consists of more than 2,400 parcels of land on islands, islets, rocks, spires, reefs and headlands of Alaska coastal waters stretching from the Chukchi Sea to southeastern Alaska.

All but five of the more than 124 islands in the Aleutians are part of the refuge. The Alaska Peninsula Unit includes Simeonof and Semidi islands, the Shumagin Islands, Sutwik Island, the islands and headlands of Paule Bay, and other lands south of the peninsula from Katmai National Park and Preserve to False Pass.

Alaska Maritime is synonymous with seabirds — millions of them. About 75 percent of Alaska's marine birds (15 million to 30 million birds among 55 species) use the refuge.

They congregate in colonies along the coast. Each species has a specialized nesting site, be it rock ledge, crevice, boulder rubble, pinnacle or burrow. This adaptation allows many birds to use a small area of land, as seen in the photo at left, where murres and kittiwakes inhabit a staircased cliff on Amak Island. (John E. Sarvis, reprinted from ALASKA GEOGRAPHIC®).

The refuge also hosts thousands of sea lions, seals, walruses and sea otters. Bird watching is popular, especially on Attu Island and on the Pribilof Islands. The refuge also offers some spectacular photo opportunities, such as the sunset on Buldir Island seen below. (T. Early)

Most lands of the refuge are extremely rugged and virtually inaccessible. There is scheduled air service to Dutch Harbor and Cold Bay, both of which have visitor facilities as well as charter aircraft available. St. Paul and St. George in the Pribilof Islands have scheduled air service from Anchorage and locally guided tours of seabird rookeries and fur seal haul-out sites.

Alaska Peninsula National Wildlife Refuge

This 3.5 million-acre refuge on the Pacific side of the Alaska Peninsula is one of the most scenically diverse, featuring active volcanoes, lakes, rivers, tundra and a beautiful stretch of rugged, rocky Pacific Ocean coastline. It extends southwest from Becharof National Wildlife Refuge to False Pass. Aniakchak National Monument and Preserve splits the refuge into two parts.

The Alaska Peninsula is dominated by the rugged Aleutian Range, part of a chain of volcanoes known as the "Ring of Fire" that encircles the Pacific Rim. Mount Veniaminoff (8,224 feet) on the refuge is one of Alaska's active volcanoes, last erupting in June 1983. Other special features of this refuge are the Ugashik Lakes, renowned for trophy grayling fishing; the Black Lake-Chignik Lake area, which has one of the densest concentrations of brown bears in North America; Castle Cape Fjords, a famous landmark to ships with its distinctive light and dark rock layers; and the needle-pointed Aghileen Pinnacles and vertical buttresses of Cathedral Valley near the recently active Pavlof Volcano.

Besides bears, wildlife on the refuge includes moose, caribou, wolves, and wolverines. Large populations of sea lions, seals and migratory whales inhabit the coastline and offshore waters. On the Pacific side of the peninsula the population of sea otters, hunted nearly to extinction in the 1880s, numbers at least 30,000 today. The entire refuge provides habitat for millions of birds — especially waterfowl — that use the area as a staging ground on their way to and from nesting grounds in the Arctic. Virtually the entire world's population of emperor geese, estimated to be 100,000 birds, migrates along the north side of the Alaska Peninsula in the spring.

This refuge is renowned for big game hunting, especially for moose, caribou and brown bear. Fishing is outstanding for king and silver salmon, arctic char, lake trout, northern pike and grayling.

Access is from King Salmon, Kodiak, Sand Point or Cold Bay, where small planes may be chartered to the refuge. There are no commercial facilities, roads or trails on the refuge.

The Meshik River flows west from Meshik Lake to Port Heiden. (George Wuerthner)

Becharof National Wildlife Refuge

This 1.2 million-acre refuge on the Alaska Peninsula is dominated by Becharof Lake, second largest lake in Alaska, which covers a quarter of the refuge. The lake is surrounded by low rolling hills, tundra wetlands in the northwest and volcanic peaks to the southeast. The refuge is sandwiched between Katmai National Park and Preserve and the Alaska Peninsula National Wildlife Refuge.

The lake area includes abandoned Kanatak village and the Kanatak Portage Trail that allowed people to traverse the Alaska Peninsula. On the south side of the lake are The Gas Rocks, which belched clouds of ash during a major eruption in 1977, and 4,835-foot Mount Peulik volcano.

The salmon spawning streams attract a large concentration of brown bears, many of which make their dens on islands in Becharof Lake. Moose inhabit the refuge in moderate numbers and about 10,000 caribou migrate through and winter on the refuge. Other mammals include wolves, wolverines, river otters, red foxes and beavers. In addition, thousands of sea mammals such as sea

Mount Peulik dominates The Gas Rocks on the south side of Becharof Lake. (R.J. Wilk)

otters, sea lions, harbor seals and migratory whales inhabit the Pacific coastline. Eagles, peregrine falcons, and thousands of seabirds inhabit the sea cliffs and islands. Waterfowl are abundant in the wetlands and coastal estuaries in the fall, often exceeding 46,000 birds. Several thousand emperor geese use refuge bays and lagoons in the spring and some lakes are spring and fall staging areas for tundra (whistling) swans, which also nest in large numbers on the refuge. About 20 species of seabirds nest in 13 colonies on the refuge; two

colonies in Puale Bay are among the largest on the Alaska Peninsula.

Becharof offers outstanding bear and caribou hunting, the most popular recreational activity. Sportfishing on the refuge so far has been light, although there are trophy-sized rainbow trout, char, grayling and salmon.

Access is by charter plane from King Salmon, Kodiak, Sand Point or Cold Bay. There are no commercial facilities or roads on the refuge; wilderness camping only.

A moose swims across Becharof Lake. (Jo Keller, U.S. Fish & Wildlife Service, reprinted from ALASKA GEOGRAPHIC®)

The rich salmon-spawning streams near Becharof Lake attract large numbers of brown bears. (Jo Keller, U.S. Fish & Wildlife Service, reprinted from ALASKA GEOGRAPHIC®)

Izembek National Wildlife Refuge

One of the older refuges in the state, the 321,000-acre Izembek is located at the tip of the Alaska Peninsula just across False Pass from Unimak Island, first in the Aleutian Chain. It faces the Bering Sea and abuts the Alaska Peninsula National Wildlife Refuge to the east.

Izembek's landscape features volcanoes with glacial caps, valleys and tundra uplands that slope into lagoons adjoining the Bering Sea, pristine streams, and sand dunes. The centerpiece of the refuge is Izembek Lagoon, protected by barrier islands from the Bering Sea. This lagoon, along with several smaller lagoons, hosts up to 300,000

Hiker sloshes his way through eelgrass beds at Izembek refuge. (Larry Rice, reprinted from ALASKA GEOGRAPHIC®)

Black brant — accompanied by a few emperor geese — cross Kinzarof Lagoon. (Larry Rice, reprinted from ALASKA GEOGRAPHIC®)

geese, 150,000 ducks and nearly all of the world's population of black brant — 120,000 to 150,000 birds — during the fall migration. These birds feed on Izembek Lagoon's 84,000-acre eelgrass bed, one of the largest in the world. Most waterfowl arrive on the refuge in late August or early September. By early November a second wave of northern waterfowl (primarily sea ducks) arrives to winter on Izembek. The colorful Steller's eider, which nests on the Arctic coast of Alaska and Siberia, is the most common wintering duck. In addition, thousands of shorebirds feed on the bay shore at low tide. At high tide they gather in such large flocks that in flight they look like smoke clouds.

Hunting is excellent for waterfowl, ptarmigan and caribou. Sportfishing for salmon and Dolly Varden also is popular.

This refuge is one of the few in Alaska accessible by a road. The refuge boundary is less than a mile from Cold Bay. The 42 miles of roads in the area lead to Frosty Peak, a 5,820-foot volcano on the refuge's eastern boundary; Grant Point, which provides an excellent overlook on Izembek Lagoon; and to the lagoon itself.

Alaska Peninsula Rivers

While not numerous, the rivers and lakes of the Alaska Peninsula still offer the raft or kayak enthusiast a good variety of excellent wilderness trips. Most popular are the following:

Alagnak and Nonvianuk rivers — The 80-mile-long Alagnak River and its 11-mile tributary, the Nonvianuk, both originate within Katmai National Preserve. The Nonvianuk and the first 67 miles of the Alagnak were included in the National Wild and Scenic River System in 1980. The Alagnak originates in Kukaklek Lake, then flows west-southwest to join the Kvichak River, which empties into Bristol Bay. Either the main branch or the Nonvianuk, which heads in Nonvianuk Lake, offers excellent boating opportunities.

Aniakchak River — The 32-mile-long Aniakchak River is unique in that it heads in a freshwater lake inside the caldera of an active volcano, which last erupted in 1931. The river, located wholly within Aniakchak National Monument, was included in the National Wild and Scenic River System in 1980.

Katmai Lakes — Several lakes and a river in Katmai National Park afford a circular trip of nearly 100 miles for kayakers and canoeists in a scenic setting amid low mountains. This trip generally starts at Brooks Camp on Naknek Lake, then skirts the shore of Naknek Lake to the Bay of Islands, where there is a mile-long portage to Grosvenor Lake. After paddling the length of Lake Grosvenor, you'll enter the relatively calm Grosvenor River which joins the Savonoski River, a braided, fairly slow glacial stream which flows 12 miles to Iliuk Arm. Iliuk Arm joins Naknek Lake just a few miles from Brooks Camp. Variations of this trip are to start at Grosvenor Camp on Lake Grosvenor or to put in at Lake Camp at the far end of Naknek Lake, paddle the length of Naknek Lake and then take the circular route.

King Salmon River — This is a slow, silty river flowing westward about 60 miles across a soggy tundra-covered coastal plain to Egegik Bay, which empties into Bristol Bay. This river's headwaters are in Katmai National Park and it flows partially through Becharof National Wildlife Refuge.

Sportfishing

Except for a few miles of road out of King Salmon, access to lakes and rivers on the Alaska Peninsula is almost solely by airplane, although those with enough time can take a boat or walk to some good spots. There are many commercial lodges in the area, but other than Brooks Camp in Katmai National Park, there are no established campgrounds.

This region offers some of the finest sportfishing in the world. Probably the most prized sport fish are the trophy-sized rainbow trout. During late August, these beauties leave the lakes and enter the streams to feast on salmon eggs and decaying salmon. Rainbows are abundant until freezeup and regularly attain 10 pounds. The Kvichak and Alagnak watersheds are within the state's Bristol Bay Wild Trout Area, which is governed by special regulations.

Big king salmon are at their best from mid-June

A kayaker on the bank of the Ukak River, which flows into Iliuk Arm of Naknek Lake. (George Wuerthner)

Salmon fishing is concentrated in the Alaska Peninsula's river systems. (George Wuerthner)

through July. These fish are not uncommon at 30 pounds and up — trophy size is 50 pounds. Chums and reds show up by July 1, pinks by mid-July (in even numbered years) and silvers by mid-August. Salmon fishing is concentrated in the river systems.

Arctic char and Dolly Varden are found throughout the peninsula region and are most abundant either in spring when some migrate to the sea, or in midsummer when large schools concentrate at river mouths to feed on outmigrating juvenile salmon. These fish usually weigh one to three pounds, but occasional nine- to 12-pound lunkers have been reported. Grayling can be caught most of the summer, but larger ones are more plentiful August through October, with record breakers found in the outlet of lower Ugashik Lake. Grayling measuring 18 inches are not uncommon and they can reach 23 inches.

Anangula

Dating back at least 8,000 years, Anangula is the oldest known settlement in the Aleut world. This site on now-uninhabited Anangula (Ananiuliak) Island in Samalga Pass off Nikolski village is at the southern terminus of a land bridge over which people migrated from Siberia across what is now the Bering Sea.

Thousands of stone artifacts have been found at Anangula that link this culture to those of northern and central Asia, particularly the Kamchatka Peninsula.

Lighthouses

There are two lighthouses in the Aleutians that are part of a chain of navigational beacons operated by the U.S. Coast Guard. Originally they had lighthouse keepers, but none are staffed today.

Cape Sarichef Light Station, located on the northwest side of Unimak Island overlooking Unimak Pass, is the most westerly lighthouse in North America. Cape Sarichef Lighthouse, along with Scotch Cap on the opposite side of the island, stands sentinel over the pass, which is a natural route through the Aleutian Islands. This station began operating in 1904. The station serves as a National Weather Service forecasting center.

Scotch Cap Light Station was the first built on the outside coast of Alaska. The station, which was automated in 1971, is a monument to many ship disasters, before and after its establishment. It began operation July 18, 1903. Partly because of the hazardous duty, each of Scotch Cap's three keepers received one year's vacation every four years. On April 1, 1946, an earthquake that registered 7.4 on the Richter Scale occurred southwest of Unimak Island, generating a 100-foot tsunami that swamped Scotch Cap and killed all five Coast Guardsmen at the station. The wave crossed the Pacific Ocean and hit the north side of the Hawaiian Islands, killing 159 people. It then continued to Chile, rebounded and hit the southern side of Hawaii, causing what is rated as Hawaii's worst natural disaster ever because it hit with no warning.

A fisherman on the upper Brooks River uses a snag for a hammock. (© Chlaus Lotscher)

111

World War II Military Sites

Several sites in the Aleutians that played a major role during World War II have been designated national historic landmarks. At least two companies offer tours to view the wartime relics.

Attu Battlefield and the U.S. Army and Navy airfields on Attu Island, site of the only World War II battle fought in North America.

Attu is at the western end of the Aleutian Chain, 1,500 air miles southwest of Anchorage and only 500 miles east of the Soviet Union. The Japanese occupation of Attu and Kiska in June 1942 coincided with the Battle of Midway. Attu was held for nearly a year before American troops launched a bitterly fought, 19-day battle which only 29 of the 2,500 Japanese troops survived. U.S. casualties were heavy, too. Of 15,000 troops, 550 were killed, 1,500 wounded and another 1,200 disabled by Attu's harsh climate. During the remaining years of the war, the U.S. flew bombing raids on Japan from Attu. Today, evidence of the desperate battle litters Attu's eastern end. There are thousands of shell and bomb craters, as well as Japanese trenches, foxholes and gun emplacements. American ammunition magazines and dumps and spent cartridges, shrapnel and shells are found at the scenes of heavy fighting. The steel-mat runways at Alexai Field and the asphalt runways at the U.S. naval air station remain. Deteriorating piers stand at Massacre Bay. Roads still can be traced, but only a few miles are maintained. The only occupants today are 24 U.S. Coast Guardsmen who operate a long range navigation station. The Aleut village of Attu, whose residents were captured and taken to Japan, was destroyed during the battle and no trace remains. The entire island is part of the Alaska Maritime National Wildlife Refuge.

Japanese Occupation Site on Kiska Island, from which the Japanese withdrew after the U.S. reclaimed Attu.

A World War II U.S. gun emplacement at East Holtz Bay on Attu Island. (Staff, reprinted from ALASKA GEOGRAPHIC®)

Kiska, one of the Rat Islands, is near the western end of the Aleutian Chain, 165 miles southeast of Attu. On June 7, 1942, a Japanese task force invaded Attu and Kiska, overrunning a U.S. weather station on Kiska. They constructed coastal and antiaircraft defenses, camps, roads, an airfield, submarine base, seaplane base, and other installations. The occupation marked the peak of Japan's military expansion in the Pacific and caused great alarm in North America that a Japanese invasion would be mounted through Alaska. As Allied forces prepared to invade Kiska, 5,183 Japanese secretly were evacuated in less than an hour under cover of fog on July 28, 1943. On Aug. 15, 34,000 U.S. and Canadian troops invaded a deserted island. The Allies subsequently established their

Unga Island Petrified Forest

Although the Aleutians are one of the most extensive treeless zones in the world, there is much evidence that trees thrived here before the ice age. Some 150 acres of beach on the northwest coast of Unga Island, located west of Sand Point, contain black, yellow and gray petrified stumps measuring two to four feet in diameter. In the photo above, blue light reflects from a quartz lens in a piece of petrified wood on Unga Island. The rock stumps are the remains of metasequoia trees, thought to be an ancestor of redwood trees. Scientists estimate they lived 11 to 25 million years ago, during the warm and humid Miocene period. Today, the only trees in the Aleutians are a few transplanted evergreens at Unalaska, Atka, Adak, Unga, Akutan and Squaw Harbor. Access to Unga Island is by charter plane or boat from Sand Point. (Andrew Gronholdt, reprinted from ALASKA GEOGRAPHIC®)

Marker honors the Japanese soldiers who died on Kiska Island. (Charles A. Simenstad, reprinted from ALASKA® magazine)

A rusting Japanese mini-sub on Kiska Island, one of many World War II relics that litter the island. (Staff, reprinted from ALASKA GEOGRAPHIC®)

own camps on the island. Kiska was abandoned after the war, but wartime relics still litter the countryside. Today, unoccupied Kiska is part of the Alaska Maritime National Wildlife Refuge.

Dutch Harbor Naval Operating Base and Fort Mears on Amaknak Island.

At the time of the Dec. 7, 1941, Japanese attack on Pearl Harbor in Hawaii, this base and fort, along with top-secret Fort Glenn on nearby Umnak Island, were the only U.S. defense facilities in the Aleutians. Shortly after Pearl Harbor, a Navy base was constructed at Unalaska. Some 60,000 men were stationed at Dutch Harbor/Unalaska, which was the target of Japanese bombing on June 3 and 4, 1942, in conjunction with the Battle of Midway. The military installations remained at Dutch Harbor and Unalaska until June 1985, when a clean-up program began. Although many of the old buildings are gone, machine gun nests, barbed wire, trenches, and bomb shelters will remain for

years to come. The hulk of the bombed-out ship, *Northwestern,* which had been used for barracks, still lies partially submerged at the head of Captain's Bay, a short drive from town.

Adak Army Base and Adak Naval Operating Base on Adak Island (nominated to the National Register of Historic Places).

Adak, one of the Andreanof Islands, is about 1,400 air miles southwest of Anchorage. The island was unoccupied at the outbreak of World War II, but became the site of Alaska's largest and most expensive wartime base after the Japanese bombings of Unalaska and Dutch Harbor and the invasion of Attu and Kiska in 1942. The need for an advance base farther west than Unalaska and

Umnak islands became urgent and Adak was selected because of its all-weather harbor. The first airstrip was built on Adak in 12 days and on Sept. 14, 1942, the first Liberators flew from Adak to bomb Japanese forces on Kiska. Permanent airfields later were built and Adak served as the command post for the invasions of Attu and Kiska in 1943. Adak continued to serve as an active base throughout the war. In 1950 the Army Air Force turned it over to the Navy. Today, Adak Naval Air Station, located on the wartime site, occupies the northern half of the island; the southern half is part of the Alaska Maritime National Wildlife Refuge. As with many of the other islands that played a major role in the war, Adak is littered with military buildings and other relics.

BERING SEA COAST

The Bering Sea coast region covers western Alaska and extends in a convex curve from the Arctic Circle south to where the Alaska Peninsula joins the mainland near Katmai National Park. It is the home of Inupiat and Yup'ik Eskimos. The region can be divided into three distinct subregions: the central Yukon-Kuskokwim river delta; the Seward Peninsula to the north; and Bristol Bay and its watershed to the south.

Offshore, three major island groups rise from the floor of the shallow Bering Sea: St. Lawrence, home to nearly 1,000 Siberian Yup'ik Eskimos; Nunivak Island, across Etolin Strait from the delta region; and uninhabited St. Matthew and Hall islands in the central Bering Sea between St. Lawrence and the Pribilof Islands.

Just south of Kotzebue Sound, the 200-mile-long Seward Peninsula stretches toward Siberia. Cape Prince of Wales at its tip points seaward to Little Diomede Island, a mere three miles (and a day) across the Bering Strait and the International Dateline from the Soviet Union's Big Diomede

A fork of the Kuskokwim River flows from the Alaska Range. (George Wuerthner)

Island. Norton Sound, a 125-mile extension of the Bering Sea, borders the southern side of the Seward Peninsula and the northern edge of the Yukon-Kuskokwim Delta.

The delta, a fan-shaped area formed mostly by centuries of deposits from the Yukon River, stretches 250 miles south to Kuskokwim Bay and inland 200 miles to the Kuskokwim Mountains. This marshy land, lake-studded and very flat, is one of the world's major coastal flood plains.

South and east of Kuskokwim Bay lies Bristol Bay, one of the richest fishing grounds in the world. The bay spans some 200 miles from its base at Port Moller on the Alaska Peninsula to its northwest boundary at Cape Newenham and stretches northeastward nearly the same distance to the mouths of the Nushagak and Kvichak rivers which drain its inland reaches. Lake Clark and Iliamna Lake are part of the Bristol Bay drainage.

The northern portion of the Bering Sea coast borders the Arctic and is subject to long harsh winters; temperatures ranging from -5°F to the low 20s are common. Summer temperatures range from the low 40s to the low 60s. Farther south, the weather moderates a bit. Highs in the 30s and lows around 0°F occur in winter; mid-30s to

Fall colors tinge a tundra blueberry patch. (© Chlaus Lotscher)

Bristol Bay set-netters prepare for opening of red salmon fishing. (©Chlaus Lotscher)

northwest of Dillingham, Wood-Tikchik State Park north of Dillingham, and the Walrus Islands State Game Sanctuary to the southwest.

Transportation along the Bering Sea coast, as in most of rural Alaska, is by plane year-round, boat in summer and snow machine in winter. Although not commonly used for transportation anymore, dog teams are still popular for sport.

There are several long-distance races, the most famous of which is the Iditarod Trail Sled Dog Race from Anchorage to Nome.

Commerce in this coastal region centers around Nome on the Seward Peninsula, Bethel in the Yukon-Kuskokwim delta and Dillingham on Bristol Bay. Nome, a booming gold rush town at the turn of the century, is today the administrative center

mid-60s are common in summer. But the wind blows often in this region and the accompanying wind chill lowers temperatures considerably. Total annual precipitation is about 20 inches, with northern regions drier than southern. North of Bristol Bay, rain and snow fall more frequently on the coast than farther inland. Near the bay, however, the opposite is true; precipitation on the coast averages less than farther inland where the highlands are influenced by the moist marine air from Cook Inlet and the Gulf of Alaska.

Much of the Bering Sea coast is treeless, carpeted by tundra. Grasses, sedges, mosses and lichens and a multitude of wildflowers cover the ground beneath scrub willows and alder. A band of forests marches over the hills on the eastern end of the Seward Peninsula and Norton Sound. White spruce and balsam poplar grow upriver on the Yukon. Inland on the Kuskokwim River, birch and spruce maintain a tenuous hold in poor soil. Near Bristol Bay the tundra once again gives way to forests.

A variety of large mammals including moose, wolves, brown/grizzly bears, caribou and occasional Dall sheep roam the coastal region. Smaller mammals — wolverines, weasels, land otters, lynx, fox, shrews, lemmings and voles — also are found. Millions of migrating birds stop over or nest in the delta, one of the most significant waterfowl breeding areas in North America. Offshore waters support walrus, whales, and several species of seals.

After being hunted out of Alaska in the last century, musk ox were reintroduced in the 1930s on Nunivak Island, which also supports a sizable reindeer herd.

Nunivak is part of the 19.6 million acre Yukon Delta National Wildlife Refuge, largest in the nation and one of several areas of the Bering Sea coast set aside as public lands. Others are Bering Land Bridge National Preserve north of Nome; Lake Clark National Park and Preserve northeast of Iliamna Lake; and Togiak National Wildlife Refuge

Top — *Musk ox viewed from the Nome-Council Road. (Tina Waisman)*

Above — *Parakeet auklets perch on St. Lawrence Island rock. (©Chlaus Lotscher)*

Bering Sea

Bering Sea

Kotlik

Emmonak

Alakanuk

Yukon

Mountain Village
St. Marys
Sheldon Point
Pitkas Point
Pilot Station

Scammon Bay

Delta

Marshall

Russian Mission

Mt. Kusilvak

pe manzof

Hooper Bay

Chevak

National

Upper Kalskag
Lower Kalskag

Tuluksak

Newtok

Nunapitchuk
Kasigluk
Atmautluak
Bethel

Akiakchak
Akiak
Kwethluk

Wildlife

Napakiak
Oscarville
Napaskiak

Baird Inlet

Nelson Island

Tununak
Toksook Bay

Nightmute

Mekoryuk

Tuntutuliak

Eek

Nunivak Island

Refuge

Chefornak

Kipnuk

Kongiganak
Kwigillingok

Quinhagak

Etolin Strait

Kanektok R.

To Nome

Anvik River

Grayling

Map continues at bottom of next page.

Alternate Iditarod Route

Shageluk

Anvik

Holy Cross

Yukon River

Kuskokwim River

Iditarod

Flat

The Iditarod National Historical Trail

Ophir

Takotna
McGrath

Nikolai

Kuskokwim Mountains

Georgetown

Red Devil
Sleetmute

Stony River

Crooked Creek

Chuathbaluk

Napaimute

Aniak
Kolmakov Redoubt

The Iditarod National Historical Trail

Stony River

Nelsons R.

Lime Village

Teladiana R.

Tikakla R.

To Anchorage

Taylor Mountains

Kisaralik River

Lake Clark National Park and Preserve

Lake Clark

Port Alsworth

Mulchatna River
Chilikadrotna R.

Nondalton

Newhalen R.

Iliamna
Newhalen

Pedro Bay

Wood-Tikchik State Park

Nuyakuk R.

Wood-Tikchik Lakes

Nushagak River

Koliganek

New Stuyahok

Ekwok

Pope & Vannoy Landing

Copper R.

Iliamna Lake

Kokhanok

Igiugig

Bering Sea Coast

Togiak River

Togiak National Wildlife Refuge

Ahklun Mountains

Goodnews Bay

Platinum

Twin Hills
Togiak

Manokotak

Portage Creek

Aleknagik

Dillingham

Nushagak
Clark's Point
Ekuk

Nushagak Bay

Levelock

Alagnak River

Kvichak River

Kvichak Bay

Togiak Bay

Cape Newenham

Hagemeister Strait

Hagemeister Island

Walrus Islands

Cape Constantine

Bristol Bay

Location

N

Cartography by David A. Shott

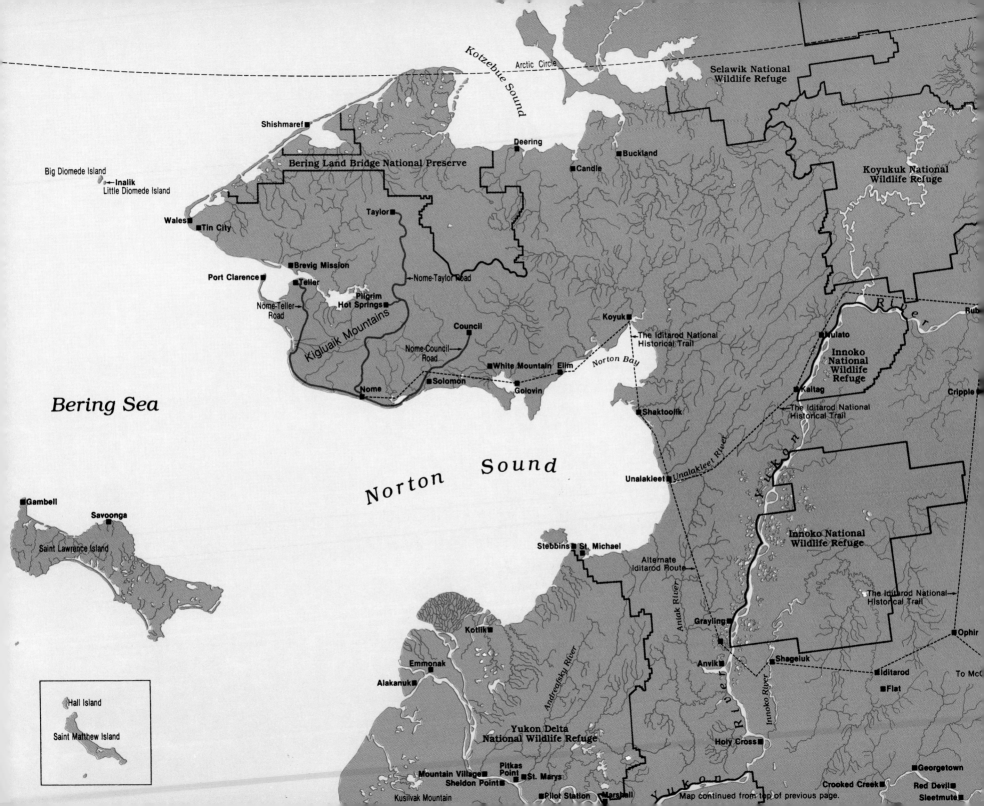

Arctic Circle

Kotzebue Sound

Selawik National
Wildlife Refuge

Shishmaref

Deering

Buckland

Candle

Koyukuk National
Wildlife Refuge

Big Diomede Island
Inalik
Little Diomede Island

Bering Land Bridge National Preserve

Taylor

Wales
Tin City

Nome-Taylor Road

Brevig Mission
Port Clarence
Teller
Pilgrim
Hot Springs

Nome-Teller
Road

Kigluaik Mountains

Council

Nome-Council
Road

Koyuk

The Iditarod National
Historical Trail

River

Rub

Nulato

Innoko
National
Wildlife
Refuge

Kaltag

Cripple

White Mountain Elim

Norton Bay

The Iditarod National
Historical Trail

Solomon

Golovin

Nome

Shaktoolik

Yukon

Bering Sea

Norton Sound

Unalakleet

Unalakleet River

Gambell

Savoonga

Saint Lawrence Island

Innoko National
Wildlife Refuge

Stebbins St. Michael

Alternate
Iditarod Route

Aniak River

Grayling

The Iditarod National
Historical Trail

Kotlik

Hall Island

Emmonak

Andreafsky River

Anvik

Shageluk

Ophir

Saint Matthew Island

Alakanuk

Innoko River

Iditarod

To McG

Flat

River

Yukon Delta
National Wildlife Refuge

Holy Cross

Georgetown

Mountain Village
Sheldon Point

Pitkas
Point
St. Marys

Crooked Creek

Red Devil

Kusilvak Mountain

Pilot Station Marshall

Yukon

Map continued from top of previous page.

Sleetmute

for the Seward Peninsula. Bethel, western Alaska's largest community, is the transfer point for passengers and freight bound for dozens of outlying villages. The salmon fishery, particularly red salmon, makes up the economy of the Bristol Bay area, with Dillingham the hub of activity during fishing season.

Visitors to this land of the Eskimo will find the very old juxtaposed with the very new. Satellite television brings up-to-the-minute news of the world and ancient legends are retold. Sled dogs clamor for a meal of dried fish and the roar of three-wheelers breaks the silence. Seal oil is eaten as enthusiastically as the frozen pizzas airlifted from Anchorage. Modern conveniences exist, but the old ways endure, a reminder that you are in a special place with much to offer.

Bristol Bay Communities

A Native woman cleans red salmon to prepare them for drying. (Staff, reprinted from ALASKA GEOGRAPHIC®*)*

ALEKNAGIK is located on the Wood River at the southeast end of Lake Aleknagik, 25 road miles north of Dillingham, 330 miles west of Anchorage. **Elevation:** 70 feet. **Transportation:** Scheduled air and taxi service from Dillingham. **Population:** 201.

Visitor Facilities: Food and lodging at Mission Lodge (seasonal). Groceries and hardware available at Quick Stop store and Moody's. Fuel (marine gas, diesel, aviation and regular gasoline) and engine repair (boat and car) are available.

Decimated by the flu epidemic of 1918, the village was reestablished about 1928 by a Seventh-day Adventist colony. The Adventists still run a summer camp on the lake. Aleknagik is a Native fishing village with a subsistence lifestyle.

As gateway to Wood-Tikchik State Park, and with a road connection to Dillingham, Aleknagik sees some visitors in summer, drawn by the fishing and boating in the park. Visitors may air charter in or take a taxi from Dillingham (although taxi costs can be as high as $100). One visitor reports:

"Fishing in the state park and surrounding watersheds is excellent, with all five species of salmon, char, grayling, northern pike and Dolly Varden. The trip from Lake Kulik to Alegnagik is about 140 miles of big lakes and short fast rivers. It is suitable for either a raft with a small outboard or kayak or canoe. It has gorgeous scenery, wildlife, amazing salmon runs, good fishing in places and very satisfying rivers and lakes to paddle."

CLARK'S POINT, on the northeast shore of Nushagak Bay, is 15 miles south of Dillingham. **Elevation:** 10 feet. **Transportation:** Scheduled air service from Dillingham. **Population:** 75.

Visitor Facilities: None. Limited selection of items available at community store.

Clark's Point was settled in 1888 when the Nushagak Packing Company cannery was established here. Since shutting down permanently in 1952, the cannery has been used as headquarters for the Alaska Packers Association fishing fleet. Clark's Point is a designated anchorage for

Village of Aleknagik sits at the threshold of Wood-Tikchik State Park. (Staff, reprinted from ALASKA GEOGRAPHIC®*)*

Village of Clark's Point is located on the east shore of Nushagak Bay, 15 miles south of Dillingham. (Staff, reprinted from ALASKA GEOGRAPHIC®)

the many scows, floaters and fishing boats which dot the bay during summer fishing season. Commercial fishing is the primary base of the economy, and residents also depend largely on subsistence activities.

DILLINGHAM is located at the north end of Nushagak Bay, 175 miles southeast of Bethel, 320 miles west of Anchorage. **Elevation:** 80 feet. **Transportation:** Scheduled airline from Anchorage. **Population:** 2,026.

Visitor Facilities: Accommodations at Bristol Inn and Dillingham Hotel. There are a laundromat, bank, restaurants, and several grocery and general merchandise stores, as well as specialty shops. Arts and crafts include grass baskets, carved ivory, Eskimo dolls and Eskimo yo-yos. Fishing and hunting licenses and guide services are available. All major engine repair, rental cars, fuel (marine

gas, diesel, propane, unleaded and regular) and moorage are available.

In 1884 the first salmon cannery in the Bristol Bay region was constructed by the Arctic Packing Co. at nearby Nushagak. Two more canneries were established in the next two years, the second one at the present city of Dillingham, then known as Snag Point. In 1903, U.S. Senator William Paul Dillingham of Vermont conducted an extensive tour through Alaska with his subcommittee. The town was named after the senator in 1904. A post office was established the same year. Dillingham is a first-class city, incorporated in 1963.

Dillingham is the economic and transportation hub of the Bristol Bay region and is headquarters for the Bristol Bay Native Corp. Northbound cargo ships unload supplies for area villages at the Dillingham dock. The city-run dock handles 10,000

tons of freight and fish annually. The city also maintains a harbor serving more than 500 boats. Bristol Bay is the world's largest producer of red salmon.

Numerous sportfishing lodges are located near Dillingham and there is a 20-mile road connecting the town with the Eskimo village of Aleknagik.

In addition to salmon, trout, grayling and arctic char are the main species of fish caught in the lakes and rivers. There is hunting for brown bear in the area and trapping for wolf, wolverine, fox, lynx, marten and beaver. Float trips down the Nushagak or Wood River systems are popular.

Much land in the Dillingham area is owned by the local Native corporation, Choggiung Ltd., which requires that a permit be obtained for any public use of its lands.

EKUK is located on the east shore of Nushagak Bay, 16 miles south of Dillingham. **Transportation:** Scheduled air service from Dillingham. **Population:** 3.

Visitor Facilities: None.

Believed to have been a major Eskimo village in prehistoric times, Ekuk means "the last village down," meaning the farthest village south on Nushagak Bay. A cannery was opened in 1903, which drew many people to the area. Floods, erosion and lack of a school caused residents to leave for more suitable locations. During summer months people return to fish and work in the cannery. St. Nicholas Chapel, a Russian Orthodox church dating from 1917, located in the village is on the National Register of Historic Places.

Much land in the Ekuk area is owned by the local Native corporation, Choggiung Ltd., which requires that a permit be obtained for any public use of its lands.

EKWOK is located on the Nushagak River 48 miles east of Dillingham and 290 miles west of Anchorage. **Elevation:** 130 feet. **Transportation:** Boat, snow machine, scheduled and charter air service from Dillingham. **Population:** 79.

Visitor Facilities: Arrangements may be made to stay at private homes. Accommodations also available during summer at Ekwok Lodge. Candy, soda pop and cigarettes can be purchased at

William Nelson Store; groceries and other supplies must be obtained from Dillingham or Anchorage. The sale and importation of alcoholic beverages is prohibited. Guide services through Ekwok Lodge. Diesel and gas available.

Ekwok is a Yup'ik Eskimo word meaning "end of the bluff" or "cut bank." Ekwok is the oldest continuously occupied village on the Nushagak River. The settlement was first used around the turn of the century as a spring and summer fish camp, and in the fall as a base for berry picking. In 1930 the Bureau of Indian Affairs established a school and mail service began.

The main source of income for the village is commercial fishing, but most residents also depend heavily on subsistence. Fish (salmon, pike, Dolly Varden, char), game (duck, moose, caribou) and wild berries (blackberries, blueberries, salmonberries and highbush cranberries) are harvested. Some of the women grow vegetable gardens. Sharing is a way of life in Ekwok and trading also takes place with other coastal communities. A few people trap beaver, mink, wolverine, otter, red fox and marten, selling the furs at the annual Beaver Roundup festival in Dillingham in early March.

Ekwok Lodge, owned by Ekwok Natives Ltd., is the main attraction in the area. This sportfishing lodge, two miles downriver from Ekwok, operates in summer and features modern accommodations and fishing for salmon, grayling, char, rainbow trout and pike. Near the lodge are the remains of several old sod houses used by previous Native residents of the area.

Much land in the area is owned by Ekwok Natives Ltd., which does not allow any public uses. The location of public easements on the Nushagak River may be obtained from the State Division of Land and Water Management in Anchorage.

IGIUGIG, on the Kvichak River at the southwest end of Lake Iliamna, 50 miles southwest of Iliamna

---

Dillingham fuel dock and cannery are bustling during the salmon season. (John and Margaret Ibbotson, reprinted from ALASKA GEOGRAPHIC®)

Above — *Clothes hang to dry on a sunny day at Igiugig, on the Kvichak River.* (Staff, reprinted from ALASKA GEOGRAPHIC®)

Below — *A line of floatplanes at Iliamna.* (© Chlaus Lotscher)

and 50 miles northeast of King Salmon. **Elevation:** 110 feet. **Transportation:** Scheduled air service from King Salmon. **Population:** 32.

Visitor Facilities: Todd's Igiugig Lodge across the river has modern facilities and guide service for fishing; tackle is sold. Igiugig Native Corp. store has some supplies. No other services available.

Igiugig began as an Eskimo fishing village around the turn of the century. Today, salmon fishing is the mainstay of this unincorporated community. Many residents leave the village to fish Bristol Bay during the red salmon season in late June and July. Sportfishing is very popular in summer in the Kvichak River/Iliamna Lake area.

The community is served by old and new Russian Orthodox churches. The old St. Nicholas Chapel is on the National Register of Historic Places.

ILIAMNA is located on the north side of Iliamna Lake at the north end of the Alaska Peninsula, 17 miles from Nondalton, 187 miles northeast of Dillingham and 225 miles southwest of Anchorage. **Elevation:** 190 feet. **Transportation:** Boat; scheduled or charter air service from King Salmon, Dillingham and Anchorage; an 8-mile gravel road connects Iliamna to Newhalen. **Population:** 90.

Visitor Facilities: Food and lodging at Iliamna Lake Lodge, Iliaska Lodge, Lakeview Lodge, Rainbow King Lodge, Red Quill Lodge and Talarik Creek Lodge. There is a laundromat. Iliamna Trading Co. carries groceries and other supplies. Fishing/hunting licenses available. Guide services available through area lodges. Aircraft mechanic available. Rental transportation includes autos and charter aircraft. Fuel available includes diesel, propane and regular gasoline.

The first of several hunting and fishing lodges opened in Iliamna in the 1930s. Commercial fishing and the area lodges are the major sources of income for this unincorporated community today. Subsistence hunting and fishing is also a significant part of life here.

Iliamna is a major gateway to the world-class fishing and hunting in the Kvichak River drainage. The system, with headwaters in Iliamna Lake and Lake Clark, is historically the most important salmon spawning and rearing habitat for sockeye or red salmon in the world and the largest contributor to the Bristol Bay fishery. State sport-fishing regulations designate the Kvichak River system as a trophy fish area. Some of the largest rainbow trout in the world can be found in these waters.

Visitors planning to hike or canoe in the area should contact the National Park Service in Anchorage; much of the land is privately owned or owned by Native corporations. The Iliamna Natives Ltd. charge fees for camping on corporation land; fees are payable in advance and are nonrefundable. Hiking, berry picking and fishing also are permitted on corporation lands; hunting in general is not. Woodcutting is not permitted.

KOKHANOK, on the south shore of Lake Iliamna, is 25 miles south of Iliamna and 210 miles west of Anchorage. **Elevation:** 50 feet. **Transportation:** Charter and air taxi service from Iliamna; by boat in summer, snow machine in winter, to Iliamna and other villages. **Population:** 80.

Visitor Facilities: Sleeping cots at the community hall. Andrew's General Store and Fennie Andrew's Store operate out of private homes. The sale and importation of alcoholic beverages is prohibited.

This primarily Aleut village relies heavily on subsistence hunting and fishing. Sled dog racing and village festivals are popular in winter. Saints Peter and Paul Orthodox Church here is on the National Register of Historic Places.

KOLIGANEK is on the Nushagak River, 65 miles northeast of Dillingham and 280 miles west of Anchorage. **Elevation:** 240 feet. **Transportation:** Scheduled air service from Dillingham. **Population:** 112.

This Eskimo village is unincorporated. Many residents spend the summer at fish camps. The village has one phone and a school.

LEVELOCK is on the west bank of the Kvichak River, 40 miles north of Naknek, 60 miles east of Dillingham and 280 miles southwest of Anchorage. **Elevation:** 60 feet. **Transportation:** Scheduled and charter air service from King Salmon. **Population:** 127.

Visitor Facilities: Accommodations at Levelock

Hotel. Meals and laundry facilities available. Two stores carry groceries. Fishing and hunting licenses may be purchased locally. Guide services arranged through area lodges. Boat and auto repair services available. Arrangements can be made to rent autos, off-road vehicles and boats. Fuel (marine gas, diesel, propane, regular gasoline) and moorage available.

Canneries operated at Levelock in 1925-26 and again in 1928-29. In 1929-30 the first school was built. A post office was established in 1939.

Nearly all residents participate in the commercial salmon fishery, with about 75 percent of the residents going to Naknek during the fishing season. The entire community also relies on subsistence hunting and fishing. Sharing is a way of life in Levelock and residents make sure that no one goes hungry.

According to one resident the best reason to come to Levelock, besides its location in the designated sport trophy fishing area, is that Alaskan artist Ted Lambert used to live here and residents still have many of Lambert's paintings and block prints, "and many stories about him are told."

MANOKOTAK is on the east bank of the Igushik River, 25 miles southwest of Dillingham and 370 miles west of Anchorage. **Transportation:** Air charter service from Dillingham. **Population:** 302.

Visitor Facilities: None. Laundry facilities are available and groceries and other supplies are available at Manokotak Co-op, Johnny's Store or Southwest Trading Co. Arts and crafts include carved ivory, grass baskets, masks, fur hats and coats. Fishing and hunting licenses available. Fuel (marine gas, diesel, regular gasoline) and moorage are available.

Manokotak is one of the newer communities in the Bristol Bay region, having become a permanent settlement in the 1940s with the consolidation of some older villages. By 1960, the community had a school and post office.

Almost everyone in Manokotak participates in the commercial salmon fishery, leaving the village during the fishing season to fish near the mouth

Top — *The "main street" of Kokhanok. (Staff, reprinted from ALASKA GEOGRAPHIC®)*

Middle — *Village of Koliganek. (Neil and Betty Johannsen, reprinted from ALASKA GEOGRAPHIC®)*

Above — *Floatplanes take visitors to remote lakes like Kontrashibuna Lake in this region. (Staff)*

of the Igushik River. A number of residents also trap fox, beaver, mink, otter, lynx, wolverine and muskrat. Furs are sold at the Beaver Roundup festival held annually in Dillingham or to furriers in Anchorage.

The entire community depends heavily on subsistence hunting and fishing. Trade with Togiak and Twin Hills brings Manokotak residents seal oil and whitefish.

NEWHALEN is located on the north shore of Iliamna Lake at the mouth of the Newhalen River, five miles southwest of Iliamna and 320 miles southwest of Anchorage. **Elevation:** 190 feet. **Transportation:** Scheduled air service to Iliamna, by road to Newhalen. **Population:** 157.

Visitor Facilities: None. There is a washeteria with showers and a store.

The village was established in the late 1800s to take advantage of the plentiful fish and game in the area. Today, it remains a fishing village. Newhalen was incorporated as a second-class city in 1971. It is connected by a nine-mile road to Iliamna.

NEW STUYAHOK is on the Nushagak River, 12 miles upriver from Ekwok, 51 miles northeast of Dillingham and 290 miles southwest of Anchorage. **Elevation:** 125 feet. **Transportation:** Boat; snow machine; scheduled or charter air service from Dillingham. **Population:** 246.

Visitor Facilities: There is a roadhouse and arrangements may also be made for accommodations in private homes. Groceries and other supplies available at Panarqukuk Co-op Store or Arctic Merchandise. Diesel and gas available.

This Eskimo village was relocated several times because of flooding, most recently to its present site in 1942. Stuyahok is an Eskimo word meaning "going downriver place." A school, post office and airstrip were established here in the 1960s. New Stuyahok was incorporated as a second-class city in 1972.

The community's economic base is the commercial salmon fishery, although a number of people trap commercially and several are employed full-time by the government or school district. Beaver, lynx, fox and mink are the primary species trapped for fur, and muskrat, otter, wolverine, bobcat, marten and weasel also are taken. Furs are sold to buyers who pass through the village, at the annual winter Beaver Roundup festival in Dillingham, or at the annual New Stuyahok Beaver Festival.

NONDALTON is located on the west shore of Six Mile Lake, 15 miles north of Iliamna and 200 miles southwest of Anchorage. **Elevation:** 250 feet. **Transportation:** Scheduled and charter air service from Iliamna. **Population:** 231.

Visitor Facilities: There are two fishing and hunting lodges here, Newhalen River Lodge and Valhalla Lodge. Supplies available at Nondalton Co-op Store and Six Mile Enterprise Store. Fishing and hunting licenses available.

Nondalton is a Tanaina Indian name, first recorded in 1909. The village originally was located on the north shore of Six Mile Lake, but was relocated to the west shore in 1940. The St. Nicholas Russian Orthodox Chapel, built in 1896 and moved with the rest of the village, is on the National Register of Historic Places.

Nondalton residents work seasonally in the commercial salmon fishery or firefighting for the Bureau of Land Management. A few other jobs are with governmental agencies and the village Native corporation. Residents also depend heavily on subsistence hunting and fishing for food.

NUSHAGAK is located on the east shore of Nushagak Bay on the north side of Bristol Bay, five air miles from Dillingham, 330 miles southwest of Anchorage. **Transportation:** Boat; charter plane from Dillingham. **Population:** Up to 100 during summer fishing season.

Visitor Facilities: None. Camp or sleep in one of several vacant huts (look for one with an intact roof). Supplies are airlifted from Dillingham.

Nushagak is a former Eskimo village established as a trading post about 1819. It was called Fort or Redoubt Alexander until a post office was established under the name Nushagak in 1899. The post office was discontinued in 1938. The area is now used seasonally as a base for set-net fishermen during the Bristol Bay salmon harvest.

The Russian Orthodox Transfiguration of Our Lord Chapel at Nushagak is on the National Register of Historic Places.

Boats line the waterfront at New Stuyahok on the Nushagak River. (Neil and Betty Johannsen, reprinted from ALASKA GEOGRAPHIC®)

Left — *Nondalton, on the shore of Sixmile Lake, is 15 miles north of Iliamna. (Staff, reprinted from ALASKA GEOGRAPHIC®)*

Below — *Nushagak is now a seasonal fishing camp. (Staff, reprinted from ALASKA GEOGRAPHIC®)*

PEDRO BAY is located at the head of Pedro Bay on Iliamna Lake, 180 miles southwest of Anchorage. **Transportation:** Scheduled or charter air service from Iliamna. **Population:** 32.

Visitor Facilities: Accommodations at a local lodge and in private homes. There is a restaurant. Groceries and some supplies available at D&G General Merchandise or Russian Creek Store. Fishing and hunting licenses and guide service available. Boats may be rented.

This village is located in one of the most attractive settings in southwestern Alaska. The Denaina Indians have occupied this area for hundreds of years. St. Nicholas Russian Orthodox Chapel, built in 1890, is on the National Register of Historic Places.

Few people in Pedro Bay have steady jobs. Some obtain short-term government jobs and a few are fishermen. Others must leave the area to earn enough money to support themselves. Most residents depend on subsistence hunting and fishing.

During the spring and summer, brown bears gather along the salmon streams near Pedro Bay. Black bears are numerous and can be a nuisance because they often wander into the village. Moose concentrate year-round in the area surrounding the village.

Pedro Bay is located within the Kvichak River system, with headwaters in Lake Clark and Iliamna Lake. This is historically the most important salmon spawning and rearing habitat for sockeye salmon in the world. Sportfishing for rainbow trout, arctic char and Dolly Varden also is excellent.

POPE & VANNOY LANDING is located on Intricate Bay on Iliamna Lake, 25 miles from Iliamna. **Transportation:** Boat; floatplane from Iliamna. **Population:** 14.

Visitor Facilities: None.

Art Pope on his home: "Our son was working for the U.S. Commissioner at Kokhonak Bay and found out a cabin was for sale here so he moved here in 1955. My wife, brother-in-law and I came up on vacation in 1957. Brother-in-law stayed and built a cabin. In 1965 my wife and I came up and built a cabin and have been here ever since. A granddaughter and family moved here in 1980. A couple from Iliamna moved here in 1983.

"Three miles from here on the Copper River Bob and Doris Walker run a fishing lodge in the summertime. There are a few moose around but hunting is poor.

"Our son and his wife, our granddaughter and husband go to Bristol Bay and salmon fish in the summer. My wife and I set-net for salmon in the summer and tend 11,000 square feet of garden too

as best we can fighting the weeds. We are both in our 70s and not as spry as in our younger days but still keep active."

PORTAGE CREEK is located 30 miles southeast of Dillingham and 320 miles southwest of Anchorage. **Elevation:** 110 feet. **Transportation:** Boat; charter air service from Dillingham. **Population:** 46.

Visitor Facilities: None.

Portage Creek was part of a summer route between the head of Nushagak Bay and the mouth of the Kvichak River which avoided the open waters of Bristol Bay and a long trip around Etolin Point. It was not until 1961 that the first residence was built. The development of Portage Creek is typical of the changes that have taken place in other villages along the Nushagak. Originally, these villages were mobile and the relocation of a few families could signal the beginning or end of a village. The passage of the Alaska Native Land Claims Settlement Act, and the construction of schools and other public institutions, have ended this mobility except for summer fish camps.

Peaceful scene at Port Alsworth on Lake Clark. (© Chlaus Lotscher)

The primary employment for Portage Creek residents is the fishing industry, but the entire population depends to some extent on subsistence hunting and fishing.

There is superb king salmon fishing from the riverbank in front of the village in June and early July. Arrangements for guided fishing in the area are best made in Dillingham.

Much land in the Portage Creek area is owned by the local Native corporation, Choggiung Ltd., which requires that a permit be obtained for any public use of its lands.

PORT ALSWORTH is located on the southeast shore of Lake Clark, 22 miles northeast of Nondalton, 40 miles from Iliamna and 180 miles from Anchorage. **Elevation:** 230 feet. **Transportation:** Boat; scheduled and charter air service from Iliamna. **Population:** 40.

Visitor Facilities: Accommodations at Alaska's Wilderness Lodge, The Farm Lodge, Lakeside Lodge and Fishing Unlimited. Meals available at lodges. Fishing and hunting licenses may be purchased at Alaska's Wilderness Lodge. Guide services through local lodges. Aircraft repair available. Rental transportation includes boats and charter aircraft. Emergency aviation fuel available from The Farm Lodge.

Early Port Alsworth was a weather reporting station and stopover for airline flights to the Bristol Bay area, according to local residents. Pioneer bush pilot "Babe" Alsworth and his wife Mary, the settlement's first postmistress, were among the early settlers in the 1940s. They homesteaded on 160 acres and developed an airstrip and flying service. They also were involved in developing the Tanalian Bible Church and Camp. Port Alsworth now has several fishing lodges and is the local headquarters for Lake Clark National Park and Preserve. One resident describes it as "one of the finest places to live and visit in rural Alaska."

Most residents make their living either directly or indirectly from tourism. Employment is through the lodges, flying service, school, commercial fishing and a few local businesses.

Local attractions include 40-mile-long Lake Clark, spawning grounds for the Bristol Bay red salmon run; the ruins of historic Kijik village, listed on the National Register of Historic Places; and picturesque Tanalian Falls. Activities include hiking, wildlife photography, bird watching, river rafting, fishing, cross country skiing, sledding, snowmobiling, and hunting for moose, caribou, bear and small game.

From Anchorage, air access to Port Alsworth is through scenic, 1,000-foot Lake Clark Pass.

TOGIAK is located 43 miles east of Goodnews Bay, 70 miles west of Dillingham and 395 miles southwest of Anchorage. **Elevation:** 12 feet. **Transportation:** Scheduled and charter air service from Dillingham. **Population:** 554.

Visitor Facilities: Some accommodations, along with a store, camping facilities and cannery tours, available at Togiak Fisheries Inc. The cannery is across the bay from Togiak. Restaurant and laundry facilities in Togiak. Togiak Co-op and Our Store carry groceries and other supplies. The sale and importation of alcoholic beverages is prohibited. Fishing and hunting licenses available. Moorage is available. Regular gasoline sometimes available.

Most people here are commercial salmon fishermen. Three fish processing facilities are located near Togiak. The entire community also depends heavily on subsistence hunting and fishing.

The major attraction near Togiak is Round Island, one of the Walrus Islands group. This is a popular place to view and photograph the 5,000 to 10,000 male walruses that summer on the island. Transportation to Round Island is by boat from Togiak or by charter plane from Dillingham or King Salmon. Visitors must bring all their own food, shelter and equipment. Access to the game sanctuary is by permit only from the Alaska Department of Fish and Game.

Fishing in the Togiak River is excellent during July, August and September for all five species of salmon, rainbow trout and Dolly Varden.

Togiak is located within the Togiak National Wildlife Refuge, a breeding and resting area for waterfowl and shorebirds.

TWIN HILLS is located two miles north of Togiak and 395 miles southwest of Anchorage. **Elevation:** 25 feet. **Transportation:** Boat from Togiak; scheduled and charter air service from Dillingham. **Population:** 67.

Visitor Facilities: Arrangements may be made to stay in private homes. Groceries available at store. Diesel, propane, unleaded and regular gasoline are available.

Twin Hills is located at the base of two hills which rise to 291 feet and 427 feet, prominent features in this generally flat coastal region. The village was established in 1965 following the 1964 flood in the upper Togiak Bay area.

"For a living we hunt off our land for subsistence," as one resident puts it. Virtually all residents of Twin Hills participate in the commercial salmon fishery. In addition, the people work at the few local jobs available, carve ivory, and trade with people from Manokotak.

There is a road leading from Twin Hills to the beach at Togiak Bay. From there it is possible to drive an auto or three-wheeler to the Togiak Fisheries cannery on the bay across from Togiak.

Twin Hills is located within the Togiak National Wildlife Refuge.

Visitors should be aware that Twin Hills Native Corporation lands are closed to sportfishing, hunting and hiking by nonmembers. Before traveling in the Twin Hills area, check with the corporation about the location of restricted lands.

Above — *Twin Hills village below its twin hills. (Staff, reprinted from* ALASKA GEOGRAPHIC®)

Right — *Togiak overlooks Togiak Bay and High Island. (Steve Westfall, reprinted from* ALASKA GEOGRAPHIC®)

Bristol Bay Attractions

Lake Clark National Park and Preserve

Magnificent Lake Clark National Park and Preserve is located north of Iliamna Lake, 150 miles southwest of Anchorage. This area where the Alaskan and Aleutian mountain ranges converge has been called "the Alaskan Alps." The 3.6 million acre park and preserve boasts a dazzling array of features including a jumble of glacier-carved peaks ranging up to 10,000 feet; two steaming volcanoes; countless glaciers; many lakes ranging in size from 40-mile-long Lake Clark to shallow tundra ponds; deep U-shaped valleys with rushing streams; open, lichen-covered uplands; three wild and scenic rivers — the Mulchatna, Tlikakila and Chilikadrotna; and a coastline along Cook Inlet full of tidal bays and rocky inlets. Lake Clark is fed by hundreds of mountain waterfalls and is part of an important red salmon spawning ground.

Wildlife includes the Mulchatna caribou herd, moose, brown and black bears, wolves, wolverines, marten, mink, land otters, weasels, beavers, lynx and red foxes. The Lake Clark mountains are the southern limit for the range of Dall

Left — *Iliamna Volcano towers over blue-green Crescent Lake. (John and Margaret Ibbotson, reprinted from* ALASKA GEOGRAPHIC®*)*

Above — *Jon Berryman and Heinz Allemann load plane at Chinitna Bay on the Cook Inlet side of the park. (© Chlaus Lotscher)*

sheep. Whales and seals swim offshore along the coast. Waterfowl are abundant along Tuxedni Bay and in the ponds and marshes of the tundra plains. Bald eagles, peregrine falcons and numerous other birds nest in the park and preserve.

Sportfishing is good for grayling, northern pike, and several trout and salmon species. Sport hunting is allowed in the preserve.

Activities in this predominantly wilderness area are primarily backpacking, river running and fishing. Wildlife and nature viewing and photography are excellent.

Access is by air from Anchorage or the Kenai Peninsula to Iliamna, which is linked by road to Nondalton at the west end of Lake Clark. There are no roads or trails in the park or preserve. Several commercial lodges operate on Lake Clark. Camping is permitted throughout the park and preserve.

Wood-Tikchik State Park

This 1.4 million acre park — largest and most remote in the state system — is located about 30 miles north of Dillingham. Wood-Tikchik is a spectacular undeveloped wilderness park featuring two separate systems of large, interconnected pristine lakes: six in the Tikchik River drainage and six in the Wood River drainage. Rugged mountains 3,000 to 5,000 feet high form a backdrop for some of the lakes on the western side of the park. Pinnacle peaks, high alpine valleys, hanging valleys and dramatic V-shaped incisions contribute to this area's fjordlike appearance. The eastern edge of the lakes overlooks numerous shoals and islands, gravel beaches and the broad tundra landscape of the Nushagak flats. Wildlife includes brown and black bears, moose, wolves, wolverines, foxes, lynx, marten and beavers. Fishing is excellent throughout the summer for arctic char, rainbow trout, northern pike, red salmon, Dolly Varden and grayling. Sport hunting also is allowed in the park.

The park offers excellent boating, hiking, sightseeing and photography opportunities. There are no restrictions on camping in the park; motorboats are allowed.

Access is primarily by charter air service from Dillingham. There is a road to Aleknagik village on Lake Aleknagik, which adjoins the southern end of the park. Several commercial lodges operate in or near the park, which has no other developed facilities or trails.

Cape Newenham, site of a major seabird colony, juts into the Bering Sea between Kuskokwim and Bristol bays. (Bill Crocker, reprinted from ALASKA GEOGRAPHIC®)

A kayaker crosses Lake Nerka in the Wood River Lakes system. (Neil and Betty Johannsen, reprinted from ALASKA GEOGRAPHIC®)

Togiak National Wildlife Refuge

Togiak National Wildlife Refuge is about 30 miles northwest of Dillingham at its closest point. The 4.3 million acre refuge is sandwiched between the huge Yukon Delta National Wildlife Refuge to the north, Wood-Tikchik State Park to the east and the Bering Sea to the west. The refuge offers outstanding scenery including glacial valleys, tundra uplands, wetlands, sand and gravel beaches, rugged mountains and coastal cliffs. The myriad lakes range in size from tundra potholes to 13-mile-long Togiak Lake. Togiak Valley is the site of a rare geological feature: a two-mile-long *tuya*, a flat-topped, steep-sided volcano formed when lava erupted under a glacier.

Togiak is a haven for migrating birds. As many as a quarter million waterfowl have been counted in the bays, lagoons and lakes along the coast of the refuge, where waterfowl await spring breakup in the Arctic. About 50 percent of the world's population of brant use the refuge — up to 50,000 birds can be seen at one time in Nanvak and Chagvan bays. Thousands of emperor geese and common and Steller's eiders migrate through refuge, along with significant numbers of king eiders, harlequin ducks and black scoters. Bald and golden eagles nest inland and on coastal cliffs. The refuge also is home to one of the largest populations of cliff-nesting seabirds in the eastern Bering Sea. Cape Newenham, Cape Peirce, Bird Rock and Shaiak Island support one million to two million seabirds, especially common murres and black-legged kittiwakes.

The refuge attracts fishermen from around the world with major concentrations of all five species of salmon, grayling, rainbow trout, Dolly Varden and arctic char in the Togiak, Kanektok and Goodnews drainages. Other fish available are lake trout, burbot and northern pike. Other recreational activities include hunting, river floating, hiking, sightseeing, camping and wildlife observation/photography.

Access is primarily by charter plane from Dillingham or Bethel. There are no campgrounds or established trail systems on the refuge.

Walrus Islands State Game Sanctuary

Hundreds of bull walruses haul out in Walrus Islands State Game Sanctuary in Bristol Bay 70 miles southwest of Dillingham. This sanctuary offers an unsurpassed opportunity to view and photograph some of the 5,000 to 10,000 male walruses that come here from May to September. Females with young are seldom seen in Bristol Bay as they remain near the edge of the ice pack as it recedes north. There are seven islands in the sanctuary, but Round Island, which may be visited with a permit from the Alaska Department of Fish and Game, is the one most used. (Rollie Ostermick, reprinted from ALASKA GEOGRAPHIC®)

Bristol Bay Rivers

The Bristol Bay region offers three wild and scenic rivers and two lake systems which provide a combination of river and lake paddling. Recreational boaters in this area should be aware that residents may be engaged in subsistence activities on the rivers and their nets and other equipment should be left undisturbed.

Chilikadrotna River — This wild and scenic river heads in Twin Lakes in Lake Clark National Park and Preserve and flows 60 miles to join the Mulchatna River 46 miles northwest of Nondalton on Lake Clark. The first 11 miles of the river are within the park and preserve. This swift river flows through the forest west of the Alaska Range.

Copper (Iliamna) River — This fast, clear-water river heads in Meadow Lake and flows 40 river miles southwest into Intricate Bay on Iliamna Lake.

Mulchatna River — This wild and scenic river heads in Turquoise Lake in the foothills of the Chigmit Mountains in Lake Clark National Park

Right — *Lothar Vollmer prepares to load raft on the Tlikakila River. (© Chlaus Lotscher)*

Rafts sometimes must be towed through shallow spots on the upper reaches of the Tlikakila River. (© Chlaus Lotscher)

Bristol Bay Sportfishing

Bristol Bay is world famous for its sportfishing, particularly for trophy-sized rainbow trout which often attain 10 pounds. These fish are at their best in late summer and early fall. The Kvichak and Alagnak watersheds are within the Bristol Bay Wild Trout area, governed by special state regulations.

Tackle-breaking king salmon are at their peak from mid-June through July. These fish are not uncommon at 30 pounds and up. Chums and reds show up by July 1, pinks by mid-July (in even-numbered years) and silvers by mid-August. Salmon fishing is concentrated in the river systems.

Arctic char and Dolly Varden are found

Happy fisherman displays king salmon caught near Port Alsworth. (Mark Lang)

and Preserve and flows some 220 miles to join the Nushagak River, 65 miles northeast of Dillingham. The first 24 miles of the Mulchatna are within the park and preserve.

Newhalen River — This is a large, clear white-water river that heads in Sixmile Lake, then flows south 22 miles to Iliamna Lake. It is a beautiful turquoise-colored river.

Nushagak River — This river flows southwest 275 miles to the head of Nushagak Bay, just south of Dillingham. The Nushagak was the first river in this area ascended by the Russians in the early 1800s. The headwaters drain the Taylor Mountains, while the major tributaries — the Nuyakuk and Mulchatna rivers — carry drainage from the western lake country and glaciers to the east.

Nuyakuk River — This river heads in Tikchik Lake in Wood-Tikchik State Park and flows about 50 miles to join the Nushagak. The upper 12 miles of the river are in the park.

Tikchik River — This clear, gravelly river heads in Nishlik Lake in the Ahklun Mountains and flows 65 river miles south to Tikchik Lake in Wood-Tikchik State Park.

Tlikakila River — This is a wild and scenic river that heads in Summit Lake and flows 51 miles to Lake Clark. It flows entirely within Lake Clark National Park and Preserve.

Togiak River — This river heads in 13-mile-long Togiak Lake on the Togiak National Wildlife Refuge and flows 60 miles to Togiak Bay.

Wood-Tikchik Lakes — The two lake systems in Wood-Tikchik State Park north of Dillingham offer a combination of lake and river paddling, very good fishing and beautiful mountain scenery. Many trip variations are possible.

A hefty arctic char from Bristol Bay area waters. (Lou Gwartney, reprinted from ALASKA GEOGRAPHIC®)

This good-sized northern pike was caught near King Salmon. (Lou Gwartney, reprinted from ALASKA GEOGRAPHIC®)

throughout this area and are most abundant in spring during migrations to the sea or in mid-summer when large schools concentrate at river mouths to feed on juvenile salmon. These usually weigh one to three pounds, but an occasional nine- to 12-pounder has been reported. Grayling can be caught most of the summer, but larger ones are more plentiful from August to October. Grayling measuring 16 inches are not uncommon and they can reach 23 inches.

Farther west, rivers and lakes on the Togiak National Wildlife Refuge provide excellent sport-fishing, with major concentrations of salmon, grayling, rainbow trout, arctic char and lake trout.

Except for a few roads around Dillingham and Iliamna, access to good fishing in the Bristol Bay region is primarily by airplane. Boats occasionally can be rented or chartered at villages along the waterways.

Arctic grayling, on top, and two rainbow trout from the Wood River Lakes system. (Don Rogers, U.W. Fisheries Research Institute, reprinted from ALASKA GEOGRAPHIC®)

Yukon-Kuskokwim Delta Communities

AKIACHAK, on the Kuskokwim River, is 15 miles northeast of Bethel and 390 miles west of Anchorage. **Transportation:** Scheduled air service from Bethel. **Population:** 378.

Visitor Facilities: Lodging available at the IRA (Indian Reorganization Act) Council Building; make arrangements through the school. There is a washeteria. Some supplies available at Akiachak Co-Op Store. Fishing and hunting licenses available.

Akiachak was founded in the early 1890s. A school was established in 1930; a post office opened in 1934; and an airstrip was built in 1967. Akiachak is located within the Yukon Delta National Wildlife Refuge. Many village residents are likely to be at fish camps during the summer.

This Eskimo community has a Moravian church and two schools.

AKIAK, on the Kuskokwim River, is 20 miles northeast of Bethel and 380 miles west of Anchorage. **Transportation:** Scheduled air service from Bethel. **Population:** 277.

Visitor Facilities: Arrangements for accommodations may be made through the city office or at the school. Supplies available at Robert Ivan's Store and Adam Kashatok's Store. Fishing and hunting licenses available.

The name Akiak reportedly means "crossing over" and refers to a trail that connected the Kuskokwim River at Akiak with the Yukon River. A school was established at Akiak in 1911 by John H. Kilbuck, co-founder in 1885 of the Moravian Mission at Bethel, the first Protestant mission on the Kuskokwim.

ALAKANUK is located eight miles southwest of Emmonak, 15 miles east of the Bering Sea and 160 miles northwest of Bethel. **Transportation:** Jet service from Bethel or Nome. **Population:** 564.

Visitor Facilities: Accommodations at city lodge through the city office. Meals available at Family Restaurant. Groceries and other supplies carried at D.F. Jorgenson Co., Alstrom's or Alakanuk Native Store. The sale and importation of alcoholic beverages is prohibited. Local arts and crafts include carved ivory, grass baskets, Eskimo boots and bead work. Washeteria with showers available. Fuel (propane, unleaded and regular gasoline) and moorage are available.

Alakanuk is a Yup'ik word meaning "wrong way," an apt description of this village's location on the maze of watercourses in the Yukon River Delta. A BIA school built in 1959 drew people here from the surrounding area. The village became a second-class city in 1973 and today has two schools.

There's a lot of fishing here, according to one resident: kings, cohos, chums, whitefish, sheefish, black fish and lush fish. Sheefish and lush can be caught by nets under the ice in winter; the rest can be caught in summer and fall. There are seals and whales to hunt in summertime. Hunting and trapping includes ptarmigan, rabbit, mink, muskrat, otters, red and white foxes, lynx, marten. Traveling is done by snowmobile in winter and boat in summer.

ANIAK is located on the south bank of the Kuskokwim River at the head of Aniak Slough, 59 miles southwest of Russian Mission, 90 miles northeast of Bethel, 325 miles west of Anchorage. **Elevation:** 80 feet. **Transportation:** Scheduled or charter air service from Bethel; by boat. **Population:** 483.

Visitor Facilities: Food and lodging at Aniak Lodge. There is a laundry and Alaska Commercial Co. and Kusko Sales carry groceries and other supplies. Fishing and hunting licenses and guide services are available. Engine repair (boats and airplanes), rental transportation (charter aircraft and taxi) and fuel (marine gas, propane and regular gasoline) are available.

Winter sun highlights village of Akiachak. (Division of Tourism)

Greased pole contest at Fourth of July celebration in Aniak. (Rob Reinhardt)

Aniak is a Yup'ik Eskimo word meaning "place where it comes out," referring to the nearby mouth of the Aniak River. Tom L. Johnson homesteaded the long-abandoned site of the old Eskimo village in 1914 and opened a general store. A post office was established and a school opened in 1936. Construction of an airfield in 1939 was followed by the erection of a White Alice radar-relay station in 1956, and the community started to grow as people from the surrounding area moved to Aniak for jobs. Today, Aniak is the transportation hub for the mid-Kuskokwim and mid-Yukon areas, as well as regional headquarters for the school district and several state and federal agencies.

The state operates a 6,000-foot runway, and float and ski planes land on Aniak Slough or on the Kuskokwim River. There's generally good flying weather, with only about a dozen days a year being weathered out. Private boats ply the waters between villages and barges out of Bethel deliver freight and fuel when the river is open. Aniak provides mail plane and charter service to several area villages and is also a transfer point for the commercial fishing industry and a staging area for firefighting crews in the summer.

The community is closely knit and has several related families. The Yup'ik language is still commonly spoken among the elders. Subsistence lifestyles are still practiced, although alongside such traditional activities cash income has brought three-wheelers, pickup trucks and VCRs to the community.

ANVIK is located on the Anvik River, just west of the Yukon River, 34 miles north of Holy Cross, 160 miles northeast of Bethel and 350 miles northwest of Anchorage. **Elevation:** 325 feet. **Transportation:** Scheduled air service or air charter; by boat. **Population:** 82.

Visitor Facilities: Accommodations at Ingalik Rentals and Chase Lodge. Meals available at Chase Lodge. Groceries and general merchandise are carried by Anvik Commerical Company and Chase Enterprises. There is a laundromat. Indian arts and crafts available locally. All major repair services and fuel are available.

One of five villages inhabited by Ingalik

Bethel is the major population center and economic heart of the Yukon-Kuskokwim Delta. (James Barker, reprinted from ALASKA GEOGRAPHIC®)

Athabascan Indians, an Episcopalian mission was established here in 1887.

Anvik has a seasonal economy, with an upswing in summer when local construction programs get under way. Most families have fish camps and rely heavily on subsistence activities such as hunting, fishing and gardening.

The remaining structures of the Christ Church Mission here are on the National Register of Historic Places. Anvik serves as a checkpoint on the Iditarod Trail Sled Dog Race in alternate years.

ATMAUTLUAK is located on the Petmigtalek River, 15 miles northwest of Bethel and 410 miles west of Anchorage. **Elevation:** 17 feet. **Transportation:** Boat, snowmachine, scheduled and charter air service from Bethel. **Population:** 261.

Visitor Facilities: Limited. Sleeping accommodations at the school and some supplies available at Atmautluak Limited Corp., Egoak's Trading Post and Moses M. Pavilla Trading. The sale and importation of alcoholic beverages is prohibited. Carved ivory and beadwork are done locally. Arrangements can be made to rent boats. Fuel (marine gas, diesel and regular) and moorage are available.

Atmautluak was incorporated in 1976. The community has two churches and a school. Atmautluak is located within the Yukon Delta National Wildlife Refuge.

BETHEL, located 90 miles from the mouth of the Kuskokwim River, 400 miles west of Anchorage. **Elevation:** 10 feet. **Transportation:**

Scheduled airline from Anchorage. **Population:** 3,681.

Visitor Facilities: Accommodations at Kuskokwim Inn, Bethel Inn, Wilson's Bed & Breakfast, TWC Hostel, and Bethel Native Corp. apartments. There are several restaurants, a laundry, banks, four grocery stores, three department stores and several specialty shops. Arts and crafts available for purchase include carved ivory, grass baskets, masks, beadwork, mukluks, kuspuks, Eskimo yo-yos, and fur coats, clothing and slippers. Fishing and hunting licenses available. Major engine repair and all types of fuel are available. Rental cars and charter aircraft; arrangements can be made to rent boats. Moorage at small-boat harbor.

The first trading post was established in the early 1870s. When the Moravian Church established a mission here in 1885, they christened the site Bethel after the scripture which commands "Arise, go up to Bethel, and dwell there."

Bethel is the largest town in western Alaska. As headquarters for various state and federal agencies, it serves as the administrative hub for the area's villages. It is also the transportation center for 57 villages in the Yukon-Kuskokwim Delta. Bethel's location at the head of Kuskokwim Bay provides access to the Bering Sea and it has the only medium-draft port in western Alaska. Bethel's flight service station is reported to be the third busiest in the state.

Commercial fishing provides a major portion of Bethel's economy and employment. While there still are many people living mainly by subsistence hunting and fishing in the surrounding villages, most of Bethel's residents work year-round in the growing private industries, Native corporations and government jobs.

The tourist industry in this area is practically nonexistent, according to the chamber of commerce. Although located within the huge (20 million acre) Yukon Delta National Wildlife Refuge, there are no formal guide services or commercial ventures to take advantage of the birdwatching or related activities.

All travel in the area is done by boat in summer, snow machine and three-wheelers in winter, and bush plane year-round.

The Kisaralik and Kwethluk Rivers, two to four hours from Bethel by boat, offer good fishing for grayling, Dolly Varden and rainbow trout, as well as silver and chum salmon. The Kisaralik also is used regularly in the summer for guided float trips sponsored by the city of Bethel.

CHEFORNAK is located at the junction of the Keguk and Kinia rivers, 100 miles southwest of Bethel, 480 miles southwest of Anchorage. **Transportation:** Scheduled air service from Bethel. **Population:** 268.

Visitor Facilities: Arrangements may be made for lodging at the high school or through Avugiak's Store. Supplies available at Yupiak Store and Avugiak's. The sale and importation of alcoholic beverages is prohibited. Fishing and hunting licenses may be purchased locally.

This Eskimo village, located within the Yukon Delta National Wildlife Refuge, was incorporated as a second-class city in 1974. Many village residents are likely to be gone to fish camps during the summer. The community is served by a church and two schools.

CHEVAK is on the north bank of the Ninglikfak River, 17 miles east of Hooper Bay, 120 miles northwest of Bethel and 500 miles west of Anchorage. **Transportation:** Boats; snow machines; scheduled or charter air service from Bethel. **Population:** 532.

Visitor Facilities: Lodging is sometimes available at the school. There is a laundry and supplies are available at Chevak Company Store, Frank Chayalkun's Store, Stone Brothers, Tomaganuk Brothers or Wayne Hill Co. Fishing and hunting licenses may be purchased locally. Marine engine repair and marine gas and regular gasoline are available.

Two former teachers describe life in Chevak: "The Eskimos lead a subsistence way of life, gathering salmonberries, cranberries, blueberries and strawberries during summer and fall. The summer can be rainy and the fall usually rainy and sunny. The winters are very cold because the wind blows constantly.

Small delta village of Chefornak. (Jerry L. Hout, reprinted from ALASKA GEOGRAPHIC®)

"The Bering Sea is 20 miles by boat or snow machine from Chevak. There the Eskimos harpoon and shoot seals, walrus and beluga whales for food. They use all portions of these animals. The birds are in abundance because the Yukon National Wildlife Refuge supports ducks and geese of all kinds during the spring and summer and fall. Cranes and swans can be seen flying over the village and on the tundra. Ptarmigans stay year-round and change color with the seasons. All birds are hunted by the Eskimos for food. Fish are plentiful in the river nearby. Whitefish, blackfish, needlefish, salmon (coho and a few kings) and devilfish are fished for by the residents."

As for visitors, as one resident puts it, "there is no tourist in the village."

CHUATHBALUK is on the north bank of the Kuskokwim River, 10 miles east of Aniak, 100 miles east of Bethel and 310 miles west of Anchorage. **Transportation:** Charter plane from Aniak. **Population:** 98.

Visitor Facilities: Lodging at the school or community center. There is a laundromat and groceries and general merchandise are available at the Little Russian Trading Post and Kelila Trading Post. Marine gas and moorage available.

The community existed as a Native settlement

The Russian Mountains rise behind the village of Chuathbaluk. (Rob Reinhardt)

as early as 1833. It has been known by several names, most recently as Little Russian Mission, but was renamed Chuathbaluk, the Yup'ik Eskimo word for "big blueberries."

The village had a small population for many years, until permission to live on the property was given by the Russian Orthodox Church. It became a second-class city in 1975. The economy depends heavily on subsistence activities, supplemented by some construction work and cottage industries such as skin sewing and basketry. The Russian Orthodox Church here was established in 1891 and is listed on the National Register of Historic Places.

CROOKED CREEK is located on the north bank of the Kuskokwim River, 50 miles northeast of Aniak, 145 miles northeast of Bethel and 280 miles west of Anchorage. **Elevation:** 130 feet.

Transportation: Scheduled air service from Bethel. **Population:** 75.

Visitor Facilities: Accommodations for 12 people at Thomas Roadhouse. Supplies available at Thomas General Store.

Crooked Creek became a supply point for the Flat and Iditarod mining camps in 1909. A post office was established in 1927.

There are few year-round employment opportunities at Crooked Creek. Government programs, the regional school district and a few support services provide the only permanent jobs. Public assistance payments and subsistence activities supplement this income.

Crooked Creek residents hunt beaver, muskrat, game birds, hare, moose, caribou and waterfowl. Income also is obtained from trapping and the sale of marten, wolverine, lynx, fox and mink. In

summer, the Kuskokwim River and Crooked Creek yield king, silver, red and chum salmon, as well as whitefish, pike, grayling, Dolly Varden, sheefish and eel.

EEK is located on the Eek River near the mouth of the Kuskokwim River on Kuskokwim Bay, 45 miles south of Bethel, 420 miles west of Anchorage. **Transportation:** Boat, snow machine, scheduled and charter air service from Bethel. **Population:** 259.

Visitor Facilities: Arrangements can be made to stay at the school by contacting the principal. There is a laundromat with bathing facilities. The sale and importation of alcoholic beverages is prohibited. Groceries and other supplies are available at Iqfijouaq Co. Store, McIntyre's Store, Carter's Store and William Pete's Trading Post. Fishing and hunting licenses are sold locally but it's best to purchase before arriving in Eek. Arrangements may be made for guide services with local hunters and fishermen. Fuel available includes marine gas, diesel, propane and regular gasoline.

Most of the Eek residents are commercial fishermen, but there also is subsistence hunting and fishing.

Eek is located within the Yukon Delta National Wildlife Refuge. Travel up the Eek River by boat is a treat, offering a real wilderness experience, according to one resident. There are birds, beavers and an occasional bear to be seen. Fish caught locally include salmon, pike, grayling, trout and smelt. Hunting is for moose, caribou, ptarmigan, rabbit and seal.

The village corporation, Iqfijouaq Co., has established no user fees or other restrictions on its lands. However, check with the corporation regarding location of private lands before traveling around Eek.

EMMONAK is located at the mouth of the Yukon River, 175 miles northwest of Bethel and 490 miles northwest of Anchorage. **Elevation:** 10 feet. **Transportation:** Scheduled and charter air service from Bethel or Nome. **Population:** 559.

Visitor Facilities: Food and lodging at Emmonak Hotel, operated by the city of Emmonak. Laundry

Cross, 85 miles southwest of McGrath and 300 miles west of Anchorage. **Elevation:** 309 feet. **Transportation:** Charter plane from Anchorage or Fairbanks. **Population:** 8 in winter, 25 in summer.

Visitor Facilities: None.

An area of mostly private mining claims, where "trespassing is carefully watched by owners," according to one resident.

GEORGETOWN is on the north bank of the upper Kuskokwim River, 16 miles northwest of Red Devil and 22 miles northwest of Sleetmute. **Transportation:** Charter air service from Bethel or Red Devil; riverboat; snow machine. **Population:** 3.

Visitor Facilities: None.

Gold was found along the George River near Georgetown in 1909. The early mining settlement and the river were named for the first three traders at the site: George Hoffman, George Fredericks and George Morgan.

The present community, across the river from the old townsite, consists of five homes and an airplane hangar. Georgetown residents travel to other communities for seasonal employment and depend on subsistence hunting and fishing. In the fall the tundra yields blueberries, blackberries and currants. Some income is obtained from trapping and selling beaver, marten, lynx, fox and mink pelts.

GOODNEWS BAY is located on Goodnews Bay on the east shore of Kuskokwim Bay, 70 miles south of Bethel and 430 miles west of Anchorage. **Transportation:** Scheduled and charter air service from Bethel or Dillingham. **Population:** 230.

Visitor Facilities: Accommodations available through Kuitsarak Inc. or the school. Kuitsarak Store, Nicolai's Varieties Store, Bayside Store and Henry Walter's General Merchandise carry groceries and other supplies. The sale and importation of alcoholic beverages is prohibited. Arts and

facilities available. Alaska Commercial Co., Kwiguk Trading Co., Emmonak Native Store and Yukon Delta Fish Marketing Co-Op carry groceries and supplies. The sale and importation of alcoholic beverages is prohibited. Arts and crafts available for purchase include carved ivory, grass baskets, fans, fur hats and spears. Fishing and hunting licenses available. Marine engine repair available. Charter aircraft and fuel available.

Commercial and subsistence fishing are the main source of income and food. Fish include king salmon, chum, coho, and sheefish. Animals caught are rabbits, foxes, otters, beavers, whales and seals. A resident describes the year in Emmonak: "During the summer most families leave the village to fish camps in the area. There they smoke fish and do their commercial fishing. When fall comes the families go berry picking for winter use. During the winter, potlatches are hosted for other nearby villages. The city basketball league along with the local high school have plenty of activities, mainly basketball which the population here is most interested in during the winter."

FLAT is located on Otter Creek, eight miles southeast of Iditarod, 59 miles northeast of Holy

Gold dredge located at isolated mining settlement of Flat. (Rob Reinhardt)

crafts available for purchase include grass baskets, carved ivory, beadwork, hand-sewn skin garments, and knitted goods. Fishing and hunting licenses and fishing guide service are available. Fuel (marine gas, diesel, propane) and moorage available.

This Eskimo community was originally known as Mumtrak. The village's present name comes from the bay on which it is located. The community grew because of nearby gold mining activities in the 1900s, according to one resident. A post office was established in 1930. Goodnews Bay was incorporated in 1970. It has a church and two schools.

GRAYLING, on the west bank of the Yukon River, is 21 miles north of Anvik and 350 miles northwest of Anchorage. **Elevation:** 90 feet. **Transportation:** Scheduled and charter air service from McGrath or Bethel. **Population:** 220.

Visitor Facilities: Arrangements can be made for accommodations in private homes. Groceries and other supplies available at Grayling Native Store or D&E Store. The sale and importation of alcoholic beverages is prohibited. Arts and crafts include birch-bark baskets, grass baskets, skin

Hooper Bay, population 525, is one of the larger communities along the Bering Sea coast. (Staff, reprinted from ALASKA GEOGRAPHIC®)

Community of Holy Cross. (Myron Wright, reprinted from ALASKA GEOGRAPHIC®)

boots, fur hats, and beadwork. Fishing and hunting licenses available. Aircraft mechanic and charter aircraft available. Fuel (diesel, propane, regular) and moorage available.

When the U.S. Revenue Service steamer *Nunivak* stopped here in 1900, Lt. J.C. Cantwell reported an Indian village of approximately 75 residents. They had a large stockpile of wood to supply fuel for steamers. When gold mining activities in the area diminished, the village was abandoned until 1962, when residents of Holikachuk on the Innoko River moved to the site because of flooding. Grayling was incorporated in 1969.

Grayling's economy is heavily dependent on subsistence activities and employment is primarily seasonal summer work in construction, road work and commercial fishing. Most families fish for salmon, whitefish, sheefish, pike and eels, and hunt for moose, black bear, small game and waterfowl. Residents also trap marten, mink, otter, beaver, wolf, lynx and wolverine and sell the pelts.

Grayling is located across the river from the Innoko National Wildlife Refuge. The community is a checkpoint on the Iditarod Trail race.

HOLY CROSS, just off the Yukon River, 34 miles southeast of Anvik and 420 miles southwest of Fairbanks. **Elevation:** 61 feet. **Transportation:** Boat; scheduled or charter air service from Bethel. **Population:** 191.

Visitor Facilities: Food and lodging at Holy Cross Lodge. Groceries and limited supplies at Holy Cross Mercantile or Linda Frank's store. The sale and importation of alcoholic beverages is prohibited. Fishing and hunting licenses available. Propane and regular gasoline available.

The community grew with the establishment of a Jesuit mission and school in 1886. Holy Cross was incorporated as a second-class city in 1968. The economy is seasonal, peaking in summer with the fishing season. People work at the school, city office, at the local corporaton office, subsistence hunt (moose) and fish (salmon, grayling, whitefish), and trap beaver and other furbearers. Summers are warm here, with temperatures to the 70s and 80s; winter temperatures range from -50°F to 50°F, with two to four feet of snow.

HOOPER BAY is 20 miles south of Cape

Blanket of snow covers village of Kipnuk. (Division of Tourism)

Romanzof and 120 miles northwest of Bethel. **Elevation:** 18 feet. **Transportation:** Scheduled and charter air service from Bethel. **Population:** 525.

Visitor Facilities: Little Flower Church serves as a guest house. Restaurant, shower and laundromat located in the Sea Lion building. Supplies available at Hooper Bay Native Store, Naneng's General Store, Tomagnuk Store and Hill's and Joe's Store. The sale and importation of alcoholic beverages is prohibited. Air charter service available. Fishing and hunting licenses sold at Hooper Bay Native Store.

The Eskimo name for Hooper Bay is "Askinuk" which refers to the mountainous area between Hooper Bay and Scammon Bay. The site was first reported in December 1878 by E.W. Nelson of the U.S. Signal Service. The present-day Eskimo name for the village is Naparagamiut meaning "stake village people." A post office was established here in 1934.

The village was incorporated in February 1966 as a second-class city. The economy is based on subsistence hunting, fishing and Native crafts, such as ivory carving and grass basket weaving.

KASIGLUK is located two miles west of Nuna-pitchuk, 20 miles northwest of Bethel and 425 miles west of Anchorage. **Elevation:** 40 feet. **Transportation:** Boat, snow machine, scheduled and charter air service from Bethel. **Population:** 355.

Visitor Facilities: Arrangements can be made for accommodations at the school. Laundry facilities available. Limited groceries at Kasigluk Cooperative Inc. The sale and importation of alcoholic beverages is prohibited. Arts and crafts include Eskimo dolls, mukluks, beaver hats and fur mittens. Fishing and hunting licenses available. Marine gas and propane are available.

"Kasigluk is an Eskimo village. It is one of the few villages that is a tundra village, others are mostly located on the ocean or a larger river," says one resident. As far as tourist attractions, there are none. "Eskimo people, tundra, birds and no reason for anyone to visit. But it is a great place to live. If you live here you travel 40 miles to the Kuskokwim to fish by net. You travel north to the Yukon by snow machine for moose. You go out on the tundra to pick berries, hunt eggs. But no one would want to spend money to come here to pick berries from plants that have one berry per plant."

Kasigluk is located within the 19.6 million acre Yukon Delta National Wildlife Refuge, a seemingly limitless expanse of wetlands that is one of the most significant waterfowl breeding areas in North America.

KIPNUK is on the bank of the Kugulik River near the Bering Sea coast, 68 miles across Kuskokwim Bay from Quinhagak, 95 miles southwest of Bethel and 500 miles west of Anchorage. **Transportation:** Scheduled air service from Bethel. **Population:** 350.

Visitor Facilities: None. Supplies available at Kipnuk Trading Post, Kashatok Brothers or Kimka Co. The sale and importation of alcoholic beverages is prohibited.

Kipnuk is located within the Yukon Delta National Wildlife Refuge. Many village residents are likely to be gone to fish camps during the summer. The community is served by a Moravian church and two schools.

KONGIGANAK is on the west shore of Kuskokwim Bay, 70 miles west of Bethel and 460 miles west of Anchorage. **Elevation:** 25 feet. **Transportation:** Scheduled air service from Bethel. **Population:** 166.

Above — A clear winter day at Kongiganak. (Division of Tourism)

Below — A clerk marks prices on items in the Alaska Commercial Co. store at Kotlik. (Staff, reprinted from ALASKA GEOGRAPHIC®)

Visitor Facilities: Lodging available at the school. There is a washeteria with bathing facilities. Supplies available at Kongiganak Trading Post and Qemirtalik Corp. Store. Arts and crafts available at Evon Asean Crafts. The sale and importation of alcoholic beverages is prohibited.

This unincorporated Eskimo village, located within the Yukon Delta National Wildlife Refuge, has a school. Many residents work seasonally in the summer commercial fishery or go to their own fish camps.

KOTLIK is on the east bank of the Kotlik Slough in the Yukon-Kuskokwim Delta, 35 miles northeast of Emmonak. **Transportation:** Scheduled and charter air service from Nome or Bethel; by boat or snow machine. **Population:** 413.

Visitor Facilities: None. Supplies available at Alaska Commercial Co., Kotlik Yup'ik Corp. general store and Bill Moore Slough Store. The sale and importation of alcoholic beverages is prohibited. Arts and crafts include grass baskets and carved ivory. Fishing and hunting licenses available from the city office. Propane and regular gasoline available.

Early in the 1960s, people from surrounding villages moved to Kotlik because a school had been built and the new site was more accessible to barges serving the delta. By 1965, Kotlik had emerged as one of the larger ports and commercial centers on the lower Yukon River, a status that it retains today.

Kotlik has a seasonal economy with its peak in the June through August fishing season. Most fishermen leave for their fish camps up the Yukon River, where they set their nets for king, silver and chum salmon. People also hunt for seals, ducks and geese for subsistence.

KWETHLUK is on the bank of the Kwethluk River near its junction with the Kuskokwim River, 10 miles east of Bethel and 385 miles west of Anchorage. **Elevation:** 28 feet. **Transportation:** Boat; snow machine or dog team; scheduled or charter air service from Bethel. **Population:** 509.

Visitor Facilities: Arrangements can be made through the city office to stay in private homes or the high school. Kwethluk Native Store and

Kwethluk lies in a bend of the Kwethluk River. (Division of Tourism)

Kwethluk Sports Store carry groceries and other supplies. The sale and importation of alcoholic beverages is prohibited. Arts and crafts include carved ivory, Eskimo dolls, ulus, baskets and fur garments. Fishing and hunting licenses available. Marine engine and boat repair available. Fuel (marine gas, diesel, regular gasoline) and moorage available.

Historically, Kwethluk stands out as the village where a Moravian church worker was killed in 1890. The men of Kwethluk, believing the lay missionary to be insane, killed him and left his body to be eaten by dogs.

"Kwethluk has been here in the past, present and hopefully in the future," as one resident puts it. "Kwethluk is termed 'bad river' in English. Most of the residents hunt and fish to survive, others work, some rely on government."

KWIGILLINGOK is located on the west side of Kuskokwim Bay across from Quinhagak, 85 miles southwest of Bethel. **Elevation:** 20 feet. **Transportation:** Scheduled air service from Bethel. **Population:** 246.

Visitor Facilities: Arrangements may be made

to stay in private homes through the IRA Council. Supplies available at Co-op Store. The sale and importation of alcoholic beverages is prohibited.

This Eskimo village, located within the Yukon Delta National Wildlife Refuge, is unincorporated. Many residents work seasonally in the summer commercial fishery or go to their own fish camps.

LIME VILLAGE is located on the south bank of Stony River, 90 miles south of McGrath, 85 miles northwest of Lake Clark and 190 miles west of Anchorage. **Elevation:** 552 feet. **Transportation:** Scheduled or charter air service from McGrath or Aniak. **Population:** 33.

Visitor Facilities: None.

Lime Village is named for the nearby Lime Hills, composed almost entirely of limestone. Year-round residents were first recorded in 1907. Other families from Lake Clark camped here in the summer to fish. A Russian Orthodox chapel, Saints Constantine and Helen, was constructed in 1923 and is on the National Register of Historic Places. A state school was established in 1974.

Income in Lime Village is primarily from government programs. This income is supplemented by public assistance and subsistence activities.

LOWER KALSKAG is located on the north bank of the Kuskokwim River, two miles southwest of Upper Kalskag, 65 miles north of Bethel and 350 miles west of Anchorage. **Elevation:** 49 feet. **Transportation:** Scheduled air service from Bethel. **Population:** 270.

Visitor Facilities: Arrangements may be made to stay at the school. The general store carries some supplies and fishing and hunting licenses may be purchased locally. Marine gas and diesel available.

The site of this Eskimo village originally was used as a fish camp for families from Upper Kalskag. Residents from the upper village, a Roman Catholic center, moved to Lower Kalskag after the Russian Orthodox chapel of St. Seraphim (now on the National Register of Historic Places) was built in 1940. Lower Kalskag is located within the Yukon Delta National Wildlife Refuge.

The economy is based primarily on subsistence activities; employment is largely limited to public programs. Hunting is for moose, black bear, rabbit,

game birds, porcupine and waterfowl. Fishing is for salmon, pike, whitefish, blackfish and eel.

MARSHALL, also known as Fortuna Ledge, is on the east bank of Poltes Slough, 75 miles north of Bethel and 400 miles northwest of Anchorage. **Transportation:** Boat; scheduled or charter air service from Bethel. **Population:** 281.

Visitor Facilities: Accommodations through Hunter Sales and Rooming. Hunter Sales, Fortuna Ledge Co-op, Marshall Enterprises and Maserculiq Inc. carry groceries and other supplies. The sale and importation of alcoholic beverages is prohibited. Hunting and fishing licenses available. Marine engine repair available. Arrangements may be made to rent boats or off-road vehicles. Marine gas, diesel, propane and regular gasoline available.

From *The History of Marshall Alaska* by the Marshall High School Journalism Class of 1984: "Marshall is named after Tom Marshall, who was vice-president of the United States during World War I. Marshall is also called Fortuna Ledge after Don Hunter's sister, Fortuna. She was the first child born in Marshall.

"Ledge refers to the rock ledge in front of the Catholic Church. The Eskimo name for Marshall is either Maserculiq, which means 'the place where salmon spawn,' or Uglouaia, which means 'little bow.' Most people today use Maserculiq."

Marshall also is known as Fortuna Ledge. (Myron Wright, reprinted from ALASKA GEOGRAPHIC®)

143

Marshall residents work primarily during the summer salmon season, either in fishing or processing. There's also firefighting in summer. A few year-round jobs are available in local government, the school, village corporation and businesses. Income is supplemented by public assistance and subsistence activities.

"In the early days of Marshall, there weren't many jobs," according to the students' history. "The men made money by cutting wood to sell to the steamboats for fuel. A cord of wood sold for $6 and it took two men two days to cut one cord.

"The people also worked in the stores, restaurants, and hotels. Exenia Fitka recalls cleaning the hotel for a dollar a day. Others would pack water with two five-gallon buckets and a yoke. They made two bits a trip.

"Some people bought food by selling and trading furs. The fur trapping was never closed, not even in the summer. Before Marshall became a town, people took their furs to St. Michaels to sell.

"There were also mink farms in Marshall and reindeer herding.

"Still, mining was the main source of income among the people. Mostly Kassags (Caucasians) worked in the mines."

MEKORYUK is located on Nunivak Island in the Bering Sea, 210 miles west of Bethel and 600 miles west of Anchorage. **Elevation:** 40 feet. **Transportation:** Scheduled and charter air service from Bethel. **Population:** 182.

Visitor Facilities: Accommodations in private homes or at the high school. Groceries and other supplies available at Nima Corp. Store, Whitman's Store and Peter Smith and Sons. The sale and importation of alcoholic beverages is prohibited. Fishing and hunting licenses available. Guide services, including lodging and meals, available locally. Private boats may be chartered. Marine gas, propane, unleaded and regular gasoline are available.

This Eskimo village is the only community on Nunivak Island, which is part of the Yukon Delta National Wildlife Refuge. The people here live mostly off the land and sea, although there are a few jobs created by the federal government. Many

Shirley Weston of Mekoryuk, the only village on Nunivak Island, holds a pair of Dolly Varden. (Glen Syzmoniak)

of the residents go to fish camps around the island during the summer. Villagers also hunt birds, walrus, seal, and red and arctic fox. The island has many rivers offering excellent fishing for salmon, trout, char and grayling. Halibut and cod are caught in the Bering Sea.

Approximately 3,000 head of reindeer roam the island, along with 600 head of musk ox, which were introduced in the 1930s. Reindeer roundups usually take place in July. People come here from all over the world to hunt musk ox during annual permit hunts.

Some of the finest ivory carving in the world is done here and villagers also make unique wooden masks and knit *qiviut* wool from musk ox into lacy garments which are sold in Anchorage.

Attractions for visitors include wilderness trips

to see and photograph musk ox, reindeer, seal, walrus and birds. Advance arrangements should be made for lodging and meals.

MOUNTAIN VILLAGE is on the north bank of the Yukon River, 20 miles west of St. Marys and 470 miles northwest of Anchorage. **Elevation:** 40 feet. **Transportation:** Scheduled or charter air service from Nome or Bethel; an 18-mile road links Mountain Village with Pitka's Point, St. Marys and Andreafsky. **Population:** 610.

Visitor Facilities: Accommodations may be arranged by contacting the city of Mountain Village. There is a restaurant and supplies may be purchased at Mountain Village Store. The sale and importation of alcoholic beverages is prohibited. Arts and crafts include grass baskets and Eskimo clothing. Fishing and hunting licenses available. Marine engine repair, rental cars, charter aircraft and fuel (marine gas, propane, regular gasoline) are available. Moorage at village marina.

Mountain Village is so named because of its location at the foot of the first mountain encountered by people traveling up the Yukon River. Originally a summer fish camp, a general store opened in 1908, prompting residents of two small upriver settlements to move here. A post office was established in 1923, a salmon saltery in 1956 and a cannery in 1964.

Mountain Village is below the first mountain seen on the way up the Yukon River. (Myron Wright, reprinted from ALASKA GEOGRAPHIC®)

Mountain Village's economy is expanding due to its relative accessibility, growing fishing industry and its function as a regional education center. The school district, the village corporation, government and local business provide year-round employment for about 70 people. This income is supplemented by public assistance and by subsistence hunting and fishing for moose, swan, geese, ducks, salmon, blackfish, sheefish, whitefish, burbot, grayling and pike.

Mountain Village is located within the Yukon Delta National Wildlife Refuge.

NAPAKIAK is located at the head of Kuskokwim Bay, 10 miles southwest of Bethel, 410 miles west of Anchorage. **Elevation:** 20 feet. **Transportation:** Scheduled air service from Bethel. **Population:** 319.

Visitor Facilities: Arrangements may be made for accommodations at the school. There is a washeteria and supplies are available at Jung's Trading Post. The sale and importation of alcoholic beverages is prohibited. Fishing and hunting licenses available. Boats may be rented at Napakiak Marina.

This Eskimo community was established around 1890 by people from a village at the mouth of the Johnson River that also was known as Napakiak. A Moravian Church chapel was dedicated in 1930; a BIA school opened in 1939; a post office was established in 1951; and the airport was completed in 1973. Napakiak is located within Yukon Delta National Wildlife Refuge. Many residents spend the summer at fish camps.

NAPASKIAK is located on the south bank of the Kuskokwim River, eight miles southeast of Bethel and 400 miles west of Anchorage. **Elevation:** 24 feet. **Transportation:** Scheduled air service from Bethel. **Population:** 289.

Visitor Facilities: Accommodations at city building. Supplies available at Napaskiak Corp. Store. The sale and importation of alcoholic beverages is prohibited.

The first Russian Orthodox priest arrived here in 1905 and baptized the entire village. St. Jacob's Chapel, listed on the National Register of Historic Places, was built in 1931.

A Bureau of Indian Affairs school opened in 1939 and an airport was completed in 1974. Napaskiak, which is located within the Yukon Delta National Wildlife Refuge, was incorporated as a second-class city in 1971. Many residents leave town during the summer season to go to fish camps.

NEWTOK is on the Kealavik River, 90 miles northwest of Bethel and 500 miles west of Anchorage. **Elevation:** 25 feet. **Transportation:** Scheduled air service from Bethel. **Population:** 187.

Visitor Facilities: None. Supplies available at Newtok Corp. Store or Nick Tom Sr. Grocery Store. The sale and importation of alcoholic beverages is prohibited.

Newtok, located within the Yukon Delta National Wildlife Refuge, is a relatively new village established around 1949. It was incorporated as a second-class city in 1976. Many residents spend the summer at fish camp.

NIGHTMUTE is on the Toksook River on Nelson Island in the Bering Sea, 105 miles west of Bethel. **Transportation:** Scheduled and charter air service from Bethel. **Population:** 134.

Visitor Facilities: Arrangements may be made through the city office for accommodations in private homes. Lodging also may be available at the school. Meals are available at the high school in winter. Groceries and other goods available at Nightmute Co-op, Post Trading, Tulik's Store or Tony's Store. Fuel (marine gas, diesel, regular gasoline) and moorage available.

Nightmute got started, according to one resident, when "someone came over to this place and stayed. Other people started to move in." A BIA school was established in the 1950s.

Nightmute doesn't get many visitors. As one person put it, "I never seen any tourists here. They probably don't know this country."

"People fish, hunt, set traps and work for living. We fish in our river and at Toksook Bay and ocean. People around here catch herring, king and red salmon, halibut, devilfish, humpies and pike. We hunt different kinds of animal, like geese and ducks, foxes and rabbits, cranes and swans, ptarmigan, beaver, muskrat, otter and mink."

Nunapitchuk on the Johnson River. (Elfrida Nord, reprinted from ALASKA GEOGRAPHIC®)

NUNAPITCHUK is in southwestern Alaska on the Johnson River, 22 miles northwest of Bethel and 425 miles west of Anchorage. **Transportation:** Boats, snow machine, scheduled air service from Bethel. **Population:** 296.

Visitor Facilities: Three rooms with kitchen area available at IRA Council building; contact the city office. Washeteria available. Groceries and other goods at Robert Nick's Store, Chaliak and Sons, Nunapitchuk Ltd. and Mojin's Store. The sale and importation of alcoholic beverages is prohibited. Hunting and fishing licenses, marine engine repair, propane and regular gasoline are available. Private off-road vehicles and boats may be rented.

In the 1930s there were only a half-dozen families in the settlement. More people moved in after the federal government built a school in the 1940s. Nunapitchuk has an IRA (Indian Reorganization Act) Council that was established in the 1940s.

"Most of the hunting and fishing that people do around here is for subsistence use, although some people have started fishing for northern pike with rod and reel the past couple of years," according to a resident.

OSCARVILLE is on the north shore of the Kuskokwim River across from Napaskiak, five miles south of Bethel and 400 miles west of Anchorage. **Transportation:** Boat, snow machine and floatplane service from Bethel. **Population:** 39.

In about 1906, a Norwegian named Oscar Samuelson and his Eskimo wife moved to Napaskiak and opened a small store. In 1908 the Samuelsons moved across the river to what became known as Oscarville. Samuelson opened another small store that he ran until his death in 1953. His daughter and subsequent owners have operated the store. The first school opened in 1964.

PILOT STATION is on the northwest bank of the Yukon River, 11 miles east of St. Marys and 26 miles west of Marshall. **Elevation:** 275 feet. **Transportation:** Scheduled and charter air service from Bethel. **Population:** 372.

Visitor Facilities: Accommodations at Pilot Station Hotel. Groceries and other supplies available at Pilot Station Native Store or Heckman Trading Post. The sale and importation of alcoholic beverages is prohibited. Fishing and hunting licenses may be purchased locally. Rental transportation includes boats and charter aircraft. Propane and regular gasoline available.

Pilot Station's beginnings, and its lifestyle today, are like those of so many other villages in the delta. As one residents sums it up: "A few people or family found it easy to get food and wood by the

Pilot Station grew on the bank of the Yukon River. (Myron Wright, reprinted from ALASKA GEOGRAPHIC®)

Yukon, so everyone's relatives stayed. People work for a living, in schools, post office, store or clinic. Some fish and hunt."

Near Pilot Station is the old village site of Kurgpallermuit, designated by the Calista Regional Corporation as a historic place because it was occupied during the wars between the Yukon and Coastal Eskimos.

Pilot Station is located within the Yukon Delta National Wildlife Refuge.

PITKAS POINT, near the junction of the Yukon and Andreafsky Rivers, is five miles northwest of St. Marys, 40 miles northwest of Marshall and 445 miles west of Anchorage. **Transportation:** Scheduled airline from Bethel to St. Marys airport; connected by an 18-mile road to St. Marys and Mountain Village; snow machine in winter. **Population:** 67.

Visitor Facilities: None. All services in St. Marys. There is a laundromat with showers in Pitkas Point.

An old Eskimo village, Pitkas Point was named for a trader who opened a general store here.

Pitkas Point is primarily a Russian Orthodox village with the principal economy being subsistence and commercial fishing and trapping.

The Andreafsky River above Pitkas provides excellent recreation for residents to enjoy camping, picnicking and fishing.

PLATINUM is located on Goodnews Bay, 11 miles southwest of Goodnews Bay village and 135 miles south of Bethel. **Elevation:** 20 feet. **Transportation:** Scheduled air service from Bethel. **Population:** 64.

Visitor Facilities: Arrangements may be made for accommodations at the school. Supplies available at Platinum Commercial Co. or Arviq Inc. store. The sale and importation of alcoholic beverages is prohibited. Fishing and hunting licenses available. Diesel, propane and regular gasoline available.

Platinum got its name from an important lode of platinum that was discovered nearby in 1926 by an Eskimo named Walter Smith. "People from a nearby village moved their families here and here they stayed," recalls one local resident.

"About 10 miles from the village of Platinum there is a mine which has been there at least 40 years. We're surrounded by mountains except on the ocean side. We have a nice long beach on which we can find most anything. For fishing we use either rod and reel or a net. We usually go up the Goodnews River or out on Goodnews Bay."

Platinum is located within the Togiak National Wildlife Refuge.

QUINHAGAK is located at the mouth of the Kanektok River on the southeast shore of Kuskokwim Bay, 46 miles northwest of Goodnews Bay, 70 miles south of Bethel and 425 miles west

mean "new formed river," which refers to the constantly changing channel of the stream on which the village is located. A post office was established here in 1905 and in 1975 Quinhagak was incorporated as a second-class city. It is located within Togiak National Wildlife Refuge.

RED DEVIL is located on the upper Kuskokwim River at the mouth of Red Devil Creek, six miles northwest of Sleetmute, 73 miles east of Aniak and 250 miles west of Anchorage. **Transportation:** Boat; scheduled and charter air service from Bethel or Aniak. **Population:** 27.

Visitor Facilities: Accommodations and meals available at Vanderpool's roadhouse. Groceries available at combination roadhouse/bar/store. Fishing/hunting licenses available. Rental transportation includes boats and charter aircraft. Marine gas, diesel and regular gasoline available.

The village was named after the Red Devil cinnabar mine, which was established in 1933 and operated under different owners until 1971, when it produced the state's total output of mercury.

Employment opportunities in Red Devil today are limited. A few residents work for the school district, post office, clinic, store and flying service. There's also firefighting in summer. This income is supplemented by public assistance and subsistence activities.

The fishing is described as "fantastic" for salmon, northern pike, trout, grayling and sheefish. There are also "lots of beautiful rivers and streams for boating."

RUSSIAN MISSION is on the west bank of the Yukon River, 25 miles southeast of Marshall, 70 miles from Bethel and 225 miles northwest of Anchorage. **Elevation:** 50 feet. **Transportation:** Scheduled and charter air service from Bethel. **Population:** 195.

Visitor Facilities: Arrangements can be made for accommodations in private homes. Lodging also may be available at the school. Groceries and other supplies available at P&K Trading Post and

Bush plane taxis on the runway at Red Devil. (Rob Reinhardt)

ANICA Inc. Arts and crafts include birch-bark baskets and masks. Fishing and hunting licenses available. Marine engine, boat repair and fuel (diesel, propane, regular gasoline) are available.

The first Russian Orthodox mission in the interior of Alaska was established here in 1851 by a Russian-Aleut priest. The village was incorporated as a second-class city in 1970.

Most residents are directly or indirectly involved in commercial fishing from June through September. There are a few full-time jobs at the two local stores, the post office and the clinic, and sporadic employment in public projects ("people work when work is available"). This income is supplemented by public assistance and subsistence activities. There's area fishing for salmon, trout, pike and lush. Game includes moose, bear, beaver, fox, marten, mink, muskrat and weasel.

of Anchorage. **Transportation:** Boat; scheduled and charter air service from Bethel. **Population:** 424.

Visitor Facilities: None. Laundry and shower facilities available. Supplies available at A&C Market, or Qanirtuuq Inc. Store. Arts and crafts include carved ivory, grass baskets and Eskimo yo-yos. Fishing and hunting licenses and guide services available. Marine engine repair, air charters, fuel (marine gas, diesel, propane, regular gasoline) are available.

This Eskimo village was first reported by Lieutenant Sarichev in 1826. The name is believed to

ST. MARYS is located on the north bank of the Andreafsky River, four miles northeast of Pitkas Point, 37 miles northwest of Marshall and 450 miles northwest of Anchorage. **Elevation:** 30 feet. **Transportation:** Boat; scheduled and charter air service from Bethel; 18 mile road to Mountain Village. **Population:** 566.

Visitor Facilities: Accommodations and meals at St. Marys Roadhouse. Laundry facilities available. Groceries and other supplies available at Alaska Commercial Co. and Yukon Traders Inc. The sale and importation of alcoholic beverages is prohibited. Arts and crafts include carved ivory, grass baskets, beaded jewelry and hand-sewn skin garments. Fishing and hunting licenses available.

St. Marys has evolved into a subregional transportation center. (James Barker, reprinted from ALASKA GEOGRAPHIC®)

Marine engine, boat and aircraft repair; charter aircraft; and fuel (marine gas, propane, regular gasoline) are available.

Present-day St. Marys was chosen in 1948 as the new site of a Jesuit mission first established downstream in 1903. Materials from an abandoned hotel built during the gold rush were used to construct the new mission and several village homes. The mission school continues to draw students from throughout the region.

Employment in St. Marys peaks during the summer fishing season when most residents are involved in some form of commercial fishing activity. Other seasonal employment, such as construction projects and firefighting, is supplemented by public assistance and subsistence activities. Other jobs are in the school, city, airlines, state government and Native corporations.

St. Marys has become a subregional center for air transportation. Its airport is capable of handling aircraft as large as a Boeing 727.

St. Marys is surrounded by the Yukon Delta National Wildlife Refuge. Locally, bird-watchers can see long-tailed jaegers, falcons and juncos. Some people sportfish on the Andreafsky River for salmon, trout and grayling.

In the slough just opposite the St. Marys dock is a burial ground for old river steamers. Rusting boilers can be seen above the water.

SCAMMON BAY is located on the south bank of the Kun River, one mile from the Bering Sea, 145 miles northwest of Bethel and 525 miles west of Anchorage. **Elevation:** 22 feet. **Transportation:** Scheduled and charter air service from Bethel; winter trail to Hooper Bay. **Population:** 296.

Visitor Facilities: Arrangements may be made for accommodations at the school. Supplies available at Askinuk Store, Aguchak Mercantile Store, Amukon Trading Post and Joey's Store. The sale and importation of alcoholic beverages is prohibited. Arts and crafts include carved ivory, grass baskets and masks. Fishing and hunting licenses available. Arrangements may be made to rent autos. Marine engine repair and fuel (marine gas, diesel, propane, unleaded, regular gasoline) are available.

The village was named after the nearby bay, which honors Captain Charles M. Scammon, marine chief of the Western Union Telegraph Expedition in Alaska in 1856-67.

Peak economic activity in Scammon Bay occurs during the summer fishing season when most residents are involved in commercial fishing. Other employment opportunities in the summer include

Most residents of Scammon Bay work in the commercial fishery. (Jerry L. Hout, reprinted from ALASKA GEOGRAPHIC®)

firefighting and construction. There are a few year-round jobs with the city, stores, school and village corporation. This income is supplemented by public assistance and subsistence activities. Residents hunt beluga whale, walrus, seal, geese, swans, cranes, ducks, loons and ptarmigan. Fishing yields salmon, whitefish, blackfish, needlefish, herring, smelt and tomcod.

Scammon Bay is located within the Yukon Delta National Wildlife Refuge.

SHAGELUK is on the east bank of the Innoko River, 20 miles east of Anvik, 34 miles northeast of Holy Cross and 330 miles west of Anchorage. **Elevation:** 70 feet. **Transportation:** Scheduled and charter air service from Bethel, Aniak, Grayling, Anvik and McGrath; trail to Anvik and Grayling. **Population:** 148.

Visitor Facilities: Accommodations at an apartment at the school. There is a washeteria with showers. Supplies available at Shageluk Native Store or The Outpost. The sale and importation of alcoholic beverages is prohibited. Fishing and hunting licenses at The Outpost. Gasoline and propane available.

Shageluk is an old Ingalik Indian village first reported by the Imperial Russian Navy in 1850. The village was relocated to its present location in the mid-1960s because of flooding. A post office was established in 1924. Shageluk, which is located about 10 miles south of the Innoko National Wildlife Refuge, was incorporated as a second-class city in 1970.

About half of the buildings in Shageluk are built of logs, including a six-sided kashim, a structure used for traditional social gatherings.

Although many residents own snow machines, dog teams are popular in Shageluk and every other year the village is a checkpoint on the Iditarod Trail Sled Dog Race from Anchorage to Nome.

SHELDON POINT is located on a south fork of the Yukon River nine miles south of Alakanuk, 18 miles southwest of Emmonak and 500 miles northwest of Anchorage. **Transportation:** Boat; scheduled or charter airline from Alakanuk or Emmonak; snow machine. **Population:** 135.

Visitor Facilities: Arrangements may be made for accommodations and meals in private homes or at the school. Supplies available at Nunam Iqua Trading Post. Arts and crafts include Native jewelry, ivory, beadwork and Eskimo clothing. Arrangements may be made with local residents for guide services and to rent off-road vehicles and boats. Diesel and gas available.

This is a relatively new village, established in the 1940s. The community is named for a man called Sheldon, who owned and operated a fish saltery at the site. It is a second-class city, incorporated in 1974. The population is exclusively Yup'ik Eskimo and the village is considered more traditionally Native than most others in the area.

Commercial fishing is the economic foundation of Sheldon Point. Fish-buying companies from the lower Yukon, Bering Sea, Fort Yukon and the Yukon Delta Fish Marketing Co-op come here to buy fish. Residents hunt beluga whale, seal, moose, geese, duck and hare and fish for salmon, whitefish, blackfish, sheefish, lush (burbot) and smelt.

There's a large summer swan population here and spring bird migration. The village is also the

Sleetmute's airfield borders the community. (Rob Reinhardt)

takeout point for rafts, canoes and kayaks coming down the Yukon.

SLEETMUTE is located on the east bank of the Kuskokwim River, 78 miles east of Aniak and 240 miles west of Anchorage. **Elevation:** 290 feet. **Transportation:** Boat; scheduled and charter air service from Bethel or Aniak. **Population:** 74.

Visitor Facilities: None.

Sleetmute, which means "whetstone people," was named for nearby slate deposits. It was founded by Ingalik Indians, and in the early 1830s, the Russians established a trading post nearby. Frederick Bishop established a trading post at Sleetmute in 1906. A school was opened in 1921, followed by a post office in 1923. Saints Peter and Paul Russian Orthodox Chapel was built in 1931. Sleetmute is unincorporated. It is also a "dry" village: the sale and importation of alcoholic beverages is prohibited.

Most income in Sleetmute is from public employment programs, the school district and summer

firefighting jobs. Some residents work in canneries in other villages during the fishing season. Residents rely on subsistence hunting and fishing.

STONY RIVER, on Stony River Island in the Kuskokwim River near its junction with Stony River, 20 miles northeast of Sleetmute, 185 miles northeast of Bethel and 245 miles northwest of Anchorage. **Elevation:** 220 feet. **Transportation:** Boat, snow machine; scheduled and charter air service from Bethel. **Population:** 43.

Visitor Facilities: Limited. Arrangements may be made for accommodations in private homes or in the IRA Council building by contacting the Traditional Council. Staple items, cigarettes and snacks available at Stony River Traditional Council Store; most supplies are obtained from Sleetmute, Red Devil, Aniak or Anchorage. Marine gas and regular gasoline available.

This Eskimo and Indian village began as a trading post and riverboat landing used to supply mining operations to the north. The first trading

Above — Super Cub takes off from runway at Stony River, located about 185 miles northeast of Bethel on the river of the same name. (Rob Reinhardt)

Below — In March a thick cloak of winter still covers the village of Toksook Bay on Nelson Island. (Alissa Crandall, reprinted from ALASKA GEOGRAPHIC®)

post was opened in 1930, followed by a post office in 1935, and a school in 1961, all of which attracted settlement.

Most income in Stony River comes from public employment programs. This income is supplemented by public assistance payments and subsistence activities. "Usually the hunting and fishing is good," says one former resident, "but more importantly it is a very untouched wilderness, wonderful for bird-watchers, especially during spring migration, or for those who just like a quiet river float trip. The Upper Stony River has some white water but the rest is good for a canoe or small skiff."

TOKSOOK BAY is on Nelson Island, 100 miles west of Bethel and 505 miles west of Anchorage. **Transportation:** Scheduled and charter air service from Bethel. **Population:** 365.

Visitor Facilities: Arrangements for accommodations may be made at the school. Supplies available at Nunakaviak Yup'ik Corp. General Store, John's Store or Jimmie's Store. The sale and importation of alcoholic beverages is prohibited. Fishing and hunting licenses may be purchased locally.

Toksook Bay was established in 1964 when most of the population of Nightmute moved to what was considered a better village site. Toksook Bay, which is located within the Yukon Delta National Wildlife Refuge, was incorporated as a second-class city in 1972 and is served by a Catholic church and a high school. Many residents may be gone to fish camps during the summer.

TULUKSAK is on the south bank of the Kuskokwim River, 45 miles northeast of Bethel, 48 miles southeast of Russian Mission and 375 miles west of Anchorage. **Transportation:** Scheduled and charter air service from Bethel. **Population:** 272.

Visitor Facilities: Arrangements for accommodations may be made through the city office. There are a washeteria and two general stores. The sale and importation of alcoholic beverages is prohibited.

This Eskimo village has been occupied continuously since early times. Outside interest in the area was generated in 1907 when gold was found along Bear Creek on the upper Tuluksak River. The first Moravian chapel was built in 1912 and a school opened in 1930.

Tuluksak, which is located within the Yukon Delta National Wildlife Refuge, was incorporated as a second-class city in 1970. Many residents may be gone to fish camps during the summer season.

TUNTUTULIAK is located on the north bank of the Kuskokwim River, 45 miles southwest of Bethel and 440 miles west of Anchorage. **Transportation:** Scheduled and charter air service from Bethel. **Population:** 203.

Visitor Facilities: Arrangements for accommodations may be made with the school. There is a washeteria. Andrew Trading Post, Peter Miller Store, Pavila Store and D&B Sales carry supplies. The sale and importation of alcoholic beverages is prohibited. Fishing and hunting licenses may be purchased locally.

Tuntutuliak, which is unincorporated, is located within the Yukon Delta National Wildlife Refuge. The community has a church and two schools. Many residents may be gone to fish camps during the summer months.

TUNUNAK is on the northwest coast of Nelson Island, 120 miles west of Bethel and 520 miles west of Anchorage. **Transportation:** Scheduled and charter air service from Bethel. **Population:** 333.

Visitor Facilities: For sleeping accommodations in the school or clinic, contact the school or the city office. There is a washeteria. Groceries and other supplies available at Tununak Native Store, Inakak Store, Herman Oscar Store or Andy Charlie Sr. Store. The sale and importation of alcoholic beverages is prohibited. Arts and crafts include carved ivory, baskets and earrings. Fishing and hunting licenses available. Arrangements may be made to rent autos and off-road vehicles. Marine gas, propane and regular gasoline available.

This Eskimo village was visited in December 1878 by E.W. Nelson of the U.S. Signal Service and reported as "Tununuk," population 6. A Roman Catholic mission was established here in 1891. Tununak was incorporated as a second-class city in 1975.

Sled dogs are still important to residents of Tuntutuliak. (Division of Tourism)

Tununak residents go to fish camps in the summer and also work on seasonal firefighting crews for the Bureau of Land Management.

The community is served by a Roman Catholic church and two schools.

UPPER KALSKAG is on the north bank of the Kuskokwim River, about 24 miles west of Aniak. **Elevation:** 49 feet. **Transportation:** Scheduled and charter air service from Aniak or Bethel. **Population:** 145.

Visitor Facilities: Arrangements for accommodations may be made at the school. Groceries and other supplies available at Commercial Store and Morgan's Trading Post. Marine gas and diesel available.

A general store was established at Upper Kalskag by a German immigrant, George Morgan, who became the first postmaster in 1932. A school was built in 1931. At that time the community owned a herd of 2,100 reindeer. Over the years, residents of Ohagamiut, Crow Village and the Yukon River communities of Russian Mission and Paimute moved to Upper Kalskag. Upper Kalskag was incorporated as a second-class city in 1975.

Most income in Upper Kalskag comes from public employment programs. Subsistence activities account for about 70 percent of the total livelihood in the village. Some residents still go to fish camps, but most fish at or near the village. Fish include king, dog, silver and red salmon, grayling, whitefish, sheefish, blackfish, pike, burbot and eel. Moose are the most important meat source, supplemented by rabbit, waterfowl and game bird. Some income also is obtained from trapping and the sale of lynx, fox, wolf, otter, muskrat, mink, marten, beaver and wolverine pelts. Berries are harvested in the fall and some residents cultivate gardens.

Upper Kalskag is located within the Yukon Delta National Wildlife Refuge.

Yukon-Kuskokwim Delta Attractions

Yukon Delta National Wildlife Refuge

At 19.6 million acres, Yukon Delta is the nation's largest wildlife refuge. It encompasses the vast, flat deltas of the Yukon and Kuskokwim rivers, two of the longest rivers in Alaska. It also includes 1.1 million acre Nunivak Island, located 20 miles off the coast. On Nunivak the terrain includes volcanic craters, sand dunes, sea cliffs and rolling tundra. This region is largely treeless and apart from the Andreafsky and Kilbuck hills is a seemingly endless expanse of wetlands. The Andreafsky River in the northern section of the refuge is a wild and scenic river within an area designated as wilderness.

This refuge is one of the most significant waterfowl breeding areas in North America. A total of 170 species have been observed and at least 136 species nest here, including more than 750,000 swans and geese, two million ducks and 100 million shore and water birds. More than half the continent's black brant population hatches on the refuge coast and all of North America's cackling

Left — *Hazen Bay is part of the Yukon Delta refuge. (Dave Spencer, U.S. Fish and Wildlife Service, reprinted from ALASKA GEOGRAPHIC®)*

Top — *Brown/grizzly bears, moose and caribou roam mainland portions of the refuge. (Steve McCutcheon, reprinted from ALASKA GEOGRAPHIC®)*

Above — *Sabine's gull is among the many species of birds that frequent the delta. (Will Troyer, reprinted from ALASKA GEOGRAPHIC®)*

Canada geese are produced in the coastal lowlands. Large populations of emperor geese, Pacific white-fronted geese and tundra swans nest near the coast and on the inland tundra.

Nunivak Island shelters introduced herds of reindeer and musk ox. Musk ox vanished from Alaska in 1865 because of overhunting. The Nunivak herd, introduced from Greenland in 1935, has provided breeding stock to establish herds elsewhere in Alaska and in the Soviet Union. The reindeer herd is a major source of food and income for residents of Mekoryuk, the only village on the island.

Other wildlife in this region include moose, caribou, grizzly and black bear, and wolves, found primarily in the northern hills and eastern mountains. Smaller mammals include beavers, muskrats, mink, land otters and foxes. On Nunivak, native land animals include only red and arctic foxes, weasels, mink, shrews, voles and lemmings. Coastal waters support harbor, ribbon, ringed and bearded seals, walruses, and many species of whales during migrations.

Fish found in refuge waters include trout, arctic char and grayling in the mountain streams and pike, sheefish, whitefish and burbot in lowland waters. Great numbers of king, silver, red, pink and chum salmon migrate through the delta rivers during the summer.

Recreational activities include wildlife observation and photography, hiking, boating, hunting and fishing.

For many centuries, the abundance of wildlife has made the delta the heart of Yup'ik Eskimo culture. Residents of at least 56 villages depend on this region for subsistence purposes.

The refuge is accessible only by boat or chartered airplane, usually from Bethel, St. Marys or Aniak. Wilderness camping is permitted on the refuge, but there are no established campgrounds or trails.

Freezeup comes to the Kuskokwim River near Aniak. (Myron Wright, reprinted from ALASKA GEOGRAPHIC®)

Yukon-Kuskokwim Area Rivers

The broad, slow-flowing Yukon and Kuskokwim rivers dominate this region, but there are other, smaller rivers which offer interesting trips for recreational boaters. The following are some of the best:

Aniak River — The Aniak flows 140 river miles to the Kuskokwim River a mile east of Aniak. Fishing on the Aniak is excellent for king, chum and coho salmon, pike, sheefish and grayling. Aniak Lake has lake trout and grayling.

Holitna River — This is a slow taiga river that was the Russians' first route into the Interior from Bristol Bay. Although it once saw much activity, today it is seldom visited.

Kanektok River — This river heads at scenic Kagati Lake in the Ahklun Mountains on the Togiak National Wildlife Refuge and flows 85 miles to Kuskokwim Bay near the village of Quinhagak. There is very good fishing for all species of salmon, arctic char, grayling and rainbow trout. The number of large fish in this river qualifies it as one of the top sportfishing rivers on the North American continent, according to the Fish and Wildlife Service.

Kisaralik River — This river heads in Kisaralik Lake in the Kilbuck Mountains and flows northwest 100 miles to the Kuskokwim River, 20 miles northeast of Bethel. There is superb mountain scenery and good hiking throughout the upper portion of the river. Seasonally there is good fishing for all varieties of salmon, rainbow trout, grayling and arctic char. Lake trout are available in Kisaralik Lake.

Kuskokwim River — This 540-mile-long river is Alaska's fourth longest. Its North Fork reaches far north to the Tanana basin and once served as a watercourse for Natives and later prospectors and trappers. Lake Minchumina is connected by a long, once well-trod portage to the North Fork. There are few travelers today, so boaters must be prepared to rely on their own resources.

Stony River — This river heads at Stony Glacier in the Alaska Range and flows southwest and northwest 190 miles to the Kuskokwim about a mile from Stony River village.

Telaquana and Necons rivers — These rivers are semiclear-water tributaries to the silt-laden Stony River. The Necons heads in Two Lakes in Lake Clark National Park and Preserve and flows 16 miles to Stony River. The Telaquana heads in Telaquana Lake, also located in Lake Clark National Park and Preserve, and flows 29 miles to the Stony.

Yukon-Kuskokwim Sportfishing

Big king salmon are at their peak in the Yukon-Kuskokwim region from mid-June through July. These fish often weigh 30 pounds or more. Chums and reds show up by July 1, pinks by mid-July (in even-numbered years) and silvers by mid-August. Salmon fishing is concentrated in the river systems.

In winter the Kuskokwim becomes a "highway" between villages for taxi cabs and other vehicles. (Staff, reprinted from ALASKA GEOGRAPHIC®)

Grayling measuring 16 inches are not uncommon in the Yukon-Kuskokwim area. (Lou Gwartney, reprinted from ALASKA GEOGRAPHIC®)

Arctic char and Dolly Varden are found throughout this area and are most abundant in late summer. These usually weigh one to three pounds, but occasionally a nine- to 12-pounder is reported. Grayling can be caught most of the summer, but larger ones are more plentiful from August to October. Grayling measuring 16 inches are not uncommon and they can reach 23 inches.

Other species found here are whitefish, which can reach five pounds; burbot (also known as lush or lingcod) which can weigh in at 10 to 12 pounds; and northern pike, which average five to eight pounds but can attain 30 pounds.

Access to good fishing in this area is primarily by airplane. Boats occasionally can be rented or chartered at villages along the waterways. There are daily commercial flights to the transportation centers of the region — Bethel, Aniak or St. Marys — where there is commuter service to smaller villages or charter service to lakes or rivers.

Kolmakov Redoubt

Built in 1841, Kolmakov Redoubt was the most important and longest occupied Russian fur trading post and settlement in inland Alaska. The stockaded Russian-American Company trading station, which at one time included about 10 buildings, was located on the south bank of the Kuskokwim River 21 miles east of present-day Aniak. The site is on the National Register of Historic Places.

The old fort was abandoned by the Russians in 1866 in anticipation of the transfer of Alaska to the United States. The station continued as a trading center until about 1917. In 1929, the best surviving structure, the station's blockhouse, was dismantled and shipped to the University of Alaska Museum, where it is on display on the Fairbanks campus.

Russian blockhouse can be seen in Fairbanks. (Courtesy of University of Alaska Museum)

Seward Peninsula/ Norton Sound Communities

BREVIG MISSION, on the Seward Peninsula, is six miles northwest of Teller, 60 miles northwest of Nome and 481 miles west of Fairbanks. Elevation: 25 feet. Transportation: Scheduled or charter air service from Nome; winter trail to Teller. Population: 159.

Visitor Facilities: Arrangements can be made to stay in private homes. There is a laundry and supplies are available at Brevig Muit Store or Brevig Co-op Store. The sale and importation of alcoholic beverages is prohibited. Fishing and hunting licenses; marine engine and boat repair; and fuel (marine gas, diesel, propane and regular gasoline)

are available. Arrangements can be made to rent boats.

Brevig Mission was established in 1892 as Teller Reindeer Station by Sheldon Jackson. Reindeer were the economic base of this community from 1892 to 1974, but they are now declining. Skin sewing for arts and crafts and seasonal construction bring in some cash income. Subsistence hunting and fishing are an important part of life here.

BUCKLAND is on the west bank of the Buckland River on the Seward Peninsula, 75 miles southeast of Kotzebue, 400 miles west of Fairbanks. Transportation: Boat; snow machine; scheduled air service from Kotzebue. Population: 249.

Visitor Facilities: Limited. Groceries and other supplies are available at three local stores, including Buckland Native Store. The sale and importation of alcoholic beverages in Buckland is prohibited. Fishing and hunting licenses may be purchased locally. Marine gas, propane and regular

gasoline are available.

This village has existed at several other locations, under various names, in the past. At one time it was known as Elephant Point, so named because fossil mastadon or mammoth bones were found at the site in 1826.

Buckland people moved repeatedly as conditions changed and the people depended at various times on reindeer or beluga whale or seal for survival.

Buckland has a primarily subsistence economy. In the fall and winter, residents hunt caribou; in spring they hunt beluga whale and seal off Elephant Point. Herring, salmon, smelt, grayling, whitefish, rabbit, ptarmigan, berries and waterfowl and their eggs supplement the local diet. Some employment is provided with a locally owned reindeer herd.

COUNCIL is located on the Niukluk River on the Seward Peninsula, 33 miles northeast of Solomon, 74 miles northeast of Nome, 470 miles west of Fairbanks. Elevation: 100 feet. Transportation: Boat, charter plane or auto from Nome. Population: 11 year-round, up to 50 in summer.

Visitor Facilities: Food and lodging in summer at Camp Bendeleben, a fishing lodge. Limited groceries and sporting goods available at a small store in a local residence; most visitors bring their own supplies. Propane and regular gasoline are available.

Council was the recording office and center of the Council gold mining district. During the summers of 1897-99, the population was estimated to be as high as 15,000 people and "Council City" was a genuine boom town with a hotel, a post office, a 20-bed hospital and numerous bars. Some 13 dredges worked streams and rivers between Solomon and Council and Council was the southern terminus of a railroad to Ophir Creek. Many of the boomers left Council in 1900 for the gold beaches of Nome, but a sizable community remained. Council was for many years the second largest community in all of western Alaska, but the flu epidemic of 1918, the Great Depression and World War II all contributed to the decline of the community and by 1950 only nine people remained. The post office closed in 1953.

Modern school dominates this view of Buckland in the southern Kotzebue Basin.
(John and Margaret Ibbotson, reprinted from ALASKA GEOGRAPHIC®)

Council, viewed from end of the Nome-Council Road across the Niukluk River. (Staff)

inhabit the area. Some placer gold mining currently takes place in the area, primarily at Ophir Creek.

DEERING is at the mouth of the Inmachuck River on Kotzebue Sound, Seward Peninsula, 57 miles southwest of Kotzebue, 150 miles north of Nome and 440 miles northwest of Fairbanks. **Transportation:** Scheduled and charter air service from Kotzebue; boat; snow machine. **Population:** 148.

Visitor Facilities: None. There is a laundromat and some supplies are available at Deering Native Store or Gil's Store. The sale and importation of alcoholic beverages is prohibited. Some carved ivory available for purchase. Fishing and hunting licenses are sold locally. Diesel, propane and regular gasoline are available.

Deering is described as "a beautiful community on the ocean" by one resident. It is built on a sand spit approximately 300 feet wide and half a mile long. The village was established in 1901 as a supply station for Seward Peninsula gold mines.

Its economy is based on subsistence hunting and fishing.

Council is one of the few villages in the region connected to Nome by a road. The road terminates across the river from Council. The river can be forded at low water periods. Three roads branch out from Council: to Ophir Creek, to Melsing Creek and the airstrip, and a third over a hill northeast to Mystery. Except for the Ophir Road, four-wheel-drive vehicles are necessary.

The countryside is dotted with old cabins, mines and dredges, including one operating dredge at Ophir Creek. Numerous old buildings in various stages of deterioration still stand among newer buildings in the settlement.

All permanent residents of Council, and many of the seasonal residents, rely in part on local hunting and fishing for food. The Niukluk River provides some of the finest fishing on the Seward Peninsula. Arctic char, grayling, pike, whitefish, and chum, pink and king salmon abound. Rabbits, ptarmigan, moose, grizzly bears and wolves all

Deering was established at the turn of the century as a supply point for mining camps. (John and Margaret Ibbotson, reprinted from ALASKA GEOGRAPHIC®)

The main sources of meat are moose, seal and beluga whale and residents go to hunting camps in the spring and fall. A local reindeer herd provides some employment.

A 20-mile road connects Deering with the mining area of Utica to the south. Also, many trails along major streams and across the tundra are used year-round for traveling to other villages, hunting and fishing.

DIOMEDE, located on the west coast of Little Diomede Island in the Bering Straits, 130 miles northwest of Nome and 650 miles west of Fairbanks. **Transportation:** Scheduled and charter floatplane from Nome; helicopter. **Population:** 153.

Visitor Facilities: Arrangements for accommodations can be made at the school or through the Inalik Village Corp. The sale and importation of alcoholic beverages is prohibited. Limited groceries at Inalik Native Store. Arrangements can be made to rent boats. Marine gas, diesel, propane and Blazo are available.

Diomede is only 2.5 miles from the Soviet Union's Big Diomede. The international boundary between the U.S. and USSR lies between the islands, which were named by Vitus Bering in 1728 in honor of Saint Diomede. The present village site was originally a spring hunting site, which was gradually inhabited as a permanent settlement.

Diomeders depend almost entirely on a subsistence economy. Blue cod, bullhead, flounder and tanner crab are harvested during the summer, and walrus, whale, seal and bear hunting occur during the spring and fall when these animals migrate through the area. Seal hides are used for mukluks, rope, harpoon lines and mittens, and walrus hides are used for boat hulls. Salmonberries, greens and some roots are found on the island. Migratory birds and their eggs supplement the subsistence diet.

The Diomede people are excellent ivory carvers, known throughout the state for the quality they produce. Many villagers market their crafts in Nome, Teller, Kotzebue and Anchorage.

ELIM, on the northwest shore of Norton Bay on the Seward Peninsula, is 96 miles east of Nome. **Elevation:** 130 feet. **Transportation:** Scheduled or charter air service from Nome. **Population:** 248.

Visitor Facilities: None. Groceries and sundry items may be purchased at Elim Native Store. The sale and importation of alcoholic beverages is prohibited. Fishing and hunting licenses are available. Fuel available includes marine gas, diesel, propane and regular gasoline.

Originally a Malemiut Eskimo village established on a federal reindeer reserve in 1911 and known as Nuviakchak, the settlement grew with the establishment of first a mission and school and later a post office. Elim became a second-class city in 1970. Its economy is based on subsistence, with seasonal employment in construction, fish processing and timber. Elim is located on the Iditarod Trail.

GAMBELL is on St. Lawrence Island in the Bering Sea, 200 miles west of Nome. **Elevation:** 30 feet. **Transportation:** Scheduled or charter air service from Nome. **Population:** 500.

Visitor Facilities: Accommodations and meals at Slwooko Lodge. Laundry facilities available. Gambell Native Store and G&E Enterprises carry supplies. The sale and importation of alcoholic beverages is prohibited. Fishing and hunting licenses available. Arrangements can be made to rent off-road vehicles or boats. Fuel available includes diesel, propane and regular gasoline.

St. Lawrence Island has been inhabited for

Little Diomede Island is only 2.5 miles across the International Dateline from the Soviet Union's Big Diomede Island. (Staff, reprinted from ALASKA GEOGRAPHIC®)

Gambell whalers watch for bowhead whales off St. Lawrence Island. (© Chlaus Lotscher)

several thousand years. The city was named in 1898 for Presbyterian missionaries and teachers Mr. and Mrs. Vene C. Gambell.

The economy in Gambell is largely based on subsistence hunting. Residents hunt walrus and bowhead and gray whales in the spring and fall. During the summer the people fish, crab, hunt birds, gather eggs and harvest various seafoods, greens, and berries. Seal, fish and crab are harvested throughout the winter. The Native people of Gambell still hunt from walrus-hide boats and follow many old customs. A whaling festival takes place in Gambell each spring.

There are four archaeological sites at Gambell which are on the National Register of Historic Places. Villagers dig up artifacts from the sites to sell.

Ivory carvings are a popular retail item and the St. Lawrence Islanders are famous for their beautiful work.

Numerous species of birds, some of them rare Asiatic species, populate the island during the summer months and draw parties of bird-watchers. Note should be made, however, of fees and restrictions for visitors which may be in effect. In 1985, the Gambell and Savoonga village corporations, which own the island, required visitors to pay a $100 land crossing fee if they wished to leave the town and tour the island. The corporation also required that any stories or photographs involving areas outside the townsite be submitted for prepublication approval.

GOLOVIN, located on a sandspit in Golovnin Bay on the Seward Peninsula, 42 miles east of Solomon, 70 miles east of Nome and 450 miles west of Fairbanks. **Elevation:** 25 feet. **Transportation:** Snow machine; scheduled and charter air service from Nome. **Population:** 122.

Visitor Facilities: None. There is a laundromat and Olson & Sons store carries limited supplies (stocks are low in the spring). The sale and importation of alcoholic beverages is prohibited.

Fishing and hunting licenses available. Aircraft mechanic and charter aircraft available. Fuel (marine gas, diesel, regular) and moorage available.

Golovin became a town in the 1890s, with the discovery of gold on the southern Seward Peninsula and the establishment of the Swedish Covenant Church mission.

Life in Golovin today is perhaps best described by the people of Golovin. With the help of their teachers, the children of the Golovin BIA School put together a book on their village, from which the following quotes have been taken.

On hunting: "In the summer we don't hunt much in Golovin. The only thing we hunt is whale when they come around. Most people fish, either to dry and eat later or sell to fish buyers. In the fall we hunt almost everything. We hunt geese, sprigs, cranes, and seals. When we go hunting we use a 12 gauge, 16 gauge, or a .22. We go hunting in a boat. In the winter all we hunt is ptarmigan, snowshoe rabbit, moose, and jack rabbit. Most of us boys always walk. You don't have to walk; you can use a ski-doo to go hunting, if you have one. I don't have one, so I always have to walk."

The reindeer industry: "Mr. Sigfried Aukongak Jr. owns the reindeer. There can be about 10 to 10,000 or maybe more. Each year they always butcher several hundred."

The fishing season: "Commercial fishing is the most important source of money in Golovin. The fishing season is short — only about four or five weeks long and the people fish four days a week. Fishing can be dangerous when you have to check your net in rough weather. The wind blows here almost all the time. Buying gas, repairing boats, motors, and nets, and just handling fish is hard work."

Things to do: "Almost everybody likes movies. Thursday and Saturday we have movies in the community hall, because there is no theater. Sometimes there are no movies. Sometimes there are too many movies so we have movies on Monday.

"Rubbery Ice is played in the fall and spring. Just before the ice gets too hard, we would run back and forth, across thin ice which is rubbery, and try not to get wet. It is not dangerous because the lakes are shallow.

"Most of the adults play bingo on Monday and Friday nights in the Community Hall.

"Every spring a lot of people go to Hot Springs and take a bath, some people stay for a week. We go up there the first week of April because of the rivers opening and takes about four to six hours to get there by snow machine."

KOYUK, on the Koyuk River at the northeast end of Norton Bay on the Seward Peninsula, 132 miles east of Nome and 75 miles north of Unalakleet. **Elevation:** 130 feet. **Transportation:** Scheduled air service from Nome. **Population:** 213.

Visitor Facilities: None. The Koyuk Native Store and Koyuk Native Corporation carry groceries and other supplies. The sale and importation of alcoholic beverages is prohibited. There's a washeteria and a pay phone. Fishing and hunting licenses may be purchased locally. Marine gas, propane and unleaded available. Guide services through Big River Hunting Lodge.

The present site was settled around 1900 as a transfer point for goods and supplies bound for Norton Bay Station upriver and coal shipments to Nome from nearby mines.

The village was incorporated as a second-class city in 1970. The economy is based on subsistence activities. Salmon, herring, grayling, beluga, seal, caribou, wildfowl, moose and berries are harvested. Some income is derived from reindeer herding, and hides and antlers are sold on the commercial market.

NOME is located on the south coast of the Seward Peninsula facing Norton Sound, 550 miles west of Fairbanks. **Elevation:** 10 feet. **Transportation:** Scheduled air service from Anchorage or Fairbanks. **Population:** 3,184.

Visitor Facilities: Accommodations at the Nome Nugget Inn and the Polaris Hotel. The Community United Methodist Church operates a youth hostel. There are banks, laundries, and several restaurants and stores. Native arts and crafts are available at several gift shops. Fishing and hunting licenses may be purchased locally. Public moorage available.

Nome owes its name to a misinterpretation of "? name" annotated on a manuscript chart prepared aboard the HMS *Herald* about 1850. The question mark was taken as a C (for cape) and the A in "name" was read as O.

Gold was found in the Nome area in September 1898 and the town got its start that winter when six miners met at the mouth of Snake River and formed the Cape Nome Mining District. News of the gold strike set off a major rush in the summer

Bundles of salmon hang on drying racks at Nome. (Division of Tourism)

of 1900. The Seward Peninsula is believed to hold 100 gold dredges from bygone days.

Nome is the oldest first-class city in Alaska and has the state's oldest first-class school district. The city acts as a transportation and commerce center for northwestern Alaska. Alaska's reindeer industry is centered in the Nome vicinity and the area has rich mineral potential. Nome also is a major stopover on arctic tours and a jumping-off point for tours to surrounding Eskimo villages.

Carrie McLain Memorial Museum, on the first floor of the building containing the museum and the Kegoayah Kozga Library on Front Street, has

exhibits on the Bering Land Bridge, natural history of the region, Eskimo cultures and the gold rush. Nearly 8,000 photographs relating to the history of northwestern Alaska, as well as newspaper archives, are stored here.

Nome's city hall, with turn-of-the-century decor, is on Front Street. A massive wood-burl arch sits next to city hall until March each year, when it is raised over Front Street for the Month of Iditarod festival celebrating the famed 1,049-mile Iditarod Trail Sled Dog Race from Anchorage to Nome.

Other events and celebrations are the annual Midnight Sun Festival in June; the Anvil Mountain Run on the Fourth of July; the Memorial Day Polar Bear Swim; and the Labor Day Bathtub Race.

There are interesting drives on three gravel roads that extend north and east from the city: The 72-mile Nome-Teller Road, the 72-mile Nome-Council Road, and the 86-mile Nome-Taylor Road. They are maintained only in summer.

ST. MICHAEL, located on the east coast of St. Michael Island on the south side of Norton Sound, 48 miles southwest of Unalakleet, 125 miles southwest of Nome and 420 miles northwest of Anchorage. **Elevation:** 30 feet. **Transportation:** Boat, snow machine, scheduled and charter air service from Unalakleet and Nome. **Population:** 279.

Visitor Facilities: Arrangements may sometimes be made for staying at the school or in private homes; contact the school principal or the city office. There is a washeteria, and supplies are available at Tachik Native Store and Alaska Commercial Co. The sale and importation of alcoholic beverages is prohibited. Fishing and hunting licenses available.

In 1833, the Russians established Redoubt St. Michael, the northernmost Russian settlement in Alaska. During the late 1800s, St. Michael became the major gateway to the interior goldfields via the

Front Street in Nome, commercial center for the Seward Peninsula. (Staff, reprinted from ALASKA GEOGRAPHIC®*)*

161

In early May, Savoonga remains tightly locked in winter's grip. (Caroline Canafax, reprinted from ALASKA® magazine)

in the village with the city, Native corporation, school and store.

St. Lawrence Islanders are famous for their ivory carvings which are a popular retail item. Artifacts found at some of the old village sites on the island also are sold for income. People here pass their time going to their camps, digging for artifacts, riding three-wheelers in summer and snow machines in winter.

The walrus herds that haul out on the island are attracting an increasing number of tourists, particularly during the annual Savoonga Walrus Festival, which takes place in May. Bird watching also is popular with visitors, who come to view and photograph the seabirds that nest on the island. Note should be made, however, of fees and restrictions for visitors which may be in effect. In 1985, the Gambell and Savoonga village corpora-

Yukon River. Remnants of St. Michael's historic past can still be seen today: Three Russian-built houses, the hulks of steamboats and several old cemeteries remain.

St. Michael is the closest deepwater port to the Yukon and Kuskokwim Rivers. It is a transfer point for freight hauled from Seattle on large ocean-going barges to be placed on smaller river barges or shipped to other Norton Sound villages.

St. Michael's economy is based on subsistence food harvest supplemented by part-time jobs. Residents harvest sea mammals, including seal and beluga whale. Moose and caribou are important winter staples.

SAVOONGA is located on the north coast of St. Lawrence Island in the Bering Sea, 39 miles southeast of Gambell, 164 miles west of Nome and 700 miles west of Fairbanks. **Transportation:** Scheduled and charter air service from Nome. **Population:** 470.

Visitor Facilities: Accommodations at Alanga Lodge. Meals at lodge or restaurant. Washeteria with showers available. Supplies available at Wayne Penayah's Store, Savoonga Native Store and Umiighham Trading Post. The sale and importation of alcoholic beverages is prohibited. Fishing and hunting licenses and guide services

are available. Arrangements may be made to rent off-road vehicles. Marine gas, diesel, propane, unleaded and regular gasoline available. Moorage on beach.

Savoonga was established as a reindeer herding station to manage the increasing numbers of animals in the early 1900s. (The federal government had introduced 70 reindeer to the island in 1891.) The continued growth of the herd, and the good hunting and trapping near Savoonga, attracted people from Gambell to Savoonga. The community is built on wet, soft tundra and boardwalks crisscross the village providing dry routes to all buildings. A post office was established in 1934, and in 1969 Savoonga was incorporated as a second-class city.

The economy of Savoonga is largely based on subsistence hunting, with some cash income. Savoonga is hailed as the "Walrus Capital of the World," and residents hunt these animals, as well as bowhead and gray whales, in the spring and fall. During the summer, the people fish, crab, hunt birds, gather eggs and harvest various seafoods, greens and berries.

Seal, fish and crab are harvested through the winter. Reindeer roam free on the island, but the herd is not really managed. There are a few jobs

Shaktoolik is a checkpoint for the Iditarod Trail Sled Dog Race. (Division of Tourism)

tions, which own the island, required visitors to pay a $100 land crossing fee if they wished to leave the town and tour the island. The corporation also required that any stories or photographs involving areas outside the townsite be submitted for prepublication approval.

SHAKTOOLIK is located two miles east of the Shaktoolik River on the east shore of Norton Sound, 33 miles north of Unalakleet, 130 miles east of Nome and 410 miles northwest of Fairbanks. **Elevation:** 20 feet. **Transportation:** Boat; scheduled and charter air service from Nome or Unalakleet. **Population:** 186.

Visitor Facilities: None. There is a laundromat with showers, and supplies are available at Shaktoolik Native Store or Air's Laufguk. The sale and importation of alcoholic beverages in Shaktoolik is prohibited. Fishing and hunting licenses are available. Arrangements may be made to rent private autos and boats. Diesel and gas are available.

The village site has been moved twice since it was first mapped in the 1800s by the Imperial Russian Navy. Shaktoolik is a second-class city, incorporated in 1969.

Its economy is based on subsistence food harvest supplemented by part-time wage earnings from jobs with the city, school, construction, store, airlines and Native corporation. Native crafts, such as carved ivory, wooden masks and berry-picking buckets, also bring in some income. A herd of about 300 reindeer provides meat and hides. Reindeer, moose, caribou, salmon, arctic char, whale, seal and waterfowl are the chief subsistence foods.

The historic Iditarod Trail passes through Shaktoolik and links the village to Unalakleet and coastal villages to the west along Norton Sound. Shaktoolik is a checkpoint during the Iditarod Trail Sled Dog Race.

Cape Denbigh, 12 miles to the northeast of Shaktoolik, is the site of Iyatayet, a national historic landmark. This archaeological site is 6,000 to 8,000 years old.

Another attraction is Besboro Island off the coast, site of a major seabird colony.

SHISHMAREF, on Sarichef Island between the Chukchi Sea and Shishmaref Inlet, is 100 miles southwest of Kotzebue, 120 miles north of Nome and 550 miles west of Fairbanks. **Elevation:** 20 feet. **Transportation:** Scheduled and charter air service from Nome. **Population:** 493.

Visitor Facilities: Accommodations in a trailer owned by Nayokpuk General Store. Washeteria available. Groceries and other supplies at ANICA Native Store, Nayokpuk's Store and Herb's Eskimo Shop. The sale and importation of alcoholic beverages is prohibited. Fishing and hunting licenses available. Diesel and gas available.

Shishmaref is 20 miles south of the Arctic Circle and 100 miles east of Siberia. The original Eskimo name for the island was "Kigiktaq." Lieutenant Otto Von Kotzebue named the inlet "Shishmarev" in 1816. The village was named after the inlet in 1900 when a supply center was established here to serve gold mines on the Seward Peninsula. A

Shishmaref, on the north coast of Seward Peninsula, faces the Chukchi Sea. (Staff, reprinted from ALASKA GEOGRAPHIC®)

post office was established in 1901 and Shishmaref was incorporated as a second-class city in 1969.

The Shishmaref economy is based on subsistence food harvest. Residents harvest oogruk, walrus, polar bear, moose, rabbit, squirrel, ptarmigan, waterfowl, eggs, various greens and plants. Fish include herring, smelt, salmon, whitefish, trout, grayling, lingcod, tomcod, flounder and sculpin. Two reindeer herds provide meat and hides. Ivory carving and skin sewing also bring in some income.

Shishmaref is the home of respected Eskimo artist Melvin Olanna and Iditarod Trail dog musher Herbie Nayokpuk.

The annual Shishmaref Spring Carnival and Seward Peninsula Open-Class Championship Sled Dog Races take place in April.

Shishmaref is surrounded by the 2.6 million acre Bering Land Bridge National Preserve.

SOLOMON, on the west bank of the Solomon River, is 32 miles east of Nome and 500 miles west of Fairbanks. **Transportation:** By auto on the Nome-Council Road; charter air service from Nome. **Population:** 4.

Visitor Facilities: None.

Solomon was originally established as a mining camp during the Nome gold rush. The town's boom was short-lived, however. Only a few people held productive mining claims and several disasters befell the remaining residents. In 1913, storms washed out the railroad, and the 1918 flu epidemic decimated the population. The post office was closed in 1925, reopened in 1928, and was closed again in 1956. Rusting narrow gauge railroad equipment, the old school and ferry docking facilities today offer mute reminders of Solomon's historic past.

The unpaved Nome-Council Road, which originated as a trail during the gold rush, runs through Solomon. Maintained only in summer, the road brings many visitors to the area, including birdwatchers, fishermen, hunters and tourists.

Only one family presently lives in Solomon year-round. Many Nome residents have seasonal homes or camps here.

STEBBINS is on the northwest coast of St. Michael Island, eight miles northwest of St. Michael, 53 miles southwest of Unalakleet and 120 miles southeast of Nome. **Elevation:** 26 feet. **Transportation:** Scheduled and charter air service from Unalakleet. **Population:** 327.

Visitor Facilities: Arrangements for lodging at a small inn or in private homes may be made through the Stebbins Native Corp. Laundry facilities and showers available. Groceries and other supplies available at Stebbins Native Store or Ferris General Store. The sale and importation of alcoholic beverages is prohibited. Fishing and hunting licenses available. Contact city office for guide services. Arrangements may be made to rent off-road vehicles and boats. Fuel (marine gas, propane, diesel, regular gasoline) and moorage available.

In 1950 Stebbins was described as a village of Eskimos who made their livelihood by hunting, fishing and herding reindeer. Stebbins was incorporated as a second-class city in 1969.

The Stebbins economy is still based on subsistence hunting and fishing, supplemented by part-time wage earnings. There is presently an unmaintained herd of reindeer on Stuart Island just off the coast. Commercial fishing in the area is on the increase.

Stebbins is located at the northern tip of the Yukon Delta National Wildlife Refuge. Bird watching is for peregrine falcons and a myriad of migratory waterfowl, according to a resident.

Recreational activities in Stebbins include basketball, bingo, Eskimo dances and an annual potlatch.

TELLER is located 72 miles north of Nome and 540 miles west of Fairbanks. **Elevation:** 10 feet. **Transportation:** By auto on the Nome-Teller Road; scheduled and charter air service from Nome. **Population:** 257.

Visitor Facilities: None. There is a washeteria and Teller Commercial Co. carries groceries and

Narrow gauge railroad engines from the gold rush lie rusting alongside the Nome-Council Road near Solomon. (Staff)

other supplies. The sale and importation of alcoholic beverages is prohibited. Fishing and hunting licenses available. Diesel and gas available.

The first permanent settlement, named for U.S. Sen. H.M. Teller, was established around 1900 following the Bluestone Placer discovery 15 miles to the south. During its boom years, Teller became a major regional trading center, attracting Native people from Diomede, Wales, Mary's Igloo and King Island. The Teller post office was established in 1900. This mostly Eskimo community was incorporated as a second-class city in 1963.

The residents live primarily a subsistence lifestyle, relying on salmon runs, moose, berries and tundra greens. Some of the Natives own reindeer herds which are corralled and butchered regularly. According to Teller's school principal, "The school serves 60 students and employs 15 people.

"Most of the people travel up Grantley Harbor to the interior of the Seward Peninsula for fishing and hunting. Salmon netting, jigging for smelt and tomcod, and moose hunting is fair close to the village. Musk ox can be seen occasionally wandering near the village and many reindeer can be seen when driving from Nome to Teller."

Teller was the landing site of the *Norge,* the first dirigible to be flown over the North Pole, piloted by Roald Amundsen. Teller's most recent claim to fame is that it is the home of Libby Riddles, winner of the 1985 Iditarod Trail Sled Dog Race. Riddles, first woman to win the grueling 1,049-mile race from Anchorage to Nome, raises and trains her dogs in Teller.

From May through October a 72-mile gravel road is open from Teller to Nome. Taxis will make the trip for $150 each way. Air taxi service is available for about $40 per person one way.

TIN CITY is located seven miles southeast of Wales, 100 miles northwest of Nome and 600 miles northwest of Fairbanks. **Elevation:** 270 feet. **Transportation:** Boat; scheduled and charter air service from Wales. **Population:** 30-50.

Visitor Facilities: None. Groceries and supplies available at Lee Trading Co. Arts and crafts

available for purchase include carved ivory, moccasins and other hand-sewn skin items from Diomede, Wales, Shishmaref, Brevig Mission and other villages. Fuel available includes marine gas and propane.

Tin City was established as a mining camp in 1903 after tin ore was discovered on Cape Mountain in 1902. Tin City Air Force Station was constructed in the early 1950s. Military personnel have since been replaced by RCA Alascom employees. An abandoned White Alice communications site is located on a nearby hill.

There still is tin mining in the area. Lee Mining Camp operated in the 1960s, but was sold to Lost River Mining Co. in the 1970s. Tin ore, jade and other minerals, can be found on the beach.

UNALAKLEET is located on the east shore of Norton Sound at the mouth of the Unalakleet River, 145 miles southeast of Nome. **Transportation:** Scheduled and charter air service from Nome; winter trail to Anvik. **Population:** 784.

Visitor Facilities: Food and lodging at Unalakleet Lodge. Meals also at The Weathered Inn and the community center snack bar. Supplies carried at Alaska Commercial Co. and Unalakleet Native Corp. General Store. Fishing and hunting licenses and guide services are available. Major engine repair available. Arrangements can be made to rent autos and boats. Fuel available includes marine gas, propane, diesel, and regular gasoline. Moorage available.

Students from Covenant High School in Unalakleet described their community in *earthlines/tidelines* (February 1983): "Unalakleet is a break-off from the first known Eskimo settlement, which was the Cape Denbigh Flint Complex, about 50 miles north of here. It is supposed to have existed more than 7,000 years ago. From there the Eskimo people moved to the site which is present-day Unalakleet.

Henry Oyoumick picks Dolly Varden from net strung beneath ice near Unalakleet. (Jim Greenough, reprinted from ALASKA GEOGRAPHIC®)

"Today, Unalakleet has modernized quite a bit. We have a mayor and city council. We have electricity, running water and flush toilets. We have no paved roads but there are quite a few trucks and cars, not to mention snow machines and ATCs, buzzing around.

Norton Sound Dream

Outside the sky is all aglow,
  the mercury dipped to ten below.
The North wind's kicking up a fuss.
  when walking bent, it makes you cuss.
The view is one of winter white,
  with blowing snow, to blind your sight.
Beyond the storm, the beauty lies,
  amid the cold and Arctic skies.
To see it all, is quite a pleasure,
  I know it well, my frozen treasure.
The Norton Sound, to me is gold,
  yet others only see the cold.
We keep it frozen for a reason,
  so fish can swim in any season.
The trout we catch, through frozen water,
  on sunny days, there's lynx and otter.
No polar bears are seen a-running,
  but seals on icebergs may be sunning.
Teams of dogs with speeds of lightening,
  at night, their bark can be so frightening.
That stately raven guards our border,
  his stance commands some law and order.
Bald eagles soar in windy currents,
  so high and free, with no deterrents.
At the night, the serenading loon,
  sings songs of magic to the moon.
The lilting tune provides esteem,
  to live this has been my dream.
              —June Degnan

"The kids in Unalakleet are no different from kids in big cities. They also enjoy listening to popular Top 40 hits, playing Scramble and Pac-Man at the Rondevous, shooting pool and playing ping-pong on lazy afternoons. A lot of people watch movies on video in their homes.

"But Unalakleet hasn't turned its back on all of its Eskimo culture. There are still men who carve ivory and hunt seal and walrus. They trap for furs and hunt moose and caribou. The women in the village, especially the older ones, still sew mukluks and make parkas. They skin *oogruk* and hang the meat to dry, saving the oil for dipping dried fish in.

"In the summer most of the people fish, many commercially. My Grandma and Grandpa Johnson still cut and hang fish for the winter months. I love eating dried fish and seal oil with Grandma while watching her sew skins."

A herd of musk oxen maintained near Unalakleet provide *qiviut,* a rich underwool, which is spun and then knitted into scarves, caps and sweaters, which are sold through the Musk Ox Producers' Co-operative in Anchorage.

"Unalakleet is a fun place to be during the Iditarod. It is the thirteenth stop, with only six more stops and 250 miles to go to the finish line at Nome.

"There is much excitement when the leaders come in from Kaltag. Planes bringing reporters and spectators land on the frozen river right in front of Leonard and Mary Brown's Unalakleet Lodge where the mushers check in.

"When the first team arrives, school is let out and the whole town races to the lodge to see who the leader is. Everyone claps and cheers and some of the older folks who know the racer go down to congratulate him. Then the rest of us gather round to pat the dogs and see what's going on."

Unalakleet is the takeoff point for sportfishing in Norton Sound and the Unalakleet and North Rivers. The Unalakleet River above the Chiroskey River has been designated a wild and scenic river and is popular for float trips. The area is administered by the Bureau of Land Management. Visitors should be aware, however, that the land surrounding Unalakleet is owned by the Unalakleet Native Corp. and trespassing laws are strictly enforced. Permits can be obtained from the corporation office in Unalakleet for camping, hunting, fishing, bird watching, boating, sledding and photography.

WALES is on the western tip of the Seward Peninsula, seven miles west of Tin City and 111 miles northwest of Nome. **Elevation: 25 feet.**

Transportation: Scheduled and charter air service from Nome; winter trail to Tin City. **Population:** 139.

Visitor Facilities: Limited accommodations in the Wales Native Corp. building. Arrangements also may be made for accommodations in private homes. Laundromat and showers available. Groceries and other supplies at Wales Native Store. The sale and importation of alcoholic beverages is prohibited. Fishing and hunting licenses available. Arrangements may be made to rent private off-road vehicles and boats. Marine gas, diesel and propane available. Moorage on beach.

Cape Prince of Wales is the farthest west point of mainland Alaska. The area has been inhabited for centuries: A burial mound of the Birnirk culture (500-900 A.D.) was discovered behind the present village and is now a national historic landmark. Wales was a major center for whale hunting until the 1918 flu epidemic claimed the lives of many of Wales' finest whalers.

A mission was established in 1890 and in 1894 a reindeer station was organized. The post office opened in 1902. Wales was incorporated as a second-class city in 1964.

The economy of Wales is based on subsistence hunting and fishing, trapping, seasonal jobs, some mining and Native arts and crafts. Wales artisans make excellent ivory carvings, especially birds, which are sold locally or marketed in Nome, Anchorage or Fairbanks. Other crafts such as skin sewing bring additional income to the community.

According to city clerk Ellen Richard, "In the spring the men go out hunting for whale, walrus, ducks and *oogruk*. Fishing consists of getting some trout, whitefish, silver salmon and red salmon. Rod and reel is done at the point of Cape Mountain and other locations are 30 miles south of Wales on York River and at the camping sites up north, such as Mint River. We have clam season in the fall, when the clams wash in with the tide. People go camping in the summer for fishing and in the fall for picking berries. We get tons of birds and especially ducks migrating north in the spring and south in the fall."

In Wales, the visitor will get a glimpse of Eskimo life relatively unaffected by outside contact. During the summer, Wales is a base for residents of remote Little Diomede Island and these Eskimos often can be seen traveling to and from their island in the large traditional skin boats. Air service and tours to Wales are available out of Nome.

The George Otenna Museum in the community center features arts and crafts and historic artifacts.

WHITE MOUNTAIN is located on the west bank of the Fish River, 15 miles northwest of Golovin, 33 miles east of Solomon and 65 miles east of Nome. **Elevation:** 50 feet. **Transportation:** Boat; snow machines; scheduled and charter air service from Nome. **Population:** 150.

Visitor Facilities: Arrangements may be made for lodging in private homes. Washeteria with showers available. Groceries and other supplies available at White Mountain Native Store. Arts and crafts include knitted gloves and caps and porcupine quill earrings. Fishing and hunting licenses available. Boat repair available. Marine gas, propane and regular gasoline available. Moorage on beach.

The Eskimo village of "Nutchirviq" was located here prior to the influx of white settlers during the turn-of-the-century gold rush. In 1899, C.D. Lane erected a log warehouse as supply headquarters for his numerous gold claims in the Council district. The name White Mountain was derived from the color of the mountain located next to the village. A post office was established in 1932. White Mountain was incorporated as a second-class city in 1969.

White Mountain residents rely both on subsistence hunting and fishing and on wages from seasonal work in commercial fishing, construction, firefighting, wood cutting, trapping, some cannery work and reindeer herding activities at Golovin. Residents spend much of the summer at fish camps.

Seward Peninsula/ Norton Sound Attractions

Bering Land Bridge National Preserve

Bering Land Bridge National Preserve is located just below the Arctic Circle on the Seward Peninsula 50 miles south of Kotzebue and 90 miles north

Visitor walks among tors in Bering Land Bridge National Preserve. (T. Newman, National Park Service, reprinted from ALASKA GEOGRAPHIC®)

Female common eider on her nest watches for intruders in the preserve. (Staff, reprinted from ALASKA GEOGRAPHIC®)

of Nome. It is a remnant of the land bridge that once connected Asia and North America 14,000 to 25,000 years ago. More than just a narrow strip across the Bering Strait, the land bridge at times was up to 1,000 miles wide. It rose during the ice age as a massive glacier formed, causing the water levels of the Bering and Chukchi seas to fall. Across this bridge people, animals and plants migrated to the New World. The preserve is considered one of the most likely regions where prehistoric hunters crossed over. An archaeological site at Trail Creek caves has yielded evidence of human occupation 10,000 years old.

Other interesting features of the 2.8 million acre preserve are lava flows around Imuruk Lake, some as recent as 1,000 years ago; low-rimmed volcanoes called maar craters, now filled with water, in the northern lowlands around Devil Mountain; and Serpentine Hot Springs, long utilized for its spiritual and medicinal values. (The springs' Inupiat Eskimo name is Iyat, which means "cooking pot.") Hillsides in the preserve are dotted with the remains of ancient stone cairns, their original purpose lost in the misty past. Also of interest are the more recent historical sites from early explorations and mining activities.

Today, Eskimos from neighboring villages pursue subsistence lifestyles and manage reindeer herds in and around the preserve.

During the short summer the preserve bursts into life and many of its 245 species of plants bloom with bright colors. From mid-August to mid-September the tiny tundra plants take on autumnal tones of yellow, orange and scarlet.

Wildlife in and around the preserve includes some 112 species of migratory birds; marine mammals such as bearded, hair and ribbon seals, walrus, and humpback, fin and bowhead whales; grizzly bears, some wolves, caribou to the north and east, some musk ox from transplanted herds, moose, red and arctic foxes, weasels and wolverines. Fish in preserve waters include salmon, grayling and arctic char.

Recreational activities include hiking, camping, fishing, sightseeing, wildlife observation and photography.

Visitors generally arrive by charter plane from Nome or Kotzebue. There is an airstrip and a public-use cabin at Serpentine Hot Springs. There are no other facilities in the preserve.

Seward Peninsula/ Norton Sound Rivers

The wild and scenic Unalakleet River flows southwest through the low, rugged Nulato Hills to the village of Unalakleet where it drains into Norton Sound.

This clear-water river is approximately 105 miles long, but only the lower 76 miles is deep enough to float. Many sand and gravel bars provide camping sites and there is a commercial fishing lodge on the lower portion of the river.

The Unalakleet flows through flat valley with marshes and oxbows. Fishing is good for salmon, arctic char, Dolly Varden and grayling. Wildlife includes moose, black and brown bears, wolves, waterfowl, beavers and foxes.

Seward Peninsula/ Norton Sound Sportfishing

Large king salmon are available in the Seward Peninsula and Norton Sound area from mid-June through July. These fish often weigh 30 pounds or more. Chums and reds show around the first of July, pinks by mid-July (in even-numbered years) and silvers by mid-August. Salmon fishing is concentrated in the river systems.

Arctic char and Dolly Varden are found throughout this area and are most abundant in the fall. These usually weigh one to three pounds, but occasionally reach nine to 12 pounds. Grayling can be caught most of the summer, but larger ones are more plentiful in late summer. Grayling measuring 16 inches are not uncommon and they can reach 23 inches.

At more northerly locations anglers can encounter the "Tarpon of the North," or sheefish, a great fighter which can reach 60 pounds. Other species that may be encountered are whitefish, which weigh up to five pounds; burbot (also called lush or lingcod) which can weigh in at 10 to 12 pounds; and northern pike, which average five to eight pounds but can attain 30 pounds.

In general the best fishing throughout the northern half of the Bering Sea Coast region is in July and August.

Except for a few roads around Nome, access to good fishing in the Seward Peninsula/Norton Sound area is primarily by airplane. Boats occasionally can be rented or chartered at villages along the waterways.

Fisherman on the wild and scenic Unalakleet River prepares to land a trout. (George Wuerthner)

Cape Denbigh

The Iyatayet archaeological site at Cape Denbigh, 12 miles west-northwest of the village of Shaktoolik on Norton Sound, is a national historic landmark. Cape Denbigh was named by English explorer Captain James Cook on Sept. 11, 1778; its Eskimo name is Nuklit.

This site, excavated by archaeologist J.L. Giddings from 1948-52, is the type site for the Norton culture and the Denbigh Flint complex and was a momentous discovery because it was older than previously known sites. The site is located on an old beach ridge and represents three cultural periods dating back as far as 5,000 B.C.

Cape Nome Roadhouse

Located just east of Cape Nome at Mile 14 on the Nome-Council Road, this historic roadhouse is listed on the National Register of Historic Places. It is the only roadhouse still standing that was used in the famous 1925 "race to Nome" to deliver serum during the diptheria epidemic. The building was used as an orphanage at one time and is now a private residence.

The original section was built in 1900 of logs hauled 70 miles from Council by horse. In 1913 after a flood destroyed the log building an abandoned government building from Safety reportedly was moved to the site and became the present roadhouse. From about 1910 it was a major stopover for dog teams traveling the Iditarod Trail.

Pilgrim Hot Springs

Above — Sunlight illuminates the roof of Our Lady of Lourdes mission church at Pilgrim Hot Springs, located on the bank of the Pilgrim River 13 miles northeast of Salmon Lake on the Seward Peninsula northeast of Nome. The springs was the site of a gold rush resort about 1900; the Catholic mission opened in 1917-18. It is on the National Register of Historic Places. Pilgrim Hot Springs is reached by charter air service from Nome or by car on a new gravel road that joins the Nome-Taylor Road at Cottonwood. (Brother Albert Heinrich, reprinted from ALASKA® magazine)

King Island

Right — The abandoned village of Ukivok clings to the rocky slope of 1,196-foot-high King Island. The island, located in the Bering Sea 40 miles west of Cape Douglas on the Seward Peninsula, is the ancestral home of the King Island Eskimos, who now live at Nome. The island was named by Captain James Cook on Aug. 6, 1778, for a member of his party. The island today is home to thousands of seabirds. Villagers began moving away in the 1950s, attracted by job opportunities and health facilities in Nome. The village was last inhabited in 1966, but King Islanders still return in late May or June each year to pick greens, gather bird eggs and hunt walrus. (Steve Leatherwood, reprinted from ALASKA GEOGRAPHIC®)

ARCTIC

An invisible line separates the Arctic from the rest of Alaska. It runs west along the crest of the Brooks Range to Mount Igikpak, near the head of the Noatak River, then curves south past the village of Kobuk to the Arctic Circle and extends west to reach the Chukchi Sea just south of Kotzebue.

Strong winds, cold temperatures and low precipitation characterize the climate. The Beaufort and Chukchi seas moderate the climate in summer somewhat, but temperatures at Barrow, near the northernmost tip of North America, average between 30° and 40°F in July and August and between -15° and -18°F in January and February. Both the Beaufort and Chukchi seas are ice-covered for up to nine months each year.

This virtually treeless country is interlaced with meandering rivers and dotted with thousands of shallow thaw lakes. Permafrost, beginning just a few inches under the surface and extending down as far as 2,000 feet, underlies most of the Arctic.

Sandpipers and other shorebirds are flushed from tundra ponds. (Peter G. Connors, reprinted from ALASKA GEOGRAPHIC®)

Most areas receive less than 10 inches of precipitation a year, but soggy tundra and bogs are common in summer because there is little evaporation and permafrost impedes drainage.

While it is covered by snow and ice much of the year and has total darkness for up to three months, there is enough sunshine in the remaining months to transform the bleak winter tundra into a summer carpet of miniature, flowering plants.

There are several varieties of tundra in the region. Higher elevations support alpine tundra: lichens, grasses, sedges, some herbs such as mountain avens and saxifrage. Cotton grass, mosses, lichens, dwarf birch and willows cover the foothills. Sedges, mosses, cotton grass and lousewort predominate on the boggy plain. Scrub willow and alder grow along major rivers.

Numerous large mammals including moose, wolves, brown/grizzly bears and Dall sheep make their homes on the northern tundra. Two major herds of caribou — Western Arctic and Porcupine — roam all but the rockiest slopes of the Brooks Range. Smaller mammals — wolverines, weasels, a few river otters, snowshoe hares, lynx, arctic and red foxes, shrews, lemmings and voles — also live in the Arctic.

A subsistence catch of chum salmon is cleaned. (John and Margaret Ibbotson, reprinted from ALASKA GEOGRAPHIC®)

Arctic

Location

N

Cartography by David A. Shott

Arctic Ocean

Barrow■

Wainwright■

Kasegaluk Lagoon

■Atqasuk

Teshekpuk Lake

■Ku

Prudh

■Tunalik Airstrip

Chukchi Sea

Point Lay■

Ulukok River

■Nuiqsut

Colville River

Umiat■

Killik R.

Anaktuvuk River

Point Hope■

DeLong Mountains

Etivluk River

Nigu R.

Noatak   River

Aniuk River

Noatak   National   Preserve

Anaktuvuk Pass■

Atalna River

John River

Endicott Mountains

Brooks Range

Kivalina■

Wulik River

Cutler River

Baird Mountains

Gates   of   the   Arctic   National   Park   and   Preserve

Cape Noatak■

Squirrel R.

Salmon River

Reedstone River

Kobuk Valley National

Arrigetch Peaks▲

Wild River

North Fork Koyukuk River

Krusenstern National Monument

Ambler■

Ambler River

Walker Lake

Hotham Inlet

Kiana■

Kobuk   River

Park

Kotzebue■

Waring Mountains

Noorvik■

Shungnak■   Kobuk■

Kotzebue Sound

Selawik National Wildlife Refuge

Selawik■

Arctic Circle

River

Beaufort Sea

Prudhoe Bay

Flaxman Island

Barter Island **Kaktovik**

Sagavanirktok River

Ivishak River

Canning River

Hulahula River

Arctic

Romanzof Mountains

Kongakut River

National

Sheenjek River

Yukon Territory

Alaska

Dalton Highway

Wildlife

Philip Smith Mountains

Refuge

Yukon   Flats   National   Wildlife   Refuge

Mount Igikpak is reflected in the calm waters of the Noatak River. (John and Margaret Ibbotson, reprinted from ALASKA GEOGRAPHIC®)

After being hunted out of Alaska, musk ox were reintroduced in the 1930s on Nunivak Island in southwestern Alaska. Part of that herd was transplanted to the mainland and now lives on the arctic slope near Kavik and on the seacoast near Cape Thompson.

Many bird species migrate to the Arctic to breed and raise their young, although few species winter here.

The frigid waters of the Beaufort and Chukchi seas support polar bears, walruses, bowhead and beluga whales, and bearded and ringed seals. In the short summer months when the ice retreats from the coast, harbor seals, harbor porpoises and killer and gray whales pass by. Rarer species of

This pingo, a large mound raised by permafrost, adds some relief to the flat coastal plain. (Steve McCutcheon, reprinted from ALASKA GEOGRAPHIC®)

great whales — fin, sei and little piked — also have been reported in Chukchi waters. Even rarer are narwhals, the males of which sport single spiraled tusks up to seven feet long.

Millions of acres in this region have been set aside as public lands. Cape Krusenstern National Monument on the Chukchi Sea coast contains ancient beach fronts created by ocean currents and storms. Artifacts dating back thousands of years have been unearthed from these beach ridges. East from the sea are Noatak National Preserve, Kobuk Valley National Park and Gates of the Arctic National Park and Preserve. Just south of Kobuk Valley National Park is Selawik National Wildlife Refuge. And in the northeastern corner of the state, the Arctic National Wildlife Refuge encompasses 18 million acres.

Transportation in the Arctic is chiefly by plane year-round, boat in summer and snow machine in winter. Dog teams, once the only form of transportation in this region, are still used by residents. Each summer a fleet of tug-pulled barges from the Lower 48 brings supplies and equipment to coastal villages and the oil-drilling operations at Prudhoe Bay.

Few settlements have been established in the Arctic. Barrow, the largest Inupiat Eskimo community in the world, is the trade center for the North Slope Borough, which includes the smaller communities of Wainwright, Point Hope, Point Lay, Atqasuk, Nuiqsut, Anaktuvuk Pass and Kaktovik and the oil complex at Prudhoe Bay. Commerce among villages in the southwestern Arctic revolves around Kotzebue, from where supplies are shipped to Kobuk, Shungnak, Ambler, Kiana, Noorvik, Noatak, Kivalina and Selawik.

Oil field development and related construction created jobs for many arctic residents and provided the economic stimulus for new houses, schools, hospitals and civic buildings. The Prudhoe Bay oil discovery was confirmed in 1968 and the 800-mile-long pipeline connecting Prudhoe Bay with the marine terminal at Valdez began operation in 1977.

Residents of the smaller villages rely on subsistence and seasonal work, usually in construc-

Seal hunter goes out by dog team near Cape Krusenstern. (Ken Ross, reprinted from ALASKA GEOGRAPHIC®)

subsistence hunting and fishing. In the summer, many residents go to Kotzebue for commercial fishing. Some local employment is provided by government, school and local businesses.

Ambler is some 20 miles from the archaeological dig at Onion Portage, 15 miles upriver from Kobuk Valley National Park and about 35 miles away from the Great Kobuk Sand Dunes. Visitors often air charter out of Ambler to Walker Lake in the Brooks Range, then float back down the Kobuk River.

According to local residents Ole Wik, Regina Randall and Sally Walker, recreation here includes: good grayling fishing (at times) in the Ambler River; good sheefishing in July (local guide recommended); and caribou hunting in September. "Many square miles of stabilized sand dunes offer glorious hiking and solitude, though mosquitoes take the edge off the charm during midsummer." Jade can be found in some streams and at Dahl Creek (above Kobuk) and near Jade Mountain (check with local people). Swimming is enjoyable at low river stages; best is in June. And bird watching is best around breakup.

tion or government projects. Caribou are important to inland Eskimos, while coastal villagers depend on fish and marine mammals such as whales, seals and walrus.

Commercial fishing, trapping, fur buying and tourism generate income in the Kotzebue area, although subsistence hunting and fishing continue to play a major role.

The Communities

AMBLER, located on the north bank of the Kobuk River near the confluence of the Ambler and Kobuk rivers, 125 miles east of Kotzebue and 320 miles northwest of Fairbanks. **Elevation:** 135 feet. **Transportation:** Scheduled airline or air charter from Kotzebue. **Population:** 262.

Visitor Facilities: Food and lodging at Kobuk River Lodge. Groceries and other supplies available at the lodge or A&M Store. Fishing and hunting licenses and guide services are available. Rental transportation includes autos, off-road vehicles, boats and charter aircraft. Marine gas, diesel, propane and regular gasoline are available. Boat moorage on riverbank.

Ambler has been described as "a beautiful village by arctic standards." On the south slope of the Brooks Range, it is surrounded by spruce and birch forest. An Inupiat village, it was settled in 1958 when people from Shungnak and Kobuk moved here for the forest and game. Ambler's economy is based on arts and crafts (birch-bark baskets, masks, mukluks, beaver hats, yo-yos) and

The Inupiat village of Ambler. (Staff, reprinted from ALASKA GEOGRAPHIC®)

Modern building at Anaktuvuk Pass in the Brooks Range. (George Wuerthner)

ANAKTUVUK PASS is on a divide between the Anaktuvuk and John rivers in the central Brooks Range, 260 miles northwest of Fairbanks. **Elevation:** 2,200 feet. **Transportation:** Scheduled airline or air charter from Fairbanks. **Population:** 233.

Visitor Facilities: There is a public campground (check with National Park Service ranger station or village store) and Nunamiut Store carries groceries. Fishing and hunting licenses may be purchased locally. Propane and gas are available.

The Native residents of Anaktuvuk Pass are the last remaining band of Nunamiut Eskimo, a semi-nomadic group whose ancestors date back to 500 B.C. They settled permanently at this location, an historic caribou migration route, in the early 1950s.

Subsistence hunting, primarily of caribou; some construction work; and arts and crafts (caribou hide masks and carvings) make up the economy. The village is located virtually in the middle of Gates of the Arctic National Park and Preserve. There is public access to parklands across nearby regional

and village Native corporation lands, but check with the park ranger about planned routes.

Temperatures here can be below freezing from September through May because of the high elevation.

ATQASUK is on the west bank of the Meade River, 58 miles southwest of Barrow. **Elevation:** 65 feet. **Transportation:** Scheduled airline or air charter from Barrow. **Population:** 214.

Visitor Facilities: Limited. Meade River Store carries groceries and some supplies. Fishing and hunting licenses may be purchased. Propane and gas are available.

The area around this Inupiat Eskimo village has traditionally been hunted and fished by the Inupiat. During World War II, subbituminous coal was mined here and freighted to Barrow. There was a post office from 1951 to 1957 under the name Meade River, and in 1977 the village was reestablished by former Barrow residents. Atqasuk (or Atkasook) was incorporated in 1982.

Atqasuk's economy is based on subsistence

hunting and fishing. Some local people trap and some residents find temporary employment in Barrow, with which Atqasuk remains closely tied. Fish in the Meade River include pike, grayling and cod. Fossils of flowers and leaves have been found in the clay rocks along the river. Subsistence hunting ranges from inland for caribou to duck hunting on the coast and harvesting sea mammals on the ice. Since outdoor life here revolves around subsistence, indoor life is devoted to recreation. Bingo is a popular activity in Atqasuk.

BARROW is located on the Chukchi Sea coast, 10 miles southwest of Point Barrow and 500 miles northwest of Fairbanks. **Elevation:** 20 feet. **Transportation:** Scheduled airline from Fairbanks. **Population:** 2,943.

Visitor Facilities: Accommodations at Top of the World Hotel, Arctic Inn and Airport Inn. There are four restaurants, a laundromat and bank. Supplies are available from Alaska Commercial Co., Arctic Coast Trading Post, Brower's Store and Arctic Cash and Carry. Arts and crafts available for purchase include baleen works, carved ivory, masks, parkas and fur mittens. Fishing and hunting licenses may be purchased locally. Major repair services include marine engine, boat, auto and aircraft mechanics. Charter aircraft available locally. All types of fuel are available.

The northernmost community in North America, Barrow is one of the largest Eskimo settlements in North America and the seat of the 88,000-square-mile North Slope Borough, the world's largest municipal government. Barrow takes its name from Point Barrow, named for Sir John Barrow of the British Admiralty by Captain Beechey of the Royal Navy in 1825. Barrow's far north location gives it long summer days and very short winter days. When the sun rises May 10, it does not set until August 2. When the sun disappears at noon November 18, it does not appear again until noon January 24.

Visitors may see Eskimo residents headed for whale camps in April and May. Despite the fact that the village is very much into the 20th century, hunting of whales and ducks is still important traditionally and to the economy. Barrow residents also

Aerial view of Barrow, North America's northernmost community. (Division of Tourism)

work for the oil companies at Prudhoe Bay, for the borough and for various local businesses.

Village life centers around the school, with its sports facilities and library. Hunting ducks and fishing is also done for recreation, along with riding ATVs and boating. A blanket toss is put on daily in summer.

The Will Rogers and Wiley Post Monument here commemorates the 1935 airplane crash of the American humorist and the pioneer world-circuiting pilot. The accident happened 15 miles south of Barrow. Two monuments, both on the National Register of Historic Places, are located where the men died.

Other area sites on the national register are the Cape Smythe Whaling and Trading Station (the oldest frame building in the Arctic) in nearby Browerville, and Birnirk archaeological site, approximately two miles north of the Barrow airfield.

KAKTOVIK is on the north coast of Barter Island in the Beaufort Sea, 390 miles north of Fairbanks. **Elevation:** 40 feet. **Transportation:** Scheduled airline or air charter from Fairbanks. **Population:** 207.

Visitor Facilities: Food and lodging at Audi Camp (through air charter service), Sims Bunkhouse and Waldo Arms Hotel. Groceries and some other supplies can be purchased at Kikiktak Store and Sims Store. Local arts and crafts include etched baleen, carved ivory and masks. Fishing and hunting licenses may be purchased locally and guide services are available. Local auto and aircraft mechanics and charter aircraft available. Fuel includes marine gas, diesel, propane, unleaded and regular.

This Inupiat Eskimo village is on the northern edge of Arctic National Wildlife Refuge, the most northerly unit of the refuge system. Access to the refuge is via private aircraft or charter aircraft from Kaktovik, Fort Yukon or Arctic Village.

The ruins of old Kaktovik can be seen from the road into the village from the airport. Hunting nearby is for Dall sheep, moose, caribou and gray fox.

KIANA, on the north bank of the Kobuk River, is located 28 miles northwest of Selawik, 57 miles east of Kotzebue and 390 miles west of Fairbanks. **Elevation:** 150 feet. **Transportation:** Scheduled airline or charter aircraft from Kotzebue; by boat except during breakup (May) and freezeup (October). **Population:** 402.

Visitor Facilities: Limited. There is a laundromat and groceries and other supplies are available from Blankenship Trading Post, Dorsey's Trading Post and Baldwin Merchandise. Fishing and hunting licenses may be purchased locally. Outboard engine repair only is available. Rental transportation includes boats and charter aircraft. Most types of fuel and boat moorage are available.

This Eskimo village probably was established as a seasonal camp or central village of the Kowagmiut Eskimos. Its name means "place where three rivers meet." It became a supply center for Squirrel River placer mines in 1909 and a post office was established in 1915. Kiana is downstream from Kobuk Valley National Park.

Kiana has a subsistence economy based on moose, caribou, rabbits and various waterfowl. Hunting is restricted by subsistence use and park rules. Fishing, which is mediocre, includes chum salmon, sheefish, whitefish and grayling. In summer, residents may go to Kotzebue, Fairbanks or Nome to work in construction or commercial fishing.

From Kiana, a network of old trading trails is still used for intervillage travel, hunting and fishing. All-terrain vehicles, snow machines and, less frequently, dog sleds are used in the winter. There are about 10 pickup trucks in town.

KIVALINA is located on an eight-mile-long barrier beach between the Chukchi Sea and Kivalina Lagoon, 43 miles northwest of Noatak, 90 miles north of Kotzebue and 465 miles west of Fairbanks. **Elevation:** 11 feet. **Transportation:**

Scheduled airline or charter aircraft from Kotzebue; boat. **Population:** 294.

Visitor Facilities: None. Accommodations sometimes available in private homes. Groceries and other supplies at Kivalina Native Store, J&J's Store, Triple S Store or Steph's Sweet Shop Store. The sale and importation of alcoholic beverages is prohibited. Arts and crafts include model skin kayaks, model dog sleds, whale bone masks, ivory carvings and baskets. Boats sometimes can be rented. Fuel available includes marine gas, diesel, propane, regular and unleaded.

Built on a flat sand and gravel spit, Kivalina has long been a stopping-off place for seasonal travelers between the Arctic coast and Kotzebue Sound. "Long ago, in the old days," as one local legend goes, "Kivalina was filled with a lot of people, ranging from one end of the island all the way past the other side of the channel. Until something terrible happened. A hunter and his son caught a whole bunch of belugas and they were supposed to give every family in Kivalina a piece of their catch. When they accidentally forgot to give this old lady shaman a piece of their catch. She was very angry then somehow more than half the population disappeared."

Its residents are described as people who have lived all their lives at Kivalina, "from generation to generation." The subsistence economy is based on bowhead and beluga whales, walruses, seals, moose and caribou. There is fishing for salmon, grayling and arctic char in rivers near the village.

The Chukchi Sea usually is open to boat traffic from about mid-June to the first of November. Winter travel is by snow machine and dog sled from late October through May.

KOBUK is on the right bank of the Kobuk River, seven miles northeast of Shungnak, 150 miles east of Kotzebue and 300 miles west of Fairbanks. **Elevation:** 140 feet. **Transportation:** Scheduled

Laundry at Kivalina dries in the wind off the Chukchi Sea. (Staff, reprinted from ALASKA GEOGRAPHIC®)

airline or air charter from Kotzebue. **Population:** 97.

Visitor Facilities: Accommodations at Kobuk Hotel. Arrangements for lodging can also be made with private homes or the clinic. There is a laundromat with showers. Bernhardt's Store and Ross' General Store carry groceries and other supplies. Fishing and hunting licenses may be purchased locally. Boat rentals, charter aircraft, most types of fuel and boat moorage are available.

This Eskimo community of log homes was founded in 1899 as a supply point for mining activities in the Cosmos Hills to the north and was then called Shungnak. Riverbank erosion forced relocation of the village in the 1920s to present-day Shungnak, 10 miles downriver. The few people who stayed and those who returned named the old village Kobuk.

People here work for the school district, the airlines, the city office and by making baskets, or in seasonal work, such as firefighting and construction. Subsistence hunting and fishing is also important. Game includes caribou, moose, black and grizzly bear, and Dall sheep. Fish are "everywhere on Kobuk River" as one resident puts it. Grayling fishing is excellent and the sheefishing in late July and August is world famous, with fish up to 60 pounds. Other species include whitefish, pike, trout, salmon, suckers and smelt. Historic trails along the river are still used for intervillage travel and hunting and fishing.

Located near the headwaters of the Kobuk River, visitors to Kobuk Valley National Park can fly into Kobuk from Nome or Kotzebue and float down the Kobuk to the national park and the Great Kobuk Sand Dunes or fly to Walker Lake in Gates of the Arctic National Park and float the river from there. Summer weather is hot, can be very wet, "and a lot of mosquitoes go along with the summer," according to the village Public Safety Officer.

Also of interest for visitors is the jade mine at Dahl Creek, three miles from Kobuk by jeep. Owned by Ivan and Oro Stewart of Anchorage, the main camp is one-half mile from Dahl Creek airstrip and operates June and July. Visitors are welcome to watch jade mining and cutting; there's

Above — The community of Kobuk lies on the Kobuk River. (U.S. Forest Service)

Below — The Stewart's jade operation at Dahl Creek is three miles from Kobuk. (Jon Osgood, reprinted from ALASKA GEOGRAPHIC®)

Kotzebue's Front Street separates homes from the rocky beach along Kotzebue Sound. (Staff, reprinted from ALASKA GEOGRAPHIC®)

A husky finds refuge from the wind off Kotzebue Sound. (Division of Tourism)

present name when a post office was established in 1899 with the name of the adjacent sound, named for Polish explorer Otto von Kotzebue.

The population is over 80 percent Eskimo. The economy is based on commercial fishing and subsistence hunting and fishing. The wage economy of the entire region is concentrated in Kotzebue, which contains the regional offices of several state and federal agencies. Government construction is one of the main sources of income in the area.

Local attractions include the NANA Museum of the Arctic, which features a two-hour program with a diorama show unequaled anywhere in Alaska. Included is a visit to the jade factory and an Eskimo blanket toss. The west end of the museum building houses the National Park Service information center. An excellent city museum, Ootukahkuktuvik or "Place Having Old Things," is open daily in summer. During the summer, tour groups are entertained with Eskimo blanket tosses and often dances and skin-sewing demonstrations.

The Fourth of July celebration is the biggest event of the year in Kotzebue, featuring traditional Native games and awards for the largest beluga whales caught during the season. The Arctic Trades Fair takes place the week following the Fourth of July. People from all over the region come to trade handicrafts and participate in traditional dances and feasts. Preliminaries to the Eskimo Olympics take place between Christmas and New Year's Day.

KUPARUK is located 30 miles west of Prudhoe Bay and 400 miles north of Fairbanks. **Transportation:** Charter plane from Prudhoe Bay. **Population:** Approximately 1,500.

Visitor Facilities: None. Kuparuk is an Atlantic Richfield Co. base camp for oil well drilling, established about eight years ago.

NOATAK, on the west bank of the Noatak River, is 55 miles north of Kotzebue and 470 miles northwest of Fairbanks. **Elevation:** 60 feet. **Transportation:** Scheduled air service or charter aircraft from Kotzebue; boat. **Population:** 355.

Visitor Facilities: Arrangements may be made for sleeping at the school and in private homes.

no charge for cabins, but bring sleeping bags and food. NANA Regional Corp. also operates a jade mine at nearby Jade Mountain.

KOTZEBUE, located on the northwest shore of Baldwin Peninsula in Kotzebue Sound, 421 miles northwest of Fairbanks, 566 miles northwest of Anchorage. **Elevation:** 10 feet. **Transportation:** Daily jet service from Nome. **Population:** 2,345.

Visitor Facilities: Accommodations at Nul-Luk-Vik Hotel. There are restaurants, a bank, several stores and other services. Among the many Eskimo arts and crafts that can be purchased here are jade items made at the local NANA Regional Corporation factory. Fishing and hunting licenses and guide services are available, as well as several air charter companies. All fuel is available.

Kotzebue is the commercial center for a 48,000-square-mile area of northwestern Alaska which includes 10 villages and a population of about 5,900. The town is on a spit that is about three miles long and 1,100 to 3,600 feet wide. The site, known as "Kikiktagruk," has been occupied for some 600 years and was a busy trading center centuries before Europeans arrived. It acquired its

Groceries and other supplies may be purchased at Noatak Native Store or D and D Trading. The sale and importation of alcoholic beverages is prohibited. Fishing and hunting licenses are available and boats may be rented. Fuel available includes marine gas, propane and regular gasoline.

A community of log and wood-frame homes 70 miles above the Arctic Circle, Noatak was established as a fishing and hunting camp in the 19th century. People here live off the land, hunting caribou, moose, and mountain sheep, and fishing for trout, whitefish, grayling, Dolly Varden, lingcod and pike. There are some jobs at the school and there is summer employment in Kotzebue or

Below — *Orderly row of painted houses in Noatak. (John and Margaret Ibbotson, reprinted from* ALASKA GEOGRAPHIC®)

Right — *Base camp at Kuparuk drilling site. (Courtesy of ARCO, reprinted from* ALASKA GEOGRAPHIC®)

Lower right — *The neatly laid-out community of Noorvik on Nazuruk Channel. (Staff, reprinted from* ALASKA GEOGRAPHIC®)

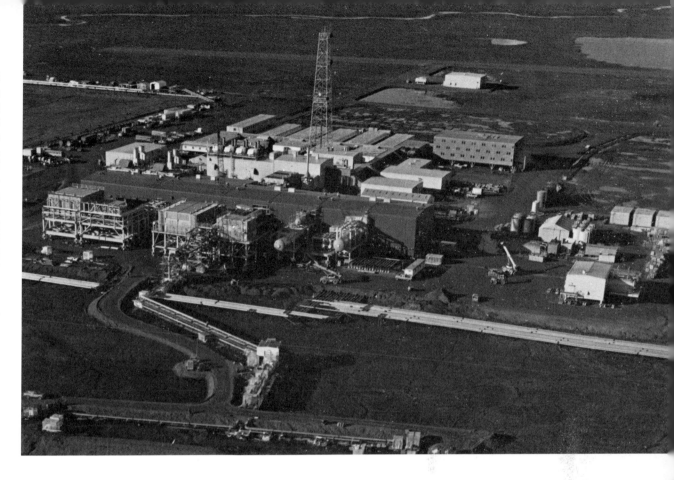

Point Hope sits at the tip of a point of land that juts into the Chukchi Sea. (Leslie Nakashima, reprinted from ALASKA GEOGRAPHIC®)

Nome. Visitors come downriver in summer by canoe. Noatak is the only settlement along the 396-mile-long Noatak River.

NOORVIK is located on the Nazuruk Channel of the Kobuk River, 33 miles northwest of Selawik, 45 miles east of Kotzebue and 400 miles west of Fairbanks. **Elevation:** 70 feet. **Transportation:** Scheduled airline or charter plane from Kotzebue; boat. **Population:** 517.

Visitor Facilities: Food and lodging at the Morris Hotel. Noorvik Native Store, Morris Trading Post and Harvey's Trading Post carry groceries and other supplies. Fishing and hunting licenses, guide services, boat engine repair and most types of fuel are available.

This village was established by Kowagmiut Eskimo fishermen and hunters from the village of Deering in the early 1900s. The economy is based primarily on subsistence hunting and fishing. There is some full-time employment with local government and businesses and seasonal employment in Kotzebue, Nome or Fairbanks. Noorvik is downstream from Kobuk Valley National Park.

NUIQSUT is located on the Nechelik Channel of the Colville River delta, about 35 miles from the Beaufort Sea coast, 60 miles west of Prudhoe Bay, 380 miles north of Fairbanks. **Elevation:** 50 feet. **Transportation:** Scheduled airline or charter plane from Prudhoe Bay or Barrow. **Population:** 305.

Visitor Facilities: Limited. There is a laundromat and groceries and other supplies are sold at Kuukpik Store, Mukluk Souvenir Shop, Joe's Jewelry & Gift or Nuiqsut Trading Post. Nuiqsut prohibits the sale and importation of alcoholic beverages. Fishing and hunting licenses available. Guiding through local airboat service. Most types of fuel available.

The Colville Delta has traditionally been a gathering and trading place for the Inupiat and has always offered good hunting and fishing. The village was constructed in 1974 under sponsorship of the Arctic Slope Regional Corp. after a winter overland move of 27 Barrow families with family ties to the Colville River delta area.

The economy is based primarily on subsistence hunting and fishing, but many residents are employed in seasonal construction work. Fish include whitefish, burbot, arctic char and grayling. Game animals include bowhead and beluga whales, caribou, seals, moose and many species of waterfowl such as swans, geese, ducks and loons. Local recreation is riding snow machines and three-wheelers and playing bingo.

POINT HOPE sits on a triangular foreland which juts into the Chukchi Sea 275 miles north of Nome and 570 miles northwest of Fairbanks. **Elevation:** 10 feet. **Transportation:** Scheduled airline or air charter from Kotzebue. **Population:** 582.

Visitor Facilities: Food and lodging at Whalers Inn. Laundry facilities are available. Point Hope Native Store carries groceries and other supplies. The sale and importation of alcoholic beverages is prohibited. Arts and crafts include carved ivory, baleen baskets, etched baleen, carved whale bone masks and animals and parkas. Fishing and hunting licenses, guide services and repair services for marine engines, boats and autos are available. Visitors may be able to rent autos, off-road vehicles or boats from local residents. All types of fuel and public moorage available.

The Point Hope peninsula is one of the longest continually occupied areas in Alaska. The remains of the sod houses of Old Tigara Village and an earlier site known as Ipiutak are found here.

In addition to the prehistoric village sites, there are old burial grounds in the area, including a cemetery marked by large whale bones. Beachcombing and rockhounding are available in the area and the wide expanse of land on the point also is home to an abundance of tiny arctic wildflowers. Other activities include boating and bird, wildlife and whale watching.

POINT LAY, located between Wainwright and Point Hope on the Chukchi Sea, 550 miles northwest of Fairbanks and 300 miles southwest of Barrow. **Elevation:** 10 feet. **Transportation:** Scheduled airline or air charter from Barrow. **Population:** 67.

Visitor Facilities: None. Some supplies carried at the Native store.

One of the more recently established Inupiat villages on the Arctic coast, Point Lay is also the smallest village in the region. The deeply indented shoreline prevented effective whaling, and the village never fully participated in the whaling culture. Residents rely heavily on subsistence hunting and fishing and there are some jobs in the school, store, clinic, and in construction.

SELAWIK is located at the mouth of the Selawik River where it empties into Selawik Lake, 70 miles southeast of Kotzebue and 375 miles west of Fairbanks. **Elevation:** 50 feet. **Transportation:** Scheduled airline or charter plane from Kotzebue. **Population:** 635.

Visitor Facilities: Accommodations in private homes or at the school may be arranged through the city office. Restaurant and laundromat available. Selawik Trading Post, Griest Trading, Rotman's Store and Savok's Store carry groceries and other supplies. Selawik prohibits the sale and importation of alcoholic beverages. Hunting and fishing licenses may be purchased locally. Repair services available for marine engines, boats and autos. Fuel available includes diesel, propane and regular gasoline.

Lieutenant L.A. Zagoskin of the Imperial Russian Navy first reported its existence in the 1840s as Chilivik. Some traditional sod houses and dog teams are still found in this Eskimo village. The post office was established in 1930.

The community of Selawik is located at the mouth of the Selawik River. (Staff, reprinted from ALASKA GEOGRAPHIC®)

Selawik's economy is based on arts and crafts (masks, baskets and caribou jawbone model dogsleds) and subsistence hunting and fishing. Some residents are employed as firefighters during the summer. Fish include whitefish, sheefish, grayling, northern pike, and arctic char. Caribou and moose are the most important game animals. Selawik is located near the more than two million acre Selawik National Wildlife Refuge. The Selawik River is classified as a wild and scenic river.

SHUNGNAK is located on the Kobuk River 10 miles west of Kobuk, 150 miles east of Kotzebue and 300 miles west of Fairbanks. **Elevation:** 140 feet. **Transportation:** Scheduled or charter airline from Kotzebue; boat. **Population:** 238.

Visitor Facilities: Accommodations at Commack's roadhouse. Cafe and laundromat available. Groceries and other supplies at Commack Store or Shungnak Native Store. Shungnak prohibits the sale and importation of alcoholic beverages. Arts and crafts available for

Present-day Point Hope, however, is very much into the 20th century, as Don Spicer Sr., of Tigara Corporation points out. "Hondas and snowmobiles have just about replaced the traditional dog team. Aluminum boats are now used to hunt seal, beluga, walrus, and for traveling upriver to fish, instead of the O'mac boats (skin boats) pulled by dog teams. There are a few dog teams left and used for winter hunting and O'mac boats are preferred in the spring whaling season. Even in these modern times, the Inupiat people still carry on much of their customary lifestyle."

Nearly every man in the village participates in the spring whale hunt, in which the traditional skin boats are still used. A festival takes place around the first of June after whaling season. Visitors are welcome. There also are village-wide celebrations on the Fourth of July, Thanksgiving and Christmas.

purchase here include birch-bark baskets, jade, beadwork, masks, mukluks, beaver hats and bone carvings. Demonstrations of Native craft work may be arranged. Fishing and hunting licenses may be purchased locally. Guide services available for river floating and dog mushing. Some small engine repair. Most types of fuel are available. Public moorage on riverbank.

The original settlement of Shungnak was 10 miles upriver at the present location of Kobuk until the 1920s, when residents relocated because of riverbank erosion. The name means "jade," and jade cutting and mining take place at the Shungnak River and Dahl Creek.

The 347-mile-long Kobuk, which begins in Gates of the Arctic National Park and Preserve, has become popular for float trips to Shungnak and beyond to Kobuk Valley National Park. According to local outfitter Jerry Dixon, the upper river is excellent for bird watching in spring and summer and fishing can be very good for sheefish and grayling. Visitors should note, however, that the river corridor is where residents make their living. River traffic has increased to the point where conflicts are beginning to arise between traditional subsistence use and recreational use. "Floaters, hunters and fishermen should be aware that there is a short period of time in which fishing must be done during the fall and make an effort not to disrupt subsistence activities." The Kobuk can freeze up as early as September and break up as late as May.

Other recreational activities in the area include camping, hiking, canoeing, gold panning and photography.

UMIAT, on the Colville River, is 75 miles south of Harrison Bay and 340 miles northwest of Fair-

Eskimo hunters butcher a 30-foot bowhead whale, still an important part of the Inupiat's subsistence lifestyle. (Staff, reprinted from ALASKA GEOGRAPHIC®)

banks. **Elevation:** 340 feet. **Transportation:** Charter aircraft from Prudhoe Bay. **Population:** About 15.

Visitor Facilities: A small hotel with food service is operated by the local air charter service. Prices are high.

Umiat is basically a gas station for small airplanes. Limited aircraft repair is available. It is a major airfield and refueling stop for flights between Fairbanks and Barrow. The Eskimo name Umiat refers to the skin boats that used to be cached nearby.

There is excellent moose and caribou hunting along the Colville River west of the village. Caribou hunting is usually best the week before moose season opens the first of September. There are good landing areas for light planes on river bars and coal from the riverbank can be used for fires.

WAINWRIGHT is on the Chukchi Sea coast, 85 miles southwest of Point Barrow and 520 miles northwest of Fairbanks. **Elevation:** 30 feet. **Transportation:** Scheduled airline or charter plane from Barrow. **Population:** 507.

Visitor Facilities: Accommodations available at Olgoonik Hotel. There is a restaurant and a laundromat. The Olgoonik Corp. Store, Wainwright Co-op Store, Shooter's Supply and Comart's carry groceries, clothing and other supplies. The sale and importation of alcoholic beverages is prohibited. Fishing and hunting licenses may be purchased and guide services arranged locally. Visitors may be able to rent vehicles and boats from local residents. Gas, diesel and other types of fuel are available.

Nearby Wainwright Inlet was named in 1826 by Capt. F.W. Beechey for his officer, Lt. John Wainwright. The present village was established in 1904 when the Alaska Native Service built a school.

"The Inupiat, who used to travel with the seasons, started building permanent homes out of sod. Today, most of the Inupiat live on subsistence and a few have permanent jobs, although rapid changes have caused some hardship," according to June Childress of the Olgoonik Corporation.

Village life revolves around whaling during the spring and summer months. A Nalukatak festival takes place in June if a whale is landed. Eskimo dances — "heartbeats of Alaska's home" — are performed weekly. Recreation includes: boating and riding snow machines and three-wheelers; smelt fishing on the lagoon in spring ("get there by walking or snowmobiles"); bird watching on the tundra in summer ("walk anywhere away from the village"); and looking for seashells on the beach. The summer weather is mild, although July can be rainy and windy. Winters are -35°F and colder.

Attractions

Cape Krusenstern National Monument

The 114 beach ridges of Cape Krusenstern, and the nearby bluffs, contain a chronological record of 6,000 years of prehistoric and historic use by man and are some of the most important prehistoric sites in the Arctic. The 660,000-acre monument is located 450 miles west-northwest of Fairbanks and 10 miles northwest of Kotzebue.

The ridges were formed by shifting sea ice, ocean currents and waves, each new one being used in succession for hunting camps. The beach ridges are about 10 feet high and nine miles long. The oldest artifacts and house sites are found in the ridges farthest from the sea. Eskimos continue to hunt seals along the cape's outermost beach. At shoreline campsites, the women process the hides, the meat and oil still vital to their diet.

Wildlife in the monument includes grizzly and black bears, caribou, moose, lynx, wolves and an occasional musk ox. Walruses, polar bears and whales can be seen offshore at various times of the year. Many species of waterfowl nest around the lagoons during the summer.

Recreational activities include camping, hiking, bird watching, fishing, and, as the Park Service puts it, "experiencing the land and elements just as those who camped here for centuries have done."

Visitors most commonly reach the monument by small chartered plane or boat from Kotzebue. There are no trails, developed facilities or campgrounds. Camping is permitted throughout most of the monument, except in archaeological zones, where it would interrupt subsistence activities, or on private land holdings, which are primarily along rivers and beachfronts.

Gates of the Arctic National Park and Preserve

The major feature of eight million acre Gates of the Arctic National Park and Preserve is the Brooks Range, an extension of the Rocky Mountains stretching across the expanse of Alaska from the Canadian border almost to the Chukchi Sea. Considered one of the finest remaining wildernesses in the world, the park and preserve combined are four times the size of Yellowstone National Park.

The Gates of the Arctic was the name given to Boreal Mountain and Frigid Crags by Robert Marshall, a forester who spent several summers

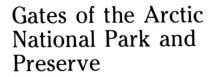

Some of the beach ridges containing evidence of several ancient cultures — for which Cape Krusenstern is famous — are visible in this aerial. (Robert Belous, National Park Service, reprinted from ALASKA GEOGRAPHIC®)

and a winter exploring the then-unmapped areas north and west of Wiseman in the 1920s and 1930s. The peaks rise like sentinels on either side of the north fork of the Koyukuk River. In the central Brooks Range the granite spires of the Arrigetch Peaks in the Alatna River drainage jut against the skyline, forming a spectacular cluster reminiscent of the Teton Range in the Rockies. Arrigetch is an Eskimo word meaning "fingers of a hand outstretched."

Mammals here range in size from lemmings to grizzly bears. Others are moose, caribou, Dall sheep, black bears, wolves, beavers, hoary marmots, wolverines, land otters, marten, mink, weasels, lynx, red foxes, porcupines and an assortment of small rodents. Eagles and many migratory birds are found within the park and preserve.

Eve Roberson fords a stream in Gates of the Arctic National Park. (George Wuerthner)

Fishing is generally good, with grayling in clear streams and lakes; lake trout in larger, deep lakes; char in streams on the North Slope; and sheefish and dog salmon in the Kobuk and lower Alatna rivers.

Access is most commonly by scheduled flights from Fairbanks to Bettles, where small aircraft may be chartered to the park or preserve. Charter flights also can begin in Fairbanks, Kotzebue or Ambler.

Some commercial lodges operate in or near the park. There are no established campgrounds, but excellent wilderness camping sites are available throughout the park and preserve. There are no roads or trails.

Six wild and scenic rivers flow within and out of Gates of the Arctic: the Noatak, Alatna, John, Kobuk, Tinayguk and North Fork Koyukuk. These, plus the Killik, Anaktuvuk and Nigu-Etivluk rivers, are considered "floatable" by the Park Service. The Arrigetch Peaks area offers superb rock and mountain climbing, as well as impressive photographic opportunities. There is excellent hiking on the open tundra at higher elevations or through the sparse shrubs and forest. Winter activities include cross-country skiing, snowshoeing and dog sledding. Sport hunting is allowed in the preserve.

Above — *Five-mile-long Chandler Lake lies near the northern boundary of the park.*

Below — *The spires of Arrigetch Peaks. (Photos by George Wuerthner)*

189

Kobuk Valley National Park

Kobuk Valley National Park totals 1.7 million acres and encompasses a mountain basin on the middle portion of the Kobuk River, 350 miles west-northwest of Fairbanks and 75 miles east of Kotzebue. Today's cold, dry climate approximates that of the ice age and supports similar plants. During the Pleistocene epoch, the Kobuk Valley provided an ice-free corridor joined to the land bridge that periodically formed, connecting Alaska and Siberia.

The valley contains artifacts dating 10,000 years of human occupation. At Onion Portage, near the eastern boundary of the park, Dr. J. Louis Giddings, the same archaeologist who made the discoveries at Cape Krusenstern, found what has been described as the most important archaeologial site ever unearthed in the Arctic. The diggings are now within a national archaeological district. Great herds of caribou still cross the Kobuk River at Onion Portage, attracting hunters today just as they did long ago.

Covering 25 square miles south of the Kobuk River are the wind-sculpted Great Kobuk Sand Dunes, some reaching 100 feet in height and over-running portions of the nearby forest. These, along with the Little Kobuk Sand Dunes near Onion Portage, and the Hunt River Dunes, are among the few dune fields in the Arctic.

Wildlife in the park includes grizzly and black bears, caribou, moose, wolves, lynx, marten, wolverines and some Dall sheep. Numerous ponds and oxbows provide excellent waterfowl habitat; more than 100 species of birds have been spotted in the area. Peregrine falcons pass through the park. Fish include five species of salmon, grayling, lake trout, pike and sheefish.

Floating the Kobuk River is one of the most popular activities in the park. The Great Kobuk Sand Dunes can be reached by an easy hike from the river. The wild and scenic Salmon River within the park also offers good canoeing and kayaking. Other activities include backpacking, fishing and photography. Sport hunting is prohibited.

Besides floating the Kobuk River, access to the park is primarily by charter aircraft from Bettles or Kotzebue. No visitor facilities, roads or trails are available in the park nor are there established campgrounds; camping is permitted throughout the park, except in archaeological zones or on private lands along the Kobuk River without consent of the owners.

A tundra pond along the Kobuk River. Floating the Kobuk River is one of the most popular activities in the park. (George Wuerthner)

Grizzly and wolf tracks along the Kobuk River. (George Wuerthner)

The meandering Noatak River bisects a broad, interior valley. (John and Margaret Ibbotson, reprinted from ALASKA GEOGRAPHIC®)

Noatak National Preserve

The 6.5 million acre Noatak National Preserve, located 350 miles northwest of Fairbanks and 16 miles northeast of Kotzebue, protects the largest untouched mountain-ringed river basin in America. Of its area, 5.8 million acres are designated wilderness. The 435-mile-long Noatak River is contained within a broad, gently sloping valley which stretches more than 150 miles east-west. The river, from its source in Gates of the Arctic National Park to its confluence with the Kelly River in Noatak National Preserve, is part of the National Wild and Scenic Rivers system. This is considered one of the finest wilderness areas in the world and UNESCO has designated it an International Biosphere Reserve.

The Noatak River passes through six fairly well-defined regions: Mountainous terrain with deeply scored canyons at its headwaters; the great Noatak Basin with its rounded mountains and plentiful wildlife; the 65-mile-long Grand Canyon of the Noatak and the much steeper, seven-mile-long Noatak Canyon; plains dotted with spruce, balsam and poplar; the rolling Igichuk Hills; and finally the flat coastal delta where tidal waters reach 40 miles upriver.

Wildlife commonly found within the Noatak drainage include the northwest Arctic caribou herd, numbering about 200,000 animals, which crosses the preserve in April and August on migrations to and from calving grounds to the north. Approximately 125 species of birds have been identified in the preserve. Fish include grayling, char, salmon, lake trout, burbot, pike and whitefish.

From Kotzebue, chartered flights provide access to the lower Noatak River. Access to the upper Noatak for float trips generally begins with a scheduled flight from Fairbanks to Bettles and a charter floatplane flight to lakes along the river's upper reaches. There are no trails, roads or established campgrounds in the preserve. Camping is permitted, however there are numerous private holdings along the lower Noatak River in the preserve and these properties should be respected.

Recreational activities in the preserve include float trips down the Noatak River, backpacking, fishing, hunting, wildlife observation and photography.

The solitary and slow-moving porcupine occurs throughout most of Alaska. (John and Margaret Ibbotson, reprinted from ALASKA GEOGRAPHIC®)

Arctic National Wildlife Refuge

The 18 million acre Arctic National Wildlife Refuge in the northeastern corner of Alaska encompasses some of the most spectacular arctic plants, wildlife and land forms in the world. Set aside to preserve migration routes of the great Porcupine caribou herd, numbering about 120,000 animals, the refuge also is home to musk ox, Dall sheep, packs of wolves and such solitary species as wolverines, polar bears and grizzly bears. Some 140 species of birds have been recorded on the refuge. Thousands of ducks, geese, swans and loons breed on coastal tundra and birds throng coastal migration routes all summer. Snowy owls and other predators can be seen along lagoons and rivers. Peregrine falcons, gyrfalcons, rough-legged hawks and golden eagles nest inland.

The refuge extends from the Porcupine River basin near the Canadian border north through the beautiful Sheenjek River valley and across the eastern Brooks Range down to the Arctic Ocean. For the most part, this land is above tree line and offers rugged, snowcapped, glaciated peaks and countless streams draining both north into the Beaufort Sea and south into the Porcupine and Yukon drainages. The refuge includes three wild and scenic rivers: the Ivishak, Sheenjek and Wind.

Winter on the refuge is long and severe; summer is brief and intense. Annual growth of trees and shrubs is slight. It may take 300 years for a white spruce to reach a diameter of five inches; small willow shrubs may be 50 to 100 years old.

This refuge has seen rapidly increasing recreational use in the last few years. Activities include kayaking and river rafting, hiking, backpacking and mountain climbing. Coastal lagoons offer excellent fishing and kayaking, plus wildlife observation and photography. Access is commonly by commercial air service from Fairbanks to Fort Yukon, Arctic Village or Kaktovik on Barter Island, the usual jumping-off points for refuge visitors. There are no lodges or other commercial facilities on the refuge; camping is permitted.

Above — *A backpacker airs his sleeping bag at a camp near Deadman Creek in Arctic National Wildlife Refuge. (George Wuerthner)*

Below — *A semipalmated plover on the gravel beds of the Jago River. (Gill Mull, reprinted from ALASKA GEOGRAPHIC®)*

Right — *The clear Junjik River, located northwest of Arctic Village. (George Wuerthner)*

Selawik National Wildlife Refuge

The 2.15 million acre Selawik National Wildlife Refuge straddles the Arctic Circle in northwestern Alaska 360 miles northwest of Fairbanks. It abuts Kobuk Valley National Park to the north and its southeastern corner adjoins Koyukuk National Wildlife Refuge. Selawik is a showcase of estuaries, lakes, river deltas and tundra slopes. Its most prominent feature is the extensive system of tundra wetlands that are nestled between the Waring Mountains and Selawik Hills.

The refuge is located near the land bridge that once connected Asia and North America and afforded a migration route for animals and humans. In later years prospectors searched these lands for gold. The refuge contains relics of both the ancient and the recent migrations.

Selawik is a vital breeding and resting area for a multitude of migratory waterbirds returning from North and South America, Asia, Africa and Australia, including the Asiatic whooper swan, whose only reported nesting area in North America is found here. Thousands of caribou winter on the refuge.

The refuge is accessible by boat, aircraft, snowmobile, dog sled, foot and cross-country skis — depending on the season and weather. Charter air service is available at Kiana, Ambler and Kotzebue. There are no roads or lodging facilities. Camping is allowed on refuge lands.

Recreation includes hiking, boating, camping, wildlife viewing and photography. Portions of the Selawik River are designated as a wild river and it provides good river rafting and sportfishing. Hunting, trapping and fishing are permitted.

Birch-lined calla cicuta mats. (Gail Corbin, Selawik National Wildlife Refuge)

Arctic Rivers

There are many arctic rivers that are suitable for travel by canoe, kayak or raft. North Slope rivers, flowing to the Beaufort Sea, usually are free-flowing by mid-June. On the south slope of the Brooks Range, rivers generally are free flowing by early June, but by mid-August water levels may be very low.

Alatna River — The upper portion of this designated wild and scenic river flows in Gates of the Arctic National Park on the south slope of the Brooks Range. River trips on the Alatna start within view of the dramatic granite spires of the Arrigetch Peaks. The Alatna then meanders through the magnificent Endicott Mountains and the Helpmejack Hills, before winding through the lowlands of the Koyukuk River.

An August sunset on the Kobuk River at a rafters camp. (Fred Dure)

Canning River — This is a fast white-water river on the Arctic National Wildlife Refuge. It heads in the Franklin Mountains and flows 125 miles northward through a scenic mountain valley and then through the arctic coastal lowlands to Camden Bay on the Beaufort Sea.

Colville River — This is Alaska's largest river north of the continental divide and is the seventh longest in the state at 428 miles. The Colville's headwaters are in the De Long Mountains, part of the Brooks Range. It bisects the arctic lowlands

The Angayuchum Mountains dwarf rafters on the Kobuk. (Fred Dure)

as it flows east-northeast into Harrison Bay on the Arctic Ocean.

Hulahula River — This seldom-run river located on the Arctic National Wildlife Refuge heads in the Romanzof Mountains and flows between some of the highest peaks in the Brooks Range: Mount Michelson and Mount Chamberlain. The Hulahula flows west and north 100 miles to Camden Bay on the Beaufort Sea, about 20 miles from Barter Island.

John River — This designated wild and scenic river in Gates of the Arctic National Park offers a rewarding voyage for the adventuresome traveler. It is possible to paddle the length of the river by starting at the Eskimo village of Anaktuvuk Pass. The John is a clear-water tributary to the Koyukuk.

Killik River — This scenic river heads in Gates of the Arctic National Park at the Continental Divide and flows northward 105 miles to the Colville River. The river passes through mountainous terrain and then into the lowlands of the Arctic Slope. The trip generally takes 10 days from Easter Creek to Umiat, on the Colville River about 70 miles downstream from the Killik River confluence.

Kobuk River — This 347-mile-long river is the ninth longest in Alaska and one of the most popular for float trips. It is designated a wild and scenic river from its headwaters at Walker Lake in Gates of the Arctic National Park to that park's western boundary. Lower stretches of the Kobuk pass through Kobuk Valley National Park.

Kongakut River — This is a seldom-run river in the Arctic National Wildlife Refuge that flows through beautiful and wild country on the North Slope of the Brooks Range. The Kongakut flows northeast from the Davidson Mountains, ending 100 miles away at Siku Lagoon, eight miles northwest of Demarcation Point in the far northeast corner of Alaska.

Nigu-Etivluk — Both the Nigu and Etivluk rivers are small, swift and clear tributaries to the Colville River. The Nigu's headwaters are in Gates of the Arctic National Park and it tumbles for 70 miles before joining the Etivluk. Then it's another 70 miles to the Colville.

Noatak River — This 425-mile-long wild and scenic river winds through Gates of the Arctic National Park and Noatak National Preserve before flowing into Kotzebue Sound. Considered by many to be the finest wilderness river in the Arctic, the Noatak flows through forest and tundra country entirely above the Arctic Circle. Highlights of this river are the mountain section along the upper river, Noatak Canyon and the run to the sea below the village of Noatak.

North Fork Koyukuk — This is a wild and scenic river in Gates of the Arctic National Park that provides a good family wilderness boating experience. The North Fork Koyukuk passes between the landmark mountains called the Gates of the Arctic by explorer Robert Marshall. The two peaks, named by Marshall, are Mount Boreal and Frigid Crags.

Wild River — This clear and fast tributary of the Koyukuk is recommended for enthusiasts of meandering streams. It flows from pristine Wild Lake, where fishing is good for grayling, pike and lake trout, to the Koyukuk.

Arctic Sportfishing

Rivers and lakes in the Arctic are accessible for sportfishing primarily by air, although riverboats occasionally can be rented or chartered at villages along the waterways. In the Far North there is virtually no sportfishing around communities such as Barrow, Kaktovik, Wainwright, Prudhoe Bay or Point Lay. However, there are lakes and rivers on the Arctic Slope that contain arctic char, which average four to six pounds, but can reach 12 to 15 pounds.

Most sportfishing in the Arctic takes place in August and September. Lakes in the Brooks Range are popular for fishing for lake trout, which can reach 30 pounds. However, these mountain lakes may not be totally ice free until July.

At other locations anglers can encounter the fighting "Tarpon of the North," or sheefish, which can reach 60 pounds in the Selawik-Kobuk area. Other species present in arctic waters are whitefish,

A lake trout is pulled from Selby Lake in Gates of the Arctic National Park. (George Wuerthner)

which can reach five pounds; burbot (also called lush or lingcod) which can weigh in at 20 pounds; northern pike, which average 20 pounds but can attain 30 pounds; and the ubiquitous arctic grayling, which occasionally reach four pounds and which fisheries biologists say can be found "everywhere it's clear and wet."

A 48-pound sheefish, the "Tarpon of the North," caught on the Kobuk. (Dick Zeldenrust, reprinted from ALASKA® magazine)

Leffingwell Camp

On southcentral Flaxman Island in the Beaufort Sea stand the remains of what is believed to be the camp established by explorer and geologist Ernest de Koven Leffingwell in 1907 to carry out important permafrost studies, mapping and other studies of arctic conditions. The camp is on the National Register of Historic Places.

Leffingwell spent several years between 1901 and 1914 in the Canning River region and compiled the first accurate maps of that part of the northern coast. A cabin at the camp site was built from the timbers of the expedition's ship the *Duchess of Bedford*, which had been damaged by the ice pack.

Kasegaluk Lagoon

Stretching southwest along the Chukchi Sea coast from just south of Wainwright to beyond Point Lay, this shallow 120-mile-long body of water is the largest barrier island-lagoon system in North America. It offers excellent wildlife viewing, as well as kayaking in quite shallow waters protected from ocean waves by the low barrier islands.

During July, August and September half a million migrating eiders, and thousands of terns, gulls, jaegers, loons, brant and oldsquaws can be seen. Many beluga whales move into the lagoon in late June. At other times of the year it is possible to see arctic foxes, lemmings, caribou, grizzly bears, seals and gray whales.

Access to the lagoon area, which has no facilities of any kind, is by chartered plane from Barrow or Kotzebue.

Teshekpuk Lake

Teshekpuk Lake lies just a few miles from the Arctic Ocean in the wet, low tundra region southeast of Barrow. This lake, which is 22 miles across, and smaller surrounding lakes, are considered critical waterfowl and caribou habitat by the Alaska Department of Fish and Game. Wildlife viewing and photography is excellent.

The region is home to migratory Canada and greater white-fronted geese and brant, which arrive in July and August from the Alaska Peninsula, Canadian Arctic and Siberia. Other birds that nest in the region include plovers, sandpipers, phalaropes, dunlins, loons, oldsquaws, jaegers, gulls and snowy owls. Caribou, arctic foxes and lemmings also can be seen.

Access to the area, which has no visitor facilities, is by charter plane from Barrow or Prudhoe Bay.

Tunalik

Tunalik is a 5,000-foot airstrip located south of Icy Cape in the vicinity of Kasegaluk Lagoon. This open tundra region offers a real arctic tundra wilderness experience, with good opportunities for wildlife viewing and photography in the summer.

The airstrip was built to supply oil exploration expeditions. It is reported to be still usable, although it is not maintained and should be inspected before a landing is attempted. There is a gravel pad on one side of the runway for camping, but no facilities.

INTERIOR

This broad lowland region was forged by great rivers in the central part of the state cradled between the Alaska Range on the south, the Brooks Range on the north, the Canadian border on the east and a transition zone with the Bering Sea coast region on the west.

The Interior is a land of superlatives. On the region's southern border stands majestic Mount McKinley, at 20,320 feet the highest peak on the continent. Alaska's longest river, the Yukon, carves a swath across the entire region. The Yukon, Tanana, Porcupine, Koyukuk and several other rivers have long been avenues of travel for Native peoples, explorers, trappers and miners and still are of major importance as summer and winter highways. South of the Yukon, the Kuskokwim River rises in the hills of the western Interior before beginning its meandering course across the Bering Sea coast region.

About 60 miles northwest of Mount McKinley in the general area of Lake Minchumina is the geographic center of Alaska: 63°50′ north, 152°

Setting up camp in Fortymile country near Glacier Mountain. (George Wuerthner)

west. The Interior's climate is primarily the effect of latitude. The Arctic Circle sweeps through the region. The summer sun shines almost 24 hours a day, but is nearly absent in winter. Fairbanks has a summer maximum of 21 hours, 49 minutes of daylight and a winter minimum of three hours, 42 minutes.

The Interior has the distinction of having both the highest and lowest temperatures in the state. In 1915, the state's record high of 100°F was recorded at Fort Yukon, while the lowest temperature, -80°F, was recorded at Prospect Creek northeast of Bettles in 1971. Winter lows of -50° and -60°F and summer highs of 80° or 90°F are not uncommon. The region is dry and the air is frequently calm. The climate is semiarid, with about 12 inches of precipitation recorded annually. The mean annual wind speed is only five miles per hour at Fairbanks, which has a high winter pollution potential from ice fog, which forms during temperature inversions and traps exhaust from vehicles, heating units and power plants.

There are two distinct environments in the Interior. The highlands (below 2,000 feet) and the river valleys are a country of boreal forests or taiga, a Russian word that means "land of little sticks."

Lynx, found throughout the Interior, prey primarily on snowshoe hare. (Steve McCutcheon, reprinted from ALASKA GEOGRAPHIC®)

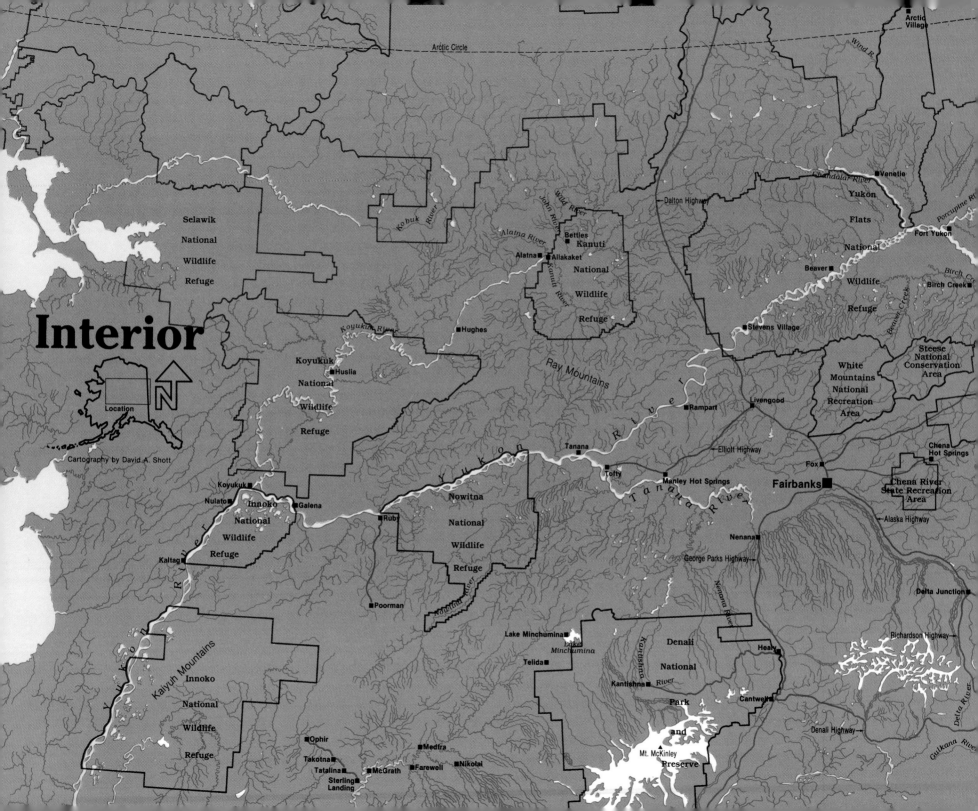

Interior

Location

N

Cartography by David A. Shott

Arctic Circle

Arctic Village

Wind R.

Selawik National Wildlife Refuge

Kobuk River

John River

Wild River

Dalton Highway

Yukon Flats National Wildlife Refuge

Venetie

Porcupine R.

Fort Yukon

Alatna River

Bettles

Kanuti

Alatna Allakaket

Kanuti River

National Wildlife Refuge

Beaver

Birch Cr.

Birch Creek

Koyukuk River

Hughes

Ray Mountains

Stevens Village

Steese National Conservation Area

Koyukuk National Wildlife Refuge

Huslia

White Mountains National Recreation Area

Yukon River

Livengood

Rampart

Chena Hot Springs

Koyukuk

Tanana

Elliott Highway

Fox

Nulato

Innoko

Galena

Tofty

Manley Hot Springs

Fairbanks

Chena River State Recreation Area

Yukon River

Kaltag

National Wildlife Refuge

Ruby

Nowitna National Wildlife Refuge

Tanana River

Nenana

Alaska Highway

George Parks Highway

Poorman

Nowitna River

Delta Junction

Nenana River

Richardson Highway

Kaiyuh Mountains

Innoko

Lake Minchumina

Lake Minchumina

Denali National

Healy

Kantishna River

Kantishna

National Wildlife Refuge

Telida

Park

Cantwell

Denali Highway

Gulkana River

Ophir

Medfra

and

Takotna

Mt. McKinley

Preserve

Tatalina

McGrath

Farewell

Nikolai

Sterling Landing

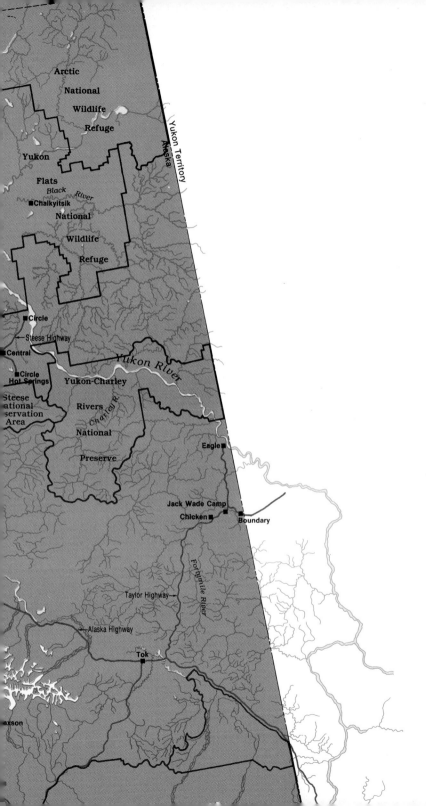

Above — *Moose calves, born in late May and early June, weigh 25 to 35 pounds at birth.* (©*Kirk Beckendorf*)

Right — *Wild iris* (I. setosa interior) *growing near Manley Hot Springs. (Staff)*

Cottonwood thrive near river lowlands; the hardy but stunted black spruce grows in muskeg and bogs; and there are also willow, alder, berries, wildflowers, grasses and sedges. In the northern and western reaches of the Interior, the forests and taiga give way to slow-growing, treeless tundra; above 4,500 feet, except for a few flowering plants and rock lichens, most mountains are bare.

This vast region spreads across nearly a third of Alaska, yet it is largely wilderness. This land shelters a large variety of wildlife and some of the prime habitat has been set aside as national parks or wildlife refuges.

Alaska's major tourist attraction — Mount McKinley — lies within 5.7 million acre Denali National Park and Preserve, which offers visitors a good chance of seeing wildlife. On the Interior's

A raft on dry land becomes a playground for children in an Athabascan village along the Chandalar River. (Fred Dure)

The black-and-white snow bunting is a common perching bird of the Interior. (Doug Murphy, reprinted from ALASKA GEOGRAPHIC®)

eastern border is Yukon-Charley Rivers National Preserve, home to endangered peregrine falcons. Other crucial habitat is protected by national wildlife refuges, including 8.6 million acre Yukon Flats and the smaller Kanuti, Koyukuk, Nowitna and Innoko refuges.

Wildlife found in this region includes millions of birds — American wigeons, pintails, green-winged teals, scoters, northern shovelers, scaup, and canvasbacks—as well as caribou, moose, grizzly and black bears, wolves, beavers, muskrats, lynx and snowshoe hares. Fish include all five species of salmon, but especially king and chum, as well as grayling, arctic char, burbot, northern pike, lake trout and several species of whitefish.

Interior residents depend on the natural resources of the land to make a living. In some communities of the Interior, guiding for hunting and for wilderness and photography treks or running lodges for visiting sportsmen and outdoor enthusiasts provide a livelihood for many residents. Some of the larger settlements such as Galena, McGrath, Bettles and Arctic Village, serve as trading centers or jumping-off points for wilderness excursions. The rest of the Interior relies primarily on a subsistence economy, sometimes combined with a cash economy where fishing or seasonal government jobs are available.

The Communities

ALATNA, on the north bank of the Koyukuk River, is two miles downriver of Allakaket and 182 miles northwest of Fairbanks. **Transportation:** Boat or snow machine from Allakaket. **Population:** 35.

Visitor Facilities: None. This small Eskimo village is situated on a high open plateau, which was a traditional meeting place of the Kobuk Eskimos and the Koyukukhotana Athabascan for trading goods.

ALLAKAKET, on the south bank of the Koyukuk River at the mouth of the Alatna River,

is two miles upriver from Alatna, 57 miles upriver from Hughes, and 180 miles northwest of Fairbanks. **Elevation:** 600 feet. **Transportation:** Scheduled air service from Fairbanks; boat or snow machine to Alatna and Hughes. **Population:** 175.

Visitor Facilities: No accommodations or meals. Allakatna Community Store and Moses Mercantile carry groceries and other supplies, along with fishing and hunting licenses. Gas and diesel available locally. There is a community laundromat which — along with the river — supplies the village with water.

Originally a meeting place where the Kobuk Eskimos and the Koyukukhotana Athabascan met to trade goods, the Eskimos settled on the north bank of the river (now Alatna) while the Athabascans settled on the south bank. In 1906, Archdeacon Hudson Stuck established a mission, and in 1925 a post office was established.

"A hard subsistence life" is how one Allakaket resident describes it here. Fish in local rivers includes sheefish, grayling and whitefish. The village has first priority for subsistence hunting, however, there are no caribou and moose are scarce. Gates of the Arctic National Park and Preserve is located to the north of the village, and Kanuti Wildlife Refuge is adjacent.

ARCTIC VILLAGE, in the Brooks Range on the east bank of the East Fork Chandalar River, 100 miles north of Fort Yukon, 290 miles north of Fairbanks. **Elevation:** 2,250 feet. **Transportation:** Scheduled air service from Fairbanks; winter trail to Venetie. **Population:** 111.

Visitor Facilities: The village council operates a bunkhouse which accommodates about a dozen people. Groceries, fuel and other supplies are available at Midnight Sun Native Store, Arctic Gas & Oil Store and Neets'aii Corp. The community laundromat has showers. Guide service available.

The Natsitkutchin Indians, a once seminomadic

people known for trading with the Barter Island Eskimos, settled Arctic Village.

Arctic Village and the surrounding Venetie Indian Reservation are bounded to the north by the Arctic National Wildlife Refuge, although recreational access to the refuge is primarily out of Kaktovik on Barter Island. A traditional Athabascan Indian village, employment is limited to the National Guard Armory, post office, clinic, school, village services, trapping and crafts. The old log Mission Church here, on the National Register of Historic Places, is under restoration.

Guided hunting for Dall sheep is available and there is sportfishing for grayling, whitefish, lake trout and pike.

BEAVER, located on the north bank of the Yukon River, 60 miles southwest of Fort Yukon, 110 miles northwest of Fairbanks. **Elevation:** 365 feet. **Transportation:** Scheduled air service from Fairbanks. **Population:** 66.

Visitor Facilities: None. The community laundromat has showers and drinking water. Limited supplies and fishing and hunting licenses are available from Innuit Co-op. Gas and diesel are also available.

Beaver is an unincorporated Eskimo and Indian village which was founded by a Japanese named Frank Yasuda. Yasuda saw Beaver as a place to relocate his Eskimo family and friends, who were facing hard times with the decline of whaling in arctic waters. Also a partner of prospectors J.T. Marsh and Tom Carter, Yasuda founded Beaver as a river landing for the Chandalar quartz mines started by them in about 1909. Present-day Beaver has two churches and a school which also houses the health clinic and community generator.

BETTLES (also known as Evansville and Bettles

Top — *Arctic Village (population 111), in the Brooks Range, is the Interior's northernmost major settlement.*

Left — *Beaver (population 66) on the Yukon River. (Both photos by Dennis and Debbie Miller, reprinted from ALASKA GEOGRAPHIC®)*

Field) is located on the south bank of the Upper Koyukuk River, 180 miles northwest of Fairbanks. **Elevation:** 850 feet. **Transportation:** Scheduled air service from Fairbanks; charter air service in Bettles; accessible by boat in summer, snow machine in winter; trail to Allakaket and Anaktuvuk Pass. **Population:** About 80.

Visitor Facilities: Food and lodging at Bettles Lodge (open year-round). Groceries and other supplies may be purchased at the trading post or at the lodge. Arts and crafts available locally include furs, gloves, hats, parkas, ivory, baskets and masks. Fishing and hunting licenses are available from the Fish & Wildlife Protection officer. Several Brooks Range outfitters and guides are headquartered here. Major repair available for aircraft; check locally for mechanics to work on

other types of engines. Local residents may lease rental transportation to visitors, such as boats and automobiles. Fuel available includes diesel, propane, aviation and regular gasoline. Unleaded gas is sometimes available. Public moorage on riverbank.

Evansville was founded by Wilfred Evans, who built a lodge there. Bettles began as a trading post in 1899 and was named for the proprietor, Gordon C. Bettles. It developed into a mining town and was eventually abandoned (it is located about six miles from the present settlement). Bettles Field, the airstrip, was built by the U.S. Navy upriver from old Bettles in 1945. Evansville was relocated to near the north end of the airfield. Employment is subsistence, state and federal jobs, construction, mining, guiding and tourism.

As gateway to Gates of the Arctic National Park and Preserve, Bettles is generally receptive to the growing number of Outside visitors, and the community sees a number of hikers and river rafters in summer. Visitors are advised, however, not to pick up souvenirs. Camps, cabins and claims that appear to be abandoned may be privately owned and still in use. Bettles is also trying to preserve some of its local mining history. There is hunting and fishing in the area, but visitors should be aware of Native subsistence claims and rules governing park and preserve lands. "Most people would welcome anyone coming to visit," says Jean Stevens, "to enjoy the country, steep themselves in the history, travel the truly pristine Brooks Range, fish the rivers, and to enjoy the isolation from the modern world while still having access to some of its conveniences."

BIRCH CREEK, on Lower Birch Creek, is 26 miles southwest of Fort Yukon and 120 miles northeast of Fairbanks. **Elevation:** 450 feet. **Transportation:** Charter plane. **Population:** 28.

Visitor Facilities: Lodging and meals at Birch Creek Enterprise Lodge. Visitors may also be able to arrange for accommodations in private homes. Supplies, including fuel, are obtained from Fort Yukon.

Birch Creek was an Athabascan Indian village in the 1800s and became a mining community with the discovery of gold. The people here hunt moose and bear, fish for northern pike, and trap furs for a living. A resident describes the climate: "Summers dry and warm, winter cold and lots of snow."

CHALKYITSIK, located 45 miles north of Fort Yukon, 170 miles northeast of Fairbanks, on the Black River. **Elevation:** 560 feet. **Transportation:** Charter or scheduled air service from Fort Yukon or Fairbanks; trail to Fort Yukon; accessible by boat. **Population:** 98.

Visitor Facilities: None. Residents may provide a place to stay in their homes if asked. The Chalkyitsik Native Corporation (CNC) Store sells groceries and some other supplies. The sale and importation of alcoholic beverages is prohibited. Propane and gasoline are available.

Bettles Lodge in Bettles, jumping-off point for Brooks Range explorers. (George Wuerthner, reprinted from The MILEPOST®)

Originally an Athabascan seasonal fish camp, Chalkyitsik means "fish with a hook at the mouth of the creek." Postmistress Geraldine Nathaniel says, "Fishhook town is small, kind of growing yet. Some people work for a long time here. The town is very quiet. Nice town to live." The only public building is the log Community Hall, which houses the clinic, council office, Native corporation office, store and post office. Geraldine says that if you need anything or can't find anything, "ask around when you enter the village." People work at the school, clinic, post office, Native store and Village Council. There is fishing for jackfish, whitefish and dog salmon; trapping; and hunting for ducks, grouse and ptarmigan.

FORT YUKON, located at a great bend of the Yukon River, just upstream from the confluence of the Porcupine and Yukon rivers; 140 miles northeast of Fairbanks and about eight miles north of the Arctic Circle. **Elevation:** 420 feet. **Transportation:** Scheduled service from Fairbanks; charter air service available; accessible by boat; connected by trail to Birch Creek, Chalkyitsik and Venetie. **Population:** 665.

Visitor Facilities: Food and lodging at Gwitchyaa Zhee Lodge and SourDough Inn. There is a laundromat and groceries and other supplies are available from Terrys Fort Yukon Store or the Alaska Commercial Company shop. The sale and importation of alcoholic beverages is prohibited. Hunting and fishing licenses may be purchased at the Alaska Commercial Company or from the Department of Fish and Game office. Local fishing trips may be arranged through the Gwitchyaa Zhee Corporation. Major marine engine, boat and auto repair is available. Charter aircraft and boats may be rented. All types of fuel are available. Public moorage on riverbank.

In 1847, Alexander Hunter Murray founded a Hudson's Bay Co. trading post near the present site of Fort Yukon. By 1873, the Alaska Commercial Company was operating a steamer on the Yukon and had established a post here run by Moses Mercier. The gold rush of 1897 dramatically increased both river traffic and the white population of Fort Yukon, while disease reduced the Indian population. Fort Yukon remained the largest settlement on the Yukon below Dawson for many years, and was headquarters for a hospital and pioneer missionary Hudson Stuck, who is buried here.

Chalkyitsik, still called Fishhook Town by some residents, is located on the Black River. (Bartz Englishoe, reprinted from ALASKA GEOGRAPHIC®)

Hub of the Yukon Flats area, Fort Yukon has just about everything the big city has except it is in the Bush. Employment is in sales and service, local, state and federal government, and also the traditional subsistence fishing (salmon, pike, etc.), hunting (moose, bear, small game), and trapping (lynx, beaver, fox). Recreation includes boating and canoeing the Yukon River, camping, softball, swimming and driving three-wheelers in summer; cross-country skiing, dog mushing, snow machining, ice skating, ice fishing and bingo in

Gwitchyaa Zhee Lodge in Fort Yukon offers food and lodging. (James Filip)

winter. The community itself is the attraction for most visitors, as city manager James Filip points out. Subsistence fish wheels, traps and garden plots exist alongside utility poles and cable television.

Native arts and crafts are displayed and sold at the Dinji Zhuu Enjit Museum. The Old Mission House is on the National Register of Historic Places.

GALENA, located on the north bank of the Yukon River near the confluence of the Yukon and Koyukuk rivers, 35 miles east of Nulato, 270 miles west of Fairbanks, 350 miles northwest of Anchorage. **Elevation:** 120 feet. **Transportation:** Scheduled air service from Fairbanks (Galena airport is the commercial air center for six surrounding villages and is also the forward Air Force base for F-15 jet fighters); accessible by boat. **Population:** 894.

Visitor Facilities: Food and lodging at the Riverside Hotel & Cafe. Meals also at Twilight's Restaurant. The local tavern is the Yukon Inn. Public laundromat and showers available. The following stores carry most supplies: Galena Commercial; Huhndorf's; Gana-A-Yoo Ltd.; and G&R Enterprises. Local arts and crafts include Indian beadwork, birch-bark baskets, skin moccasins, fur hats, and ivory work. Fishing and

Sled dogs staked out in back of a cabin are a common sight in the Interior. (Staff, reprinted from ALASKA GEOGRAPHIC®)

Galena, on the Yukon River, is transportation hub for several villages. (Chris Stall, Stone Flower Studio, reprinted from ALASKA GEOGRAPHIC®)

Fuel drums dot the yards of log cabin homes in Hughes, population 97. (Joseph Agnese, reprinted from ALASKA GEOGRAPHIC®)

hunting licenses available from the local Department of Fish and Game officer and at Gana-A-Yoo Ltd. Check with local air charter operators regarding guided hunting or fishing. All types of fuel and repair service are available. Automobiles and boats may be rented. Public moorage available.

Galena was founded as a supply point for nearby galena (lead ore) prospects in 1919. The airstrip was built in 1940 by the U.S. Army. Today, Galena is the site of Campion Air Force Base, with approximately 300 military personnel, adjacent to the airport. Koyukon Athabascans comprise most of the town's population. There is some construction and commercial fishing (fish wheels for chum and silver salmon) in summer, and year-round employment in government jobs, but traditional subsistence hunting and fishing support many residents. There is sportfishing for salmon, grayling, whitefish, sheefish, burbot and pike in nearby clear-water lakes and streams, but sport hunting

is frowned on by local Natives who depend on this resource for their subsistence. Koyukuk National Wildlife Refuge lies to the north of Galena and the northern portion of the Innoko refuge lies across the Yukon to the south.

Galena is transportation hub for several outlying villages. There's quite a bit of river traffic in summer, and in winter, when the Yukon is frozen solid, neighbors come in by dog sled or snow machine. Galena is the turnaround point for the Yukon 800 boat race from Fairbanks, held in June.

HUGHES is situated on the Koyukuk River, 120 miles northeast of Galena and 215 miles northwest of Fairbanks. **Elevation:** 550 feet. **Transportation:** Scheduled air service from Galena; accessible by boat; trails to Allakaket, Alatna, Huslia and Indian Mountain. **Population:** 97.

Visitor Facilities: Lodging at Hughes School or visitors may arrange with local residents to stay in private homes for a fee. Meals are not available, so visitors should bring their own food. Some

supplies may be purchased at Hughes General Store. Native beadwork, and sometimes snowshoes, baskets and baby sleds, may be available for purchase. If you can catch Alfred S. Attla Sr., in town, you can purchase a fishing or hunting license from him. If he's not around, the nearest outlet is the Department of Fish and Game office in Galena. Visitors can rent the town pickup, three-wheelers, automobiles or boats. Regular gasoline, diesel and propane available. Public moorage on the riverbank.

Some of the older citizens here remember when Hughes was a riverboat landing and supply point for gold mining camps in the nearby mountains about 1910. It was named for Charles Evan Hughes (1862-1948), then governor of New York. A post office was established in 1914, but the gold was mined out about 1915 and the post office was gone in 1916. The store remained here and Hughes became a Koyukuk Indian village. The post office was reestablished in 1942 and the city was incorporated in 1973. There are about 27 military personnel stationed at Indian Mountain Air Force Station, 15 miles east of Hughes. Employment in Hughes is in local services with seasonal firefighting and trapping. There is fishing for grayling, chum, sheefish and salmon.

HUSLIA is located on the Koyukuk River, 70 miles north of Galena and 250 miles northwest of Fairbanks. **Elevation:** 180 feet. **Transportation:** Scheduled air service from Galena; accessible by boat. **Population:** 283.

Visitor Facilities: Food and lodging at Min-Googa Lodge. Most supplies available at R&M Mercantile and Husler Community Store. There is a laundromat. Beadwork, yarn gloves and other arts and crafts may be purchased locally. Fishing and hunting licenses, diesel, propane and regular gasoline are available.

Originally settled in the late 1940s by Koyukuk Indians from Cutoff trading post. The post office was established at Huslia in 1952. The community takes its name from a nearby stream. Employment here includes seasonal firefighting and trapping,

along with positions at the school, church and in local government. Many local residents spend the summer at fish camp.

KALTAG, on the Yukon River, is 33 miles southwest of Nulato, 90 miles southwest of Galena and 330 miles west of Fairbanks. **Elevation:** 200 feet. **Transportation:** Scheduled air service from Galena; trails to Nulato and Galena; accessible by boat. **Population:** 262.

Visitor Facilities: None. Some supplies available from Kaltag Co-op or Visitor's store. Marine gas, diesel, propane and regular gasoline may be purchased.

An Indian village, called Kaltag by the Russians. An 1880 census listed a Lower Kaltag and Upper Kaltag here. The present village is believed to be the former Upper Kaltag, while Lower Kaltag is now referred to as the Old Kaltag site. A post office was established here in 1903. Kaltag was incorporated in 1969.

Cecelia Solomon on her community: "The people still rely on subsistence for their living. They fish during the summer (for salmon and grayling)

Autumn colors touch the trees in Kaltag in late summer. (John D. Lyle, reprinted from ALASKA® magazine)

and stay out at fish camps; they sell the fish or put some away for the winter; they also go hunting for moose, bear and other animals for food. They set traps in the winter for animals such as marten, rabbits or beaver. They sell the fur or make clothing out of it for themselves. The people mostly make a living for themselves and raise their families."

KOYUKUK is located at the confluence of the Koyukuk and Yukon rivers, 16 miles northeast of Nulato, 30 miles northwest of Galena, 300 miles west of Fairbanks. **Elevation:** 115 feet. **Transportation:** Scheduled air service from Galena; accessible by boat. **Population:** 98.

Visitor Facilities: Limited. Visitors may arrange to stay in private homes or at the school. There are showers and a laundromat at the community watering facility. Some supplies available at Kateel Enterprises in town, or at Last Chance Trading Post, located six miles downriver on the way to Nulato. Arts and crafts done in the village include beadwork, marten hats, moose skin gloves and sleds. Fishing and hunting licenses and propane and gasoline may be purchased locally.

Originally a Koyukukhotana Indian village, a trading post was established here in the late 1800s. The village served the growing number of miners

Huslia (population 283) on the Koyukuk River. (Staff, reprinted from ALASKA® magazine)

Above — Salmon dries in the summer sun at the village of Koyukuk. (Betsy Hart, reprinted from ALASKA GEOGRAPHIC®)

Right — McGrath is a hub of commerce on the Kuskokwim. (Staff, reprinted from ALASKA GEOGRAPHIC®)

in the area and the increasing river traffic. Today, people here make a living as trappers and fishermen; in seasonal construction or in local clerical and maintenance jobs; or they commute to larger communities for work. Fishing for salmon in the Yukon and Koyukuk rivers is done both commercially and for subsistence, and local summer fish camps are active. Local people do occasional guiding, but visitors should be well-prepared with equipment and supplies since none are available locally. Moose hunting is good in the fall and black bear are prevalent.

LAKE MINCHUMINA, on the northwest shore of Lake Minchumina, is 205 miles northwest of

Anchorage and 150 miles southwest of Fairbanks. **Elevation:** 700 feet. **Transportation:** Scheduled air service from Fairbanks. **Population:** 22.

Visitor Facilities: None. Groceries may be available at Cache Merchandise. Originally a Tanana Indian village, a post office was established here in 1930. The area saw further settlement with construction of the airstrip in 1941. Minchumina Lake yields some pike. Locals recommend trying the spit at the southeast end of the lake. Beautiful view of Mount McKinley from here.

McGRATH is located on the Upper Kuskokwim River opposite its junction with the Takotna River, 202 miles northwest of Anchorage, 250 miles northeast of Bethel, and 280 miles southwest of Fairbanks. **Elevation:** 337 feet. **Transportation:** Scheduled air service from Anchorage and Yukon River communities via several carriers; air charter service; river travel except during breakup (May) and freezeup (November). **Population:** 499.

Visitor Facilities: Overnight accommodations available at McGrath Roadhouse and Takusko House. Meals available at the roadhouse and at Miner's Cafe and Game Room. The local tavern is McGuire's and there is also a bar at the roadhouse. Groceries, gas and other supplies are available at Alaska Commercial Co., BJ's Pik-n-Pak and Vinasale Enterprises. Hardware available from General Services. The laundromat has shower facilities. Fishing and hunting licenses may be purchased locally and there are local guides and outfitters. All types of fuel and major repair service are available.

Originally settled by Upper Kuskokwim Athabascans, gold discoveries in the Innoko district and later Ganes Creek brought miners into the area in the early 1900s. By 1904, a trading post had been opened here and by 1907 a town was established and named for Peter McGrath, a U.S. marshall stationed in the area. In 1924, McGrath became the first city in Alaska to receive regular

The Yukon River becomes an ice road in winter at Nulato. (Matthew Donohoe, reprinted from ALASKA GEOGRAPHIC®)

airmail service, provided by pioneer aviator Carl Ben Eielson from Fairbanks. During World War II, McGrath was a fuel stop for lend-lease aircraft.

The majority of employment is in government jobs and local services, such as the school, radio station and stores. A number of residents also rely on subsistence activities, such as fishing, hunting, vegetable gardening and harvesting berries and timber for food and fuel.

In its role as a transportation and supply center, McGrath offers little in the way of conventional tourist attractions, although it does offer many urban amenities not generally available in rural Alaska. There is some big game guiding, but the Kuskokwim is too slow and silty for river runners, and fishing in the area is generally subsistence. McGrath does have its share of special events, the biggest being the arrival of the Iditarod sled dog racers in March on their way to Nome. An official checkpoint on the Iditarod trail, McGrath is filled with media, race officials, volunteers and spectators during the race. The dog teams and drivers normally reach McGrath five to seven days after leaving Anchorage. McGrath is also a mandatory

layover point for racers taking part in the Gold Rush Classic snow machine race, which takes place a few weeks prior to the Iditarod Trail Sled Dog Race and covers roughly the same route. According to KSKO general manager Chuck Hinde, "There are many social events held in conjunction with winter sports competitions, including a curious form of fund-raising known as 'Chinese Auctions,' which are more easily witnessed than described." The annual KSKO Bluegrass Music Festival is held in mid-July and the McGrath State Fair is in late August.

Visitors may wish to explore Old McGrath, a collection of abandoned log cabins located along a former channel of the Takotna River, where the town was originally located before moving to its present site in the 1940s.

NIKOLAI, at the junction of the South Fork Kuskokwim and Little Tonzona rivers, is 40 miles northeast of McGrath and 195 miles northwest of Anchorage. **Elevation:** 450 feet. **Transportation:** Scheduled air service from McGrath and Anchorage; charter air service based in McGrath; winter trails to McGrath, Medfra and Telida;

accessible by river (May to October). **Population:** 110.

Visitor Facilities: A city-owned hotel/apartment building (referred to as the Nikolai Inn) provides limited accommodations for visitors. A large community building, under construction, will house the post office, clinic, a laundromat and showers (replacing the traditional bathhouse). Supplies are available at the general store and fishing and hunting licenses may be purchased locally. Villagers use three-wheelers, snow machines and dog teams for transportation. Limited fuel is available.

As with other communities in this region, Nikolai was an Athabascan Indian village in the late 1800s and has been relocated since its original settlement. A trading post and roadhouse served miners during the Innoko gold rush. The Russian Orthodox church here was built in 1927.

More heavily subsistence than McGrath, Nikolai residents depend on hunting (moose, caribou, rabbits, ptarmigan and waterfowl) and fishing (king, chum, coho, whitefish, sheefish and grayling). Some residents spend the summer at Medfra at fish camp. There is also trapping and vegetable gardening. There are about a dozen jobs locally with federal and state agencies and some seasonal construction and firefighting jobs.

NULATO, located on the Yukon River, 25 miles west of Galena, 310 miles west of Fairbanks. **Elevation:** 2,100 feet. **Transportation:** Scheduled air service; local air charter; accessible by boat. **Population:** 388.

Visitor Facilities: Limited. Visitors may arrange for accommodations in private homes. Some supplies available at Sommer General Store, H&H Enterprise and at the Last Chance Trading Post (on the way to Koyukuk). There is a laundromat with showers at the safe-water facility. Fishing and hunting licenses are available locally, but there are no registered guides (ask local people about fishing). Diesel, propane and gasoline are available, and visitors may be able to rent boats and automobiles from residents. Charter aircraft available.

Nulato is the site of one of the most chronicled

Fisherman checks his set net near Rampart on the Yukon River. (Harry Walker, reprinted from ALASKA GEOGRAPHIC®)

events in Alaskan history, the murder of Lt. John J. Barnard by Koyukuk Indians in 1851. Barnard came to Alaska as part of the British search party sent after Sir John Franklin. While staying with the agent in charge of the Russian-American Company's post at Nulato, the Koyukuk Indians attacked the Russian fort, killing both Barnard and the Russian (Darabin), and the Indian village below the fort, killing 53 inhabitants. Barnard's gravesite is about one-half mile downriver from present-day Nulato.

RAMPART is on the south bank of the Yukon River, 61 miles northeast of Tanana and 85 miles northwest of Fairbanks. **Elevation:** 380 feet. **Transportation:** Scheduled air service from Fairbanks; charter air service; river travel except during breakup and freezeup. **Population:** 53.

Visitor Facilities: None. Some supplies available at Rampart City Trading Post. Regular gasoline, marine gas, diesel and propane are also available

and hunting and fishing licenses may be purchased locally.

Originally an Indian village, the community grew with the influx of miners following the 1896 gold discovery on Minook Creek. Today, Rampart is an Athabascan village where some residents trap and fish for a living. There are still gold mines in the area. Employment also includes commercial fishing and fish processing. Residents fish for salmon in the summer. A picturesque community, Rampart's location also makes it a good stop for anyone traveling the Yukon River, although one resident warns that there are many bears in the area.

RUBY, located on the Yukon River south of its junction with the Melozitna River, is 50 miles east of Galena and 220 miles west of Fairbanks. **Elevation:** 710 feet. **Transportation:** Scheduled air service; river travel except during breakup and freezeup; dog sled, snow machine or skis in winter. **Population:** 283.

Visitor Facilities: Food and lodging at Ruby Roadhouse. Groceries and other supplies available at Ruby Trading Company. There is a laundromat and most types of fuel are available. Automobiles may be rented and there are charter aircraft. Fishing and hunting licenses available for purchase and there is one registered guide. Public moorage on river.

Gold was discovered on Ruby Creek near the present-day townsite in 1907, but the gold rush to the area took place in 1911 with a second gold discovery on Long Creek. A post office was established in 1912 and the population for several years numbered over 1,000. Part of the Ruby Roadhouse dates from 1913. Today's residents make their living in commercial fishing, subsistence fishing, hunting, trapping (marten, beaver, mink, fox, wolf), logging, and working for the school, city or private businesses. There are some summer jobs in construction and at the sawmill.

Most supplies to Ruby arrive by barge on the Yukon River. (Chris Stall, Stone Flower Studio, reprinted from ALASKA GEOGRAPHIC®)

Recreation for residents in summer includes swimming, waterskiing, or fishing in clear pools on the Melozi River. In winter there are races by dog sled, snowshoe, snow machine or skis. Ruby is also a checkpoint for the annual Iditarod Trail Sled Dog Race in alternate years.

STEVENS VILLAGE, on the north bank of the Yukon River, is 90 miles north of Fairbanks and 54 miles southwest of Beaver. **Elevation:** 310 feet. **Transportation:** Bush airline schedule from Fairbanks; river travel except during breakup and freezeup. **Population:** 94.

Visitor Facilities: None. Visitors may arrange with villagers to stay in private homes. There are two stores and a laundromat with showers. The sale and importation of alcoholic beverages is prohibited. Marine gas and regular gasoline are available. Boat rentals and boat repair are available.

According to local tradition, this Indian village was founded by three brothers: Old Jacob, Gochonayeeya, and Old Stephen. When Old Stephen was elected chief in 1902, the village was named for him. A post office was established here in 1936. Residents make their living working in the post office or store, the Native corporation clinic, in maintenance, or the school. Villagers also do some trapping and spend summers at fish camp.

TAKOTNA is located on the north bank of the Takotna River, 17 miles west of McGrath, 230 miles northwest of Anchorage. **Elevation:** 825 feet. **Transportation:** Scheduled passenger and mail plane from McGrath; scheduled service to Anchorage from Tatalina's airport; charter plane; river travel June through September; snow machine and dogs. Takotna has more roads than most Interior communities: About 90 miles of road connect the community with Tatalina Air Force Station; Sterling Landing, on the Kuskokwim River, where the barge docks; Ophir, an old mining community with a few occupants in summer; and other mining areas. **Population:** 48.

Visitor Facilities: The community hall has beds for rent. Limited groceries are available at the Takotna General Store, which also houses the post office. There is a laundromat with showers. Marine gas and diesel are available.

Takotna started as a supply town for gold mines in the upper Innoko region and prospered through the 1930s until mining declined and McGrath replaced Takotna as supply center. Tatalina Air Force Station, established in 1949, employs some Takotna residents. Community capital improvement projects have employed many residents in construction during the summer, although as these projects slow down, some residents may have to go to Anchorage for summer work. Most residents are involved in subsistence activities. Moose hunting is excellent and moose is the staple red meat. There is some duck hunting and fishing for grayling, pike and trout. Residents also grow vegetable gardens and harvest wild berries.

This small community gets few visitors. One resident cautions that miners working the surrounding area are not particularly friendly to visitors. People here enjoy Takotna's beautiful setting — with its view of Takotna Mountain — good moose hunting and proximity to McGrath businesses. But with almost half the normal precipitation occurring between July and September, summers are "more wet than dry" as one resident puts it.

The village of Tanana, located at the junction of the Yukon and Tanana rivers, is one of the largest on the Yukon. (Staff, reprinted from ALASKA GEOGRAPHIC®)

TANANA, near the confluence of the Yukon and Tanana rivers, is 135 miles northwest of Fairbanks. **Elevation:** 227 feet. **Transportation:** Scheduled service from Fairbanks; local air charter services; river travel in summer; snow machine and dogs in winter. **Population:** 444.

Visitor Facilities: Food and lodging at Tanana Lodge. Supplies available at Alaska Commercial Co. and Tanana Store. Beadwork, parkas, mukluks, birch-bark baskets and other crafts may be available for purchase. Fishing and hunting licenses are also available. There is a laundromat. Charter aircraft are the only rental transportation available. Diesel, propane, regular gasoline and major marine engine repair are available.

Tanana is located at a historic Indian trading locality known as Nuchalawoya, meaning "place where the two rivers meet." A Nuchalawoya Indian festival, with potlatch and contests, is held in Tanana every June. Arthur Harper established an Alaska Commerical Co. trading post here in 1880, and in 1891 the U.S. Army built Fort Gibbon (the fort was abandoned in 1923). A post office was established in 1898 and in 1961 Tanana was incorporated as a first-class city. Residents make their living trapping and fishing and in government jobs.

Under restoration here is the wood-plank Mission of Our Savior Church, which overlooks the Yukon and Tanana rivers. The church was part of an Episcopal mission established in 1891 by Rev. J.L. Prevost.

Residents cite the mission, Indian festival and Tanana's sled dog races as some of its attractions. One resident says September (sunny and cool) and March and April (cold and sunny) are the best months to visit weatherwise. The Yukon River sled dog championships are held in early April, and there are also several outfitters locally for sled dog trips or for freighting on ski trips in winter. In summer, the Yukon River is swimmable ("65 °F and silty in July"), and fish wheels can be seen operating, especially in August and September. Boating is good throughout the area, and boat races are held over Labor Day weekend. There is canoeing on tributary streams.

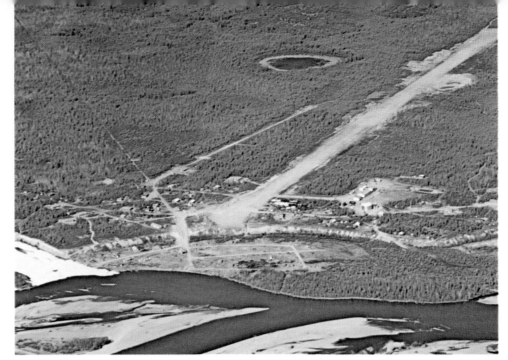

The Chandalar River breaks up in early May at Venetie. (Dennis and Debbie Miller, reprinted from ALASKA GEOGRAPHIC®)

TELIDA is located on the Swift Fork of the North Fork Kuskokwim River, 43 miles northeast of Nikolai, 80 miles northeast of McGrath, 46 miles southwest of Minchumina, l85 miles northwest of Anchorage. **Elevation:** 650 feet. **Transportation:** Charter plane; small riverboat; winter trail to Nikolai. **Population:** 29.

Visitor Facilities: None. Supplies are obtained from McGrath and Anchorage. Some beadwork is done in the village. Gasoline is available and boats may be rented.

This old Indian village has had three locations since white men first camped in the village in 1899. The village's second location, four or five miles upstream from present-day Telida, was abandoned and is now referred to as Old Telida. New Telida was settled by the Carl Sesuie family. The lifestyle here is heavily subsistence. Residents hunt moose, bear, waterfowl and small game; fish for whitefish, sheefish, chum salmon, grayling, pike and Dolly Varden; and trap fox, lynx, wolverine, beaver, muskrat, marten and mink. There is some vegetable gardening and families harvest wild berries in late summer and fall.

VENETIE, located on the Chandalar River, is 140 miles north of Fairbanks. **Elevation:** 620 feet. **Transportation:** Scheduled air service from Fairbanks; by boat; winter trail from Arctic Village and Fort Yukon. **Population:** 132.

Visitor Facilities: None. Some supplies at Venetie Native Store and Dan's Trap 'N Fur. Boats and charter aircraft are available.

An Indian village settled in 1900, a post office and school were established here in 1938. Venetie is one of two Indian villages located within the 1.8 million acre Venetie Indian Reservation. Residents are employed in seasonal trapping and firefighting. Caribou are a mainstay of the subsistence economy. There is some year-round employment in the school, store and Native corporation. Some excellent beaded work (gloves, boots, jewelry, etc.) is done here.

Unlike its sister city, Arctic Village, Venetie does not encourage tourism.

Attractions

Chena River State Recreation Area

Below — *Fishermen try their luck in the Chena River, one of the most popular arctic grayling fisheries in the state and centerpiece of the 254,080-acre Chena River State Recreation Area 40 miles east of Fairbanks. The area also is popular for camping and hiking. Established trails include the Granite Tors Loop Trail to two groups of tors, monoliths of jointed granite which jut skyward from the tundra-covered hills; the Chena Dome Loop Trail across alpine ridges that offer wildflowers in July, blueberries in August and scenic views all year; and the Angel Rocks Trail to a group of spectacular rock outcroppings. (Staff, reprinted from* The MILEPOST®)

View of Mount McKinley from Eielson visitor center in Denali National Park. (©John W. Warden, reprinted from The MILEPOST®)

Denali National Park and Preserve

Alaska's most-visited national park is located 120 miles south of Fairbanks and 240 miles north of Anchorage. The crown jewel of Denali National Park is Mount McKinley, tallest peak on the North American continent and a magnet for climbers from all over the globe. The north summit reaches a height of 19,470 feet; the south, 20,320 feet. The massive mountain is the centerpiece of the glacier-strewn Alaska Range, which has many peaks exceeding 10,000 feet in height. The Athabascan Indians called McKinley "Denali," meaning "the High One," and in 1980 the name of the park itself became Denali. That year, too, the park was enlarged from 1.9 million acres to six million acres to protect Mount McKinley on all sides and to preserve wildlife habitat.

After Mount McKinley, this park is most famous for its abundant wildlife. In the mountain's shadow live 37 species of mammals including caribou, grizzly bears, wolves, wolverines, moose, Dall sheep, red foxes, lynx, ground squirrels, snowshoe hares and voles. At least 155 species of birds have been recorded in the park. Resident species include great horned owls, ravens, and white-tailed, rock and willow ptarmigan. The majority, however, visit the park only during summer. These include sandhill cranes and oldsquaws, sandpipers, plovers, gulls, buffleheads and goldeneyes. Fish in park waters include lake trout and grayling.

Other interesting features of the park are: Wonder Lake, a superb reflecting pond for Mount McKinley; the Savage River Canyon which cuts through the Outer Range, exposing some of Alaska's oldest rocks called Birch Creek Schist; Muldrow Glacier, largest on the north side of the Alaska Range, which flows for 32 miles and descends 16,000 feet from just beneath Mount McKinley's summit; and the Kantishna Hills, which were first mined in 1906 and where mining continues today on claims that predate the park expansion.

Accommodations are available at Denali National Park Hotel and a youth hostel. Two wilderness lodges and a roadhouse are located in the Kantishna area. Campsites are available at seven National Park Service campgrounds on a first-come, first-served basis. Several motels are located outside the park along the George Parks Highway. There are several established trails in the "front country" — the area near the park entrance — or hikers may travel along the park road or set off across the tundra. A permit is required for hiking and camping in wilderness areas. Other activities include ice and rock climbing, photography and wildlife viewing, nature walks, slide programs, sled dog demonstrations, cross-country skiing, and bus and flightseeing tours.

Above — *Visitors to Denali National Park have a good chance of seeing Dall sheep. (George Wuerthner)*

Right — *Backpackers hike one of the few established trails in the national park. (Staff, reprinted from* The MILEPOST®*)*

Steese National Conservation Area

Hikers amble toward the trailhead of the Pinnell Mountain National Recreation Trail, only recreational development in the 1.2 million acre Steese National Conservation Area. The 27-mile trail, marked by rock cairns, winds along mountain ridges and through high passes above 3,500 feet; vantage points offer views of the White Mountains, Tanana Hills, Brooks Range and the Alaska Range. The conservation area, which straddles the Steese Highway near Fairbanks, also includes the drainage of Birch Creek, a wild and scenic river. (Staff)

White Mountains National Recreation Area

The White Mountains, viewed from the summer hiking trail, are the main feature of the 1 million acre White Mountains National Recreation Area near Fairbanks. From the Elliott Highway, the summer trail and a separate winter trail lead to a Bureau of Land Management public recreation cabin on Beaver Creek, a national wild and scenic river. The winter trail follows an old route that once extended to Chandalar. The summer trail leads over Wickersham Dome, which offers views of Mount McKinley, the White Mountains and the Alaska Range. (Mick Shay, reprinted from The MILEPOST®)

Yukon-Charley Rivers National Preserve

The 2.2 million acre Yukon-Charley Rivers National Preserve is flanked to the north and northwest by the Brooks Range and to the southwest by the Alaska Range; the eastern side of the preserve borders Canada. The preserve includes a 128-mile stretch of the Yukon River, as well as the entire 106 miles of the wild and scenic Charley River.

The broad, swift Yukon flows brown with glacial silt. Old cabins and relics from mining camps on its banks recall the river's importance for transportation in the gold rush era. Gold discoveries at Circle, Woodchopper Creek, Nation and other eastern Yukon localities preceded the Klondike gold rush. By contrast, the Charley River watershed is virtually untouched by modern man. It flows crystal clear and is considered to be one of Alaska's finest recreational streams. The two rivers merge between the early-day boom towns of Eagle and Circle.

River runners camp near the Nation River in Yukon-Charley Rivers National Preserve. (George Wuerthner)

The golden eagle is common in the Interior. (Rick McIntyre, reprinted from ALASKA GEOGRAPHIC®)

Wildlife in the preserve include caribou from the Fortymile herd, which migrates to Canada and back. A moderate number of moose browse along streams and lowland areas, while Dall sheep occupy heights above the Charley River. Other wildlife includes grizzly and black bears, wolves and many small mammals.

More than 200 species of birds have been recorded in the preserve, including bald and golden eagles, rough-legged hawks and gyrfalcons. In its cliffs and rocky peaks the preserve contains some of North America's finest habitat for peregrine falcons, an endangered species. Yukon-Charley lies along a major flyway for waterfowl breeding on the Yukon Flats and wintering in the continental United States.

Sportfishing centers primarily on arctic grayling. Other fish caught in preserve waters include king salmon, chum salmon, sheefish, whitefish, northern pike, burbot, and Dolly Varden.

The preserve is reached primarily by small plane or boat from Eagle, on the Taylor Highway 12 river miles south of the preserve, or Circle, 14 river miles to the north on the Steese Highway. Floating the 158 miles of the Yukon River between Eagle and Circle is the most popular means of visiting the preserve, which has no roads or maintained trails. The preserve has no lodging facilities or formal campgrounds, but camping is permitted on any federally owned land.

Other recreational activities include hiking, fishing, hunting, wildlife observation and photography, cross-country skiing, dog sledding, snowmobiling, and snowshoeing.

Innoko National Wildlife Refuge

Below — *The 4 million acre Innoko National Wildlife Refuge, located about 300 miles northwest of Anchorage in the central Yukon River valley, is renowned for its beaver population. In some years 40 percent of all beaver trapped in Alaska originate here; the annual harvest is about 20,000 pelts. Other furbearers include muskrats, martens, wolverines, lynx, river otters and red foxes. About 80 percent of the refuge is wetlands also used by waterfowl and shorebirds. (Martin Grosnick, reprinted from ALASKA GEOGRAPHIC®)*

Kanuti National Wildlife Refuge

Right — *Lou Swenson lands his catch from the Kanuti River, located in the 1.4 million acre Kanuti National Wildlife Refuge, which straddles the Arctic Circle approximately 150 miles northwest of Fairbanks and south of Bettles. Fish found in refuge lakes and rivers include four species of salmon, char, grayling, whitefish, sheefish, lake trout, burbot and northern pike. Other recreational activities in this remote area include photography, camping, boating, gold panning and rockhounding.*

Above — *A white-fronted goose, one of the most abundant species that nest on Kanuti Refuge, flaps its wings as it scoots along the Kanuti River. Some of the other 139 species of birds that have been observed on the Kanuti are Canada geese, pintails, wigeons, scaups and scoters. (Both photos by Jo Keller, U.S. Fish and Wildlife Service, reprinted from ALASKA GEOGRAPHIC®)*

Koyukuk National Wildlife Refuge

A special feature of the 3.5 million acre Koyukuk National Wildlife Refuge is the 10,000-acre Nogahabara Dune Field, one of the only two large, active dune fields in northern Alaska. (The other is in Kobuk Valley National Park.) Both were formed by windblown deposits some 10,000 years ago. The rest of the refuge, located 320 miles northwest of Fairbanks, is heavily forested and contains wetlands that provide ideal nesting grounds for some 400,000 ducks, geese and shorebirds. Moose are abundant and the entire region is part of the winter range of the Western Arctic caribou herd. (Jo Keller, U.S. Fish and Wildlife Service, reprinted from ALASKA GEOGRAPHIC®)

Nowitna National Wildlife Refuge

The forested lowlands of the 1.6 million acre Nowitna National Wildlife Refuge, located approximately 200 miles west of Fairbanks in the central Yukon River valley, provide habitat for a variety of fish and waterfowl. More than a quarter million birds, including trumpeter swans, breed on the refuge. Fishing for northern pike and sheefish is excellent. A dominant feature of the refuge is the Nowitna River, part of which is classified as a wild and scenic river. (Dave Patterson, reprinted from ALASKA GEOGRAPHIC®)

Yukon Flats National Wildlife Refuge

The large Yukon Flats National Wildlife Refuge about 100 miles north of Fairbanks encompasses 8.6 million acres in a vast basin in east-central Alaska. This area is primarily a complex wetlands which includes more than 40,000 lakes, ponds and sloughs. The refuge lies between the Brooks Range to the north and the White-Crazy Mountains to the south. The trans-Alaska pipeline corridor runs along the refuge's western boundary, while the eastern boundary extends to within 30 miles of the Canadian border.

The refuge is bisected by 300 miles of the Yukon River, America's fifth largest river. Here the Yukon spreads out through the vast floodplain. In the

The Yukon Flats are one of the last footholds of endangered peregrine falcons. (Myron Wright, reprinted from ALASKA GEOGRAPHIC®)

spring millions of migrating birds converge on the flats before the ice moves from the river, coming from four continents to raise their young. By August lakes and ponds are alive with scurrying ducklings and molting adults. The refuge has one of the highest nesting densities of waterfowl in North America and contributes more than two million ducks and geese to the continent's flyways.

Mammals on the refuge include a substantial population of moose, as well as Dall sheep in the White Mountains, caribou, wolves, grizzly and black bears, martens, lynx, snowshoe hares, beavers, muskrats and some red foxes and wolverines.

Interior Rivers

The Interior's rivers have long served as highways for Athabascan travelers. In recent years, they have become a playground for visitors from other parts of Alaska — and the world. While the Yukon River is the major draw for river floaters, others offer white water and untrammeled wilderness. The following are a few of the best:

Birch Creek — This national wild and scenic river originates about 70 miles northeast of Fairbanks and flows generally east then north into the Yukon River. Most of Birch Creek is within the Steese National Conservation Area. Extensive mining above the put-in point and outside the river corridor has muddied the water of this stream.

Chandalar River — Both main forks head in the Brooks Range and flow south to become the Chandalar River, which empties into the Yukon River south of the village of Venetie.

Charley River — All 106 miles of this wild and scenic river flow within Yukon-Charley Rivers National Preserve. The watershed of this pristine, free-flowing tributary of the Yukon River is virtually undisturbed by modern man and provides an outstanding wilderness experience. The river flows through an open upland valley draining mountains up to 6,000 feet high, a region of bluffs and cliffs overlooking the river and then the open Yukon floodplain.

Runs of king, coho and chum salmon from the Bering Sea pass through and spawn in the flats each summer — the longest salmon run in the United States. Other fish found in refuge waters include Dolly Varden, grayling, whitefish, sheefish, cisco, burbot and northern pike.

Most of the refuge is a pristine and remote wilderness with no facilities. Camping is permitted throughout the region.

Canoeists paddle on the Yukon River through the very flat Yukon Flats.
(George Wuerthner)

Delta River — The Delta flows north out of Tangle Lakes along the Denali Highway. The upper portion of this national wild and scenic river is clear water; below Eureka Creek it is cold, silty glacial water with some floating debris.

Fortymile River — This clear-water wild and scenic river is located in east-central Alaska. It is fed by numerous creeks and streams and flows

Right — *Shooting Canyon Rapids on the Fortymile River. (George Wuerthner)*

Below — *Accessible Birch Creek has been muddied by mining. (Staff)*

221

Alaska's best known and longest river is the Yukon, still a major transportation corridor. (Fred Dure)

Sportfishing

Access to good fishing in the Interior can be as simple as climbing in your car and driving down the highway to the nearest bridge crossing. However the vast majority of the best fishing locations are reached only by small plane or by boat. This is a land of thousands of lakes and thousands of miles of streams. Lurking within a great many of them are ferocious northern pike, which average two to five pounds and occasionally attain trophy status of 15 pounds. Some lucky anglers have even caught 25- to 30-pound pike. Watch out for their sharp teeth! Use a wire leader and carry pliers for unhooking your catch.

Another enthusiastic fighter commonly found in this region is the sheefish, often called the "Tarpon of the North" because of its resemblance to that sport fish of more southerly climes. Sheefish average seven to 12 pounds in the Interior, but occasionally attain 30 pounds.

Grayling are another popular sport fish in the Interior. These fish prefer clear, cold water; any grayling over three pounds is considered trophy size. Other fish encountered by Interior anglers are whitefish, which average one to two pounds, and burbot (also called lush or lingcod) which average two to five pounds, but can attain 20 pounds.

Northern pike occasionally attain trophy status in Interior waters. (George Wuerthner)

eastward into the Yukon River at Fortymile in Canada. Historic relics from the gold rush may still be seen along the banks of this excellent waterway.

Nenana River — The Nenana River heads at Nenana Glacier in the Alaska Range and flows north 140 miles to the Tanana River at the town of Nenana. This river is easily accessible at several locations on the Denali and George Parks highways and the Alaska Railroad.

Porcupine River — This river heads in Canada and flows westward 460 miles to the Yukon River, just north of Fort Yukon. The Porcupine is considered suitable for families with older children. The remote, scenic wilderness and relics from the river's historic past offer a rewarding experience. This river has long served as a major travel route and was important in the 19th century fur trade and during the gold rush to the Klondike.

Yukon River — The Yukon River, fifth largest river in North America, originates in the coastal mountains of Canada and flows 2,300 miles in a great, wide arc to the Bering Sea. Historically, travelers on the Yukon have used all manner of watercraft from log rafts to stern-wheelers. Today, most visitors use canoes, kayaks, inflatable rafts or outboard-powered riverboats. Freight-loaded barges also are often seen on this major transportation corridor.

The Kink

Rafters portage around The Kink on the North Fork Fortymile River, 40 miles southwest of Eagle. Originally the name of a sharp bend in the river, The Kink came to mean a 15-foot-wide channel (eroded to 50 feet by the 1970s) that was blasted 100 feet through the ridge that formed the neck in the bend. The channel was created in 1904 to divert the river and expose 2.75 miles of riverbed for mining. It was abandoned just a year later. The Kink, now on the National Register of Historic Places, was a major engineering feat in its time and place and is considered a permanent monument to man's undertakings in the pursuit of gold at the turn of the century. (George Wuerthner)

Minto Flats

Minto Flats, a marshy area about the size of the state of Connecticut located about 40 miles northwest of Fairbanks, is a prime nesting area, but also a staging area for waterfowl from the Yukon Flats and the North Slope during the fall migration. It is the third most popular duck hunting spot in the state. Hunters reach the flats primarily by chartered floatplane from Fairbanks or by boat from Minto. (June Mackie, reprinted from ALASKA GEOGRAPHIC®)

Alaska Geographic® Back Issues

One Man's Wilderness, Vol. 1, No. 2. The story of a dream shared by many, fulfilled by a few; a man goes into the Bush, builds a cabin and shares his incredible wilderness experience. Color photos. 116 pages, $9.95.

Admiralty . . . Island in Contention, Vol. 1, No. 3. An intimate and multifaceted view of Admiralty; it's geological and historical past, its present-day geography, wildlife and rare human population. Color photos. 78 pages, $5.

Fisheries of the North Pacific: History, Species, Gear & Processes, Vol. 1, No. 4. Out of print. (Book edition available)

The Alaska-Yukon Wild Flowers Guide, Vol. 2, No. 1. Out of print. (Book edition available)

Glacier Bay: Old Ice, New Land, Vol. 3, No. 1. The expansive wilderness of southeastern Alaska's Glacier Bay National Monument (recently proclaimed a national park and preserve) unfolds in crisp text and color photographs. Records the flora and fauna of the area, its natural history, with hike and cruise information, plus a large-scale color map. 132 pages, $11.95.

Richard Harrington's Antarctic, Vol. 3, No. 3. The Canadian photojournalist guides readers through remote and little understood regions of the Antarctic and subantarctic. More than 200 color photos and a large fold-out map. 104 pages, $8.95.

Southeast: Alaska's Panhandle, Vol. 5, No. 2. Explores southeastern Alaska's maze of fjords and islands, mossy forests and glacier-draped mountains — from Dixon Entrance to Icy Bay, including all of the state's fabled Inside Passage. Along the way are profiles of every town, together with a look at the region's history, economy, people, attractions and future. Includes large fold-out map and seven area maps. 192 pages, $12.95.

Alaska Whales and Whaling, Vol. 5, No. 4. The wonders of whales in Alaska — their life cycles, travels and travails — are examined, with an authoritative history of commercial and subsistence whaling in the North. Includes a fold-out poster of 14 major whale species in Alaska in perspective, color photos and illustrations, with historical photos and line drawings. 144 pages, $12.95.

The Aurora Borealis, Vol. 6, No. 2. The northern lights — in ancient times seen as a dreadful forecast of doom, in modern days an inspiration to countless poets. What causes the aurora, how it works, how and why scientists are studying it today and its implications for our future. 96 pages, $7.95.

Alaska's Native People, Vol. 6, No. 3. Examine the varied worlds of the Inupiat Eskimo, Yup'ik Eskimo, Athabascan, Aleut, Tlingit, Haida and Tsimshian. Included are sensitive, informative articles by Native writers, plus a large, four-color map detailing the Native villages and defining the language areas, 304 pages, $24.95.

The Stikine, Vol. 6, No. 4. River route to three Canadian gold strikes in the 1800s, the Stikine is the largest and most navigable of several rivers that flow from northwestern Canada through southeastern Alaska on their way to the sea. Illustrated with contemporary color photos and historic black-and-white; includes a large fold-out map. 96 pages, $9.95.

Alaska's Great Interior, Vol. 7, No. 1. Alaska's rich Interior country, west from the Alaska-Yukon Territory border and including the huge drainage between the Alaska Range and the Brooks Range, is covered thoroughly. Included are the region's people, communities, history, economy, wilderness areas and wildlife. Illustrated with contemporary color and black-and-white photos. Includes a large fold-out map. 128 pages, $9.95.

A Photographic Geography of Alaska, Vol. 7, No. 2. An overview of the entire state — a visual tour through the six regions of Alaska: Southeast, Southcentral/Gulf Coast, Alaska Peninsula and Aleutians, Bering Sea Coast, Arctic and Interior. Plus a handy appendix of valuable information — "Facts About Alaska." Revised in 1983. Approximately 160 color and black-and-white photos and 35 maps. 192 pages, $15.95.

The Aleutians, Vol. 7, No. 3. Home of the Aleut, a tremendous wildlife spectacle, a major World War II battleground and now the heart of a thriving new commercial fishing industry. Contemporary color and black-and-white photographs, and a large fold-out map. 224 pages, $14.95.

Klondike Lost: A Decade of Photographs by Kinsey & Kinsey, Vol. 7, No. 4. An album of rare photographs and all-new text about the lost Klondike boom town of Grand Forks, second in size only to Dawson during the gold rush. $12.95.

Wrangell-Saint Elias, Vol. 8, No. 1. Mountains, including the continent's second- and fourth-highest peaks, dominate this international wilderness that sweeps from the Wrangell Mountains in Alaska to the southern Saint Elias range in Canada. Includes a large fold-out map. 144 pages, $9.95.

Alaska Mammals, Vol. 8, No. 2. From tiny ground squirrels to the powerful polar bear, and from the tundra to the magnificent whales inhabiting Alaska's waters, this volume includes 80 species of mammals found in Alaska. 184 pages, $12.95.

The Kotzebue Basin, Vol. 8, No. 3. Examines northwestern Alaska's thriving trading area of Kotzebue Sound and the Kobuk and Noatak river basins, lifelines of the region's Inupiat Eskimos, early explorers, and present-day, hardy residents. 184 pages, $12.95.

Alaska National Interest Lands, Vol. 8, No. 4. Following passage of the bill formalizing Alaska's national interest land selections (d-2 lands), longtime Alaskans Celia Hunter and Ginny Wood review each selection, outlining location, size, access, and briefly describing the region's special attractions. 242 pages, $14.95.

Alaska's Glaciers, Vol. 9, No. 1. Examines in depth the massive rivers of ice, their composition, exploration, present-day distribution and scientific significance. 144 pages, $10.95.

Sitka and Its Ocean/Island World, Vol. 9, No. 2. From the elegant capital of Russian America to a beautiful but modern port, Sitka, on Baranof Island, has become a commercial and cultural center for southeastern Alaska. 128 pages, $9.95.

Islands of the Seals: The Pribilofs, Vol. 9, No. 3. Great herds of northern fur seals drew Russians and Aleuts to these remote Bering Sea islands where they founded permanent communities and established a unique international commerce. 128 pages, $9.95.

Alaska's Oil/Gas & Minerals Industry, Vol. 9, No. 4. Experts detail the geological processes and resulting mineral and fossil fuel resources that are now in the forefront of Alaska's economy. Illustrated with historical black-and-white and contemporary color photographs. 216 pages, $12.95.

Adventure Roads North: The Story of the Alaska Highway and Other Roads in The MILEPOST®, Vol. 10, No. 1. From Alaska's first highway — the Richardson — to the famous Alaska Highway, first overland route to the 49th state, text and photos provide a history of Alaska's roads and take a mile-by-mile look at the country they cross. 224 pages, $14.95.

ANCHORAGE and the Cook Inlet Basin, Vol. 10, No. 2. "Anchorage country" . . . the Kenai, the Susitna Valley, and Matanuska. Heavily illustrated in color and including three illustrated maps . . . one an uproarious artist's forecast of "Anchorage 2035." 168 pages, $14.95.

Alaska's Salmon Fisheries, Vol. 10, No. 3. The work of ALASKA® magazine Outdoors Editor Jim Rearden, this issue takes a comprehensive look at Alaska's most valuable commercial fishery. 128 pages, $12.95.

Up the Koyukuk, Vol. 10, No. 4. Highlights the Koyukuk region of north-central Alaska . . . the wildlife, fauna, Native culture and more. 152 pages. $14.95.

Nome: City of the Golden Beaches, Vol. 11, No. 1. The colorful history of Alaska's most famous gold rush town has never been told like this before. Illustrated with hundreds of rare black-and-white photos, the book traces the story of Nome from the crazy days of the 1900 gold rush. 184 pages, $14.95.

Alaska's Farms and Gardens, Vol. 11, No. 2. An overview of the past, present, and future of agriculture in Alaska, and a wealth of information on how to grow your own fruit and vegetables in the north. 144 pages, $12.95.

Chilkat River Valley, Vol. 11, No. 3. This issue explores the mountain-rimmed valley at the head of the Inside Passage, its natural resources, and those hardy residents who make their home along the Chilkat. 112 pages, $12.95.

Alaska Steam, Vol. 11, No. 4. A pictorial history of the Alaska Steamship Company pioneering the northern travel lanes. Compiled by Lucile McDonald. More than 100 black-and-white historical photos. 160 pages. $12.95.

Northwest Territories, Vol. 12, No. 1. An in-depth look at some of the most beautiful and isolated land in North America. Compiled by Richard Harrington. 148 color photos. 136 pages. $12.95.

Alaska's Forest Resources, Vol. 12, No. 2 examines the majestic and valuable forests of Alaska. Nearly 200 historical black-and-white and color photos. 200 pages. $14.95.

Alaska Native Arts and Crafts, Vol. 12, No. 3. An in-depth look at the art and artifacts of Alaska's Native people. More than 200 full color photos. 215 pages. $17.95.

Our Arctic Year, Vol. 12, No. 4. Vivian and Gil Staender's simple, compelling story of a year in the wilds of the Brooks Range of Alaska, with only birds, nature and an unspoiled land. They share their discoveries, and their reactions to a year of isolation with time to sense their surroundings. Over 100 color photos. 150 pages. $12.95.

Where Mountains Meet the Sea: Alaska's Gulf Coast, Vol. 13, No. 1. Alaskan's first-hand descriptions of the 850-mile arc that crowns the Pacific Ocean from Kodiak and surrounding islands to Cape Yakataga. Included is a historical overview of this area, and a close look at the geological forces that constantly reshape its landscape. More than 300 photos. 191 pages. $14.95.

FORTHCOMING ISSUE:
British Columbia Coast/The Canadian Inside Passage, Vol. 13, No. 3. Where to go, how to get there, what you'll find on the B.C. Coast west of the Coast Mountain divide, including Vancouver Island and the Queen Charlottes. Brief historical background (indigenous residents, fur trade, exploration, European settlers) and current conditions. Includes large fold-out map. $14.95.

ALL PRICES SUBJECT TO CHANGE.

Your $30 membership in the Alaska Geographic Society includes 4 subsequent issues of ALASKA GEOGRAPHIC®, the Society's official quarterly. Please add $4 for non-U.S. membership.

Additional membership information available upon request. Single copies of the ALASKA GEOGRAPHIC® back issues are also available. When ordering, please make payments in U.S. funds and add $1 postage/handling per copy. To order back issues send your check or money order and volumes desired to:

The Alaska Geographic Society

P.O. Box 93370, Anchorage, Alaska 99509